NEW SIXTEENTH CENTURY MANOR HOUSE WITH FIELDS STILL OPEN, GIDEA HALL, ESSEX.

Nichols: *Progresses of Queen Elizabeth.*

An Introduction

to the

Industrial and Social History of England

BY

EDWARD P. CHEYNEY
PROFESSOR OF EUROPEAN HISTORY IN THE UNIVERSITY
OF PENNSYLVANIA

New York
THE MACMILLAN COMPANY
LONDON: MACMILLAN & CO., LTD.
1919

All rights reserved

COPYRIGHT, 1901,
BY THE MACMILLAN COMPANY.

Set up and electrotyped. Published April, 1901.

PREFACE

This text-book is intended for college and high-school classes. Most of the facts stated in it have become, through the researches and publications of recent years, such commonplace knowledge that a reference to authority in each case has not seemed necessary. Statements on more doubtful points, and such personal opinions as I have had occasion to express, although not supported by references, are based on a somewhat careful study of the sources. To each chapter is subjoined a bibliographical paragraph with the titles of the most important secondary authorities. These works will furnish a fuller account of the matters that have been treated in outline in this book, indicate the original sources, and give opportunity and suggestions for further study. An introductory chapter and a series of narrative paragraphs prefixed to other chapters are given with the object of correlating matters of economic and social history with other aspects of the life of the nation.

My obligation and gratitude are due, as are those of all later students, to the group of scholars who have within our own time laid the foundations of the study of economic history, and whose names and books will be found referred to in the bibliographical paragraphs.

EDWARD P. CHEYNEY.

UNIVERSITY OF PENNSYLVANIA,
    January, 1901.

CONTENTS

CHAPTER I

GROWTH OF THE NATION TO THE MIDDLE OF THE FOURTEENTH CENTURY

		PAGE
1.	The Geography of England	1
2.	Prehistoric Britain	4
3.	Roman Britain	5
4.	Early Saxon England	8
5.	Danish and Late Saxon England	12
6.	The Period following the Norman Conquest	15
7.	The Period of the Early Angevin Kings, 1154-1338	22

CHAPTER II

RURAL LIFE AND ORGANIZATION

8.	The Mediæval Village	31
9.	The Vill as an Agricultural System	33
10.	Classes of People on the Manor	39
11.	The Manor Courts	45
12.	The Manor as an Estate of a Lord	49
13.	Bibliography	52

CHAPTER III

TOWN LIFE AND ORGANIZATION

14.	The Town Government	57
15.	The Gild Merchant	59
16.	The Craft Gilds	64
17.	Non-industrial Gilds	71
18.	Bibliography	73

CHAPTER IV

Mediæval Trade and Commerce

		PAGE
19. Markets and Fairs	.	75
20. Trade Relations between Towns	.	79
21. Foreign Trading Relations	.	81
22. The Italian and Eastern Trade	.	84
23. The Flanders Trade and the Staple	.	87
24. The Hanse Trade	.	89
25. Foreigners settled in England	.	90
26. Bibliography	.	94

CHAPTER V

The Black Death and the Peasants' Rebellion

Economic Changes of the Later Fourteenth and Early Fifteenth Centuries

27. National Affairs from 1338 to 1461	.	96
28. The Black Death and its Effects	.	99
29. The Statutes of Laborers	.	106
30. The Peasants' Rebellion of 1381	.	111
31. Commutation of Services	.	125
32. The Abandonment of Demesne Farming	.	128
33. The Decay of Serfdom	.	129
34. Changes in Town Life and Foreign Trade	.	133
35. Bibliography	.	134

CHAPTER VI

The Breaking up of the Mediæval System

Economic Changes of the Later Fifteenth and the Sixteenth Centuries

36. National Affairs from 1461 to 1603	.	136
37. Enclosures	.	141
38. Internal Divisions in the Craft Gilds	.	147
39. Change of Location of Industries	.	151
40. The Influence of the Government on the Gilds	.	154
41. General Causes and Evidences of the Decay of the Gilds	.	159
42. The Growth of Native Commerce	.	161
43. The Merchants Adventurers	.	164
44. Government Encouragement of Commerce	.	167

		PAGE
45.	The Currency	169
46.	Interest	171
47.	Paternal Government	173
48.	Bibliography	176

CHAPTER VII

THE EXPANSION OF ENGLAND

Economic Changes of the Seventeenth and Early Eighteenth Centuries

49.	National Affairs from 1603 to 1760	177
50.	The Extension of Agriculture	183
51.	The Domestic System of Manufactures	185
52.	Commerce under the Navigation Acts	189
53.	Finance	193
54.	Bibliography	198

CHAPTER VIII

THE PERIOD OF THE INDUSTRIAL REVOLUTION

Economic Changes of the Later Eighteenth and Early Nineteenth Centuries

55.	National Affairs from 1760 to 1830	199
56.	The Great Mechanical Inventions	203
57.	The Factory System	212
58.	Iron, Coal, and Transportation	214
59.	The Revival of Enclosures	216
60.	Decay of Domestic Manufacture	220
61.	The *Laissez-faire* Theory	224
62.	Cessation of Government Regulation	228
63.	Individualism	232
64.	Social Conditions at the Beginning of the Nineteenth Century	235
65.	Bibliography	239

CHAPTER IX

THE EXTENSION OF GOVERNMENT CONTROL

Factory Laws, the Modification of Land Ownership, Sanitary Regulations, and New Public Services

66.	National Affairs from 1830 to 1900	240
67.	The Beginning of Factory Legislation	244

Contents

		PAGE
68. Arguments for and against Factory Legislation	. . .	249
69. Factory Legislation to 1847	. .	254
70. The Extension of Factory Legislation .	. . .	256
71. Employers' Liability Acts . . .	. . .	260
72. Preservation of Remaining Open Lands	. . .	262
73. Allotments	. . .	267
74. Small Holdings	. . .	269
75. Government Sanitary Control . .	. . .	271
76. Industries Carried on by Government .	. . .	273
77. Bibliography	. . .	276

CHAPTER X

THE EXTENSION OF VOLUNTARY ASSOCIATION

Trade Unions, Trusts, and Coöperation

78. The Rise of Trade Unions	277
79. Opposition of the Law and of Public Opinion. The Combination Acts	279
80. Legalization and Popular Acceptance of Trade Unions. .	281
81. The Growth of Trade Unions	288
82. Federation of Trade Unions	289
83. Employers' Organizations	293
84. Trusts and Trade Combinations	294
85. Coöperation in Distribution	295
86. Coöperation in Production	300
87. Coöperation in Farming	302
88. Coöperation in Credit	306
89. Profit Sharing	307
90. Socialism	310
91. Bibliography	311

An Introduction to the Industrial and
Social History of England

INDUSTRIAL AND SOCIAL HISTORY OF ENGLAND

CHAPTER I

GROWTH OF THE NATION

To the Middle of the Fourteenth Century

1. The Geography of England. — The British Isles lie northwest of the Continent of Europe. They are separated from it by the Channel and the North Sea, at the narrowest only twenty miles wide, and at the broadest not more than three hundred.

The greatest length of England from north to south is three hundred and sixty-five miles, and its greatest breadth some two hundred and eighty miles. Its area, with Wales, is 58,320 square miles, being somewhat more than one-quarter the size of France or of Germany, just one-half the size of Italy, and somewhat larger than either Pennsylvania or New York.

The backbone of the island is near the western coast, and consists of a body of hard granitic and volcanic rock rising into mountains of two or three thousand feet in height. These do not form one continuous chain but are in several detached groups. On the eastern flank of these mountains and underlying all the rest of the island is a series of stratified rocks. The harder portions of these strata still stand up as long ridges, — the "wolds," "wealds," "moors," and "downs" of the more eastern and southeastern parts of England. The softer strata have been worn away into great broad valleys, furnishing the central and eastern plains or lowlands of the country.

The rivers of the south and of the far north run for the most part by short and direct courses to the sea. The rivers of the midlands are much longer and larger. As a result of the gradual sinking of the island, in recent geological periods the sea has extended some distance up the course of these rivers, making an almost unbroken series of estuaries along the whole coast.

The climate of England is milder and more equable than is indicated by the latitude, which is that of Labrador in the western hemisphere and of Prussia and central Russia on the Continent of Europe. This is due to the fact that the Gulf Stream flows around its southern and western shores, bringing warmth and a superabundance of moisture from the southern Atlantic.

These physical characteristics have been of immense influence on the destinies of England. Her position was far on the outskirts of the world as it was known to ancient and mediæval times, and England played a correspondingly inconspicuous part during those periods. In the habitable world as it has been known since the fifteenth century, on the other hand, that position is a distinctly central one, open alike to the eastern and the western hemisphere, to northern and southern lands.

Her situation of insularity and at the same time of proximity to the Continent laid her open to frequent invasion in early times, but after she secured a navy made her singularly safe from subjugation. It made the development of many of her institutions tardy, yet at the same time gave her the opportunity to borrow and assimilate what she would from the customs of foreign nations. Her separa-

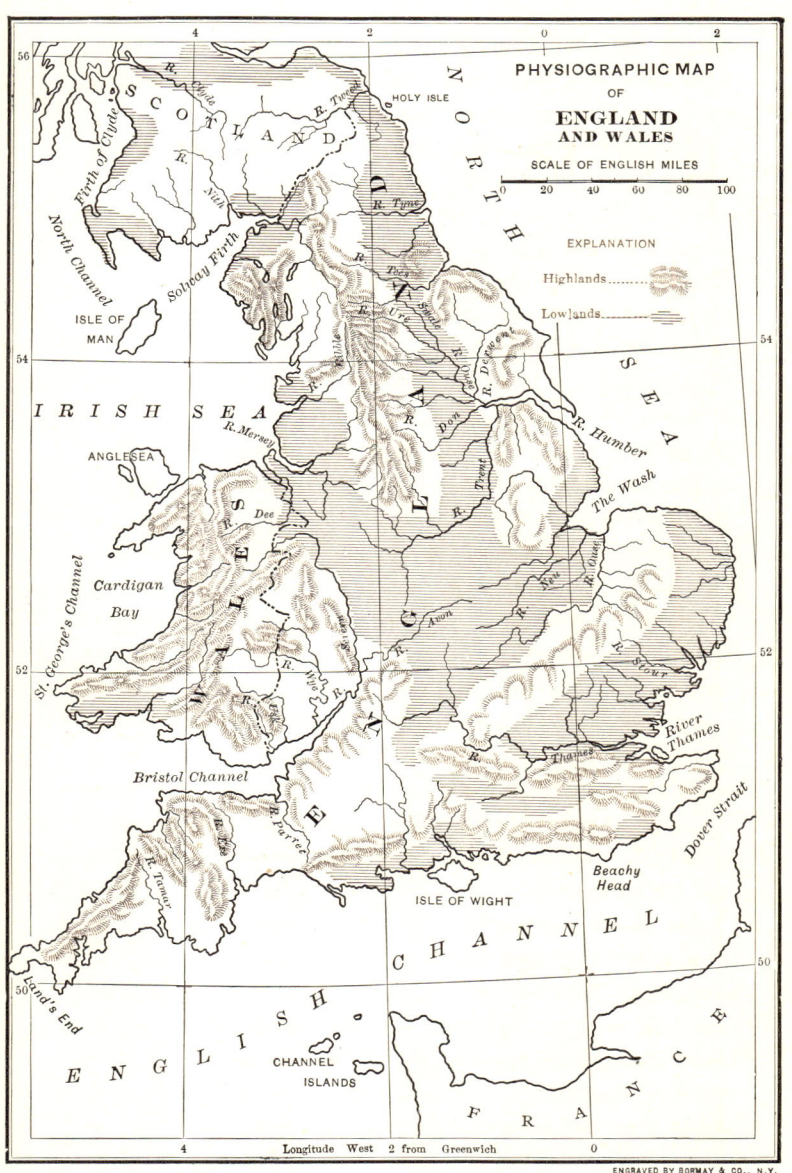

tion by water from the Continent favored a distinct and continuous national life, while her nearness to it allowed her to participate in all the more important influences which affected the nations of central Europe.

Within the mountainous or elevated regions a variety of mineral resources, especially iron, copper, lead, and tin, exist in great abundance, and have been worked from the earliest ages. Potter's clay and salt also exist, the former furnishing the basis of industry for an extensive section of the midlands. By far the most important mineral possession of England, however, is her coal. This exists in the greatest abundance and in a number of sections of the north and west of the country. Practically unknown in the Middle Ages, and only slightly utilized in early modern times, within the eighteenth and nineteenth centuries her coal supply has come to be the principal foundation of England's great manufacturing and commercial development.

The lowlands, which make up far the larger part of the country, are covered with soil which furnishes rich farming areas, though in many places this soil is a heavy and impervious clay, expensive to drain and cultivate. The hard ridges are covered with thin soil only. Many of them therefore remained for a long time covered with forest, and they are devoted even yet to grazing or to occasional cultivation only.

The abundance of harbors and rivers, navigable at least to the small vessels of the Middle Ages, has made a seafaring life natural to a large number of the people, and commercial intercourse comparatively easy with all parts of the country bordering on the coast or on these rivers.

Thus, to sum up these geographical characteristics, the insular situation of England, her location on the earth's surface, and the variety of her material endowments gave her a tolerably well-balanced if somewhat backward economic position during the Middle Ages, and have enabled her since the fifteenth century to pass through a continuous and rapid development, until she has obtained within the nineteenth century, for the time at least, a distinct economic precedency among the nations of the world.

2. Prehistoric Britain. — The materials from which to construct a knowledge of the history of mankind before the time of written records are few and unsatisfactory. They consist for the most part of the remains of dwelling-places, fortifications, and roadways; of weapons, implements, and ornaments lost or abandoned at the time; of burial places and their contents; and of such physical characteristics of later populations as have survived from an early period. Centuries of human habitation of Britain passed away, leaving only such scanty remains and the obscure and doubtful knowledge that can be drawn from them. Through this period, however, successive races seem to have invaded and settled the country, combining with their predecessors, or living alongside of them, or in some cases, perhaps, exterminating them.

When contemporary written records begin, just before the beginning of the Christian era, one race, the Britons, was dominant, and into it had merged to all appearances all others. The Britons were a Celtic people related to the inhabitants of that part of the Continent of Europe which lies nearest to Britain. They were divided into a dozen or more separate tribes, each occupying a distinct part of the country. They lived partly by the pasturing of sheep and cattle, partly by a crude agriculture. They possessed most of the familiar grains and domestic animals, and could weave and dye cloth, make pottery, build boats, forge iron, and work other metals, including tin. They had, however,

Growth of the Nation

no cities, no manufactures beyond the most primitive, and but little foreign trade to connect them with the Continent. At the head of each tribe was a reigning chieftain of limited powers, surrounded by lesser chiefs. The tribes were in a state of incessant warfare one with the other.

3. Roman Britain. — This condition of insular isolation and barbarism was brought to a close in the year 55 B.C. by the invasion of the Roman army. Julius Cæsar, the Roman general who was engaged in the conquest and government of Gaul, or modern France, feared that the Britons might bring aid to certain newly subjected and still restless Gallic tribes. He therefore transported a body of troops across the Channel and fought two campaigns against the tribes in the southeast of Britain. His success in the second campaign was, however, not followed up, and he retired without leaving any permanent garrison in the country. The Britons were then left alone, so far as military invasion was concerned, for almost a century, though in the meantime trade with the adjacent parts of the Continent became more common, and Roman influence showed itself in the manners and customs of the people. In the year 44 A.D., just ninety years after Cæsar's campaigns, the conquest of Britain was resumed by the Roman armies and completed within the next thirty years. Britain now became an integral part of the great, well-ordered, civilized, and wealthy Roman Empire. During the greater part of that long period, Britain enjoyed profound peace, internal and external trade were safe, and much of the culture and refinement of Italy and Gaul must have made their way even to this distant province. A part of the inhabitants adopted the Roman language, dress, customs, and manner of life. Discharged veterans from the Roman legions, wealthy civil officials and merchants, settled permanently in Britain. Several bodies of turbulent tribesmen who had been defeated on the German frontier were transported by the government into Britain. The population must, therefore, have become very mixed, containing representatives of most of the races which had been conquered by the Roman armies. A permanent military force was maintained in Britain with fortified stations along the eastern and southern coast, on the Welsh frontier, and along a series of walls or dikes running across the island from the Tyne to Solway Firth. Excellent roads were constructed through the length and breadth of the land for the use of this military body and to connect the scattered stations. Along these highways population spread and the remains of spacious villas still exist to attest the magnificence of the wealthy provincials. The roads served also as channels of trade by which goods could readily be carried from one part of the country to another. Foreign as well as internal trade became extensive, although exports were mostly of crude natural products, such as hides, skins, and furs, cattle and sheep, grain, pig-iron, lead and tin, hunting-dogs and slaves. The rapid development of towns and cities was a marked characteristic of Roman Britain. Fifty-nine towns or cities of various grades of self-government are named in the Roman survey, and many of these must have been populous, wealthy, and active, judging from the extensive ruins that remain, and the enormous number of Roman coins that have since been found. Christianity was adopted here as in other parts of the Roman Empire, though the extent of its influence is unknown.

During the Roman occupation much waste land was reclaimed. Most of the great valley regions and many of the hillsides had been originally covered with dense forests, swamps spread along the rivers and extended far inland from the coast; so that almost the only parts capable of tillage were the high treeless plains, the hill tops, and certain favored stretches of open country. The reduction of these waste lands to human habitation has been an age-long task. It was begun in prehistoric times, it has been carried further by each successive race, and brought to final completion only within our own century. A share in this work and the great roads were the most permanent results of the Roman period of occupation and government. Throughout the fourth and fifth centuries of the Christian era the Roman administration and society in Britain were evidently disintegrating. Several successive generals of the Roman troops stationed in Britain rose in revolt with their soldiers, declared their independence of Rome, or passed over to the Continent to enter into a struggle for the control of the whole Empire. In 383 and 407 the military forces were suddenly depleted in this way and the provincial government disorganized, while the central government of the Empire was so weak that it was unable to reëstablish a firm administration. During the same period barbarian invaders were making frequent inroads into Britain. The Picts and Scots from modern Scotland, Saxon pirates, and, later, ever increasing swarms of Angles, Jutes, and Frisians from across the North Sea ravaged and ultimately occupied parts of the borders and the coasts. The surviving records of this period of disintegration and reorganization are so few that we are left in all but total ignorance as to what actually occurred. For more than two hundred years we can only guess at the course of events, or infer it from its probable analogy to what we know was occurring in the other parts of the Empire, or from the conditions we find to have been in existence as knowledge of succeeding times becomes somewhat more full. It seems evident that the government of the province of Britain gradually went to pieces, and that that of the different cities or districts followed. Internal dissensions and the lack of military organization and training of the mass of the population probably added to the difficulty of resisting marauding bands of barbarian invaders. These invading bands became larger, and their inroads more frequent and extended, until finally they abandoned their home lands entirely and settled permanently in those districts in which they had broken the resistance of the Roman-British natives. Even while the Empire had been strong the heavy burden of taxation and the severe pressure of administrative regulations had caused a decline in wealth and population. Now disorder, incessant ravages of the barbarians, isolation from other lands, probably famine and pestilence, brought rapid decay to the prosperity and civilization of the country. Cities lost their trade, wealth, and population, and many of them ceased altogether for a time to exist. Britain was rapidly sinking again into a land of barbarism.

4. Early Saxon England. — An increasing number of contemporary records give a somewhat clearer view of the condition of England toward the close of the sixth century. The old Roman organization and civilization had disappeared entirely, and a new race, with a new language, a different religion, another form of government, changed institutions and customs, had taken its place. A number of petty kingdoms had been formed during the fifth and early sixth centuries, each under a king or chieftain, as in the old Celtic times before the Roman invasion, but now of Teutonic or German race. The kings and their followers had come from the northwestern portions of Germany. How far they had destroyed the earlier inhabitants, how far they had simply combined with them or enslaved them, has been a matter of much debate, and one on which discordant opinions are held, even by recent students. It seems likely on the whole that the earlier races, weakened by defeat and by the disappearance of the Roman control, were gradually absorbed and merged into the body of their conquerors; so that the petty Angle and Saxon kings of the sixth and seventh centuries ruled over a mixed race, in which their own was the most influential, though not necessarily the largest element. The arrival from Rome in 597 of Augustine, the first Christian missionary to the now heathen inhabitants of Britain, will serve as a point to mark the completion of the Anglo-Saxon conquest of the country. By this time the new settlers had ceased to come in, and there were along the coast and inland some seven or eight different kingdoms. These were, however, so frequently divided and reunited that no fixed number remained long in existence. The Jutes had established the kingdom of Kent in the southeastern extremity of the island; the South and the West Saxons were established on the southern coast and inland to the valley of the Thames; the East Saxons had a kingdom just north of the mouth of the Thames, and the Middle Saxons held London and the district around. The rest of the island to the north and inland exclusive of what was still unconquered was occupied by various branches of the Angle stock grouped into the kingdoms of East Anglia, Mercia, and Northumbria. During the seventh and eighth centuries there were constant wars of conquest among these kingdoms. Eventually, about 800 A.D., the West Saxon monarchy made itself nominally supreme over all the others. Notwithstanding this political supremacy of the West Saxons, it was the Angles who were the most numerous and widely spread, and who gave their name, England, to the whole land.

Agriculture was at this time almost the sole occupation of the people. The trade and commerce that had centred in the towns and flowed along the Roman roads and across the Channel had long since come to an end with the Roman civilization of which it was a part. In Saxon England cities scarcely existed except as fortified places of defence. The products of each rural district sufficed for its needs in food and in materials for clothing, so that internal trade was but slight. Manufactures were few, partly from lack of skill, partly from lack of demand or appreciation; but weaving, the construction of agricultural implements and weapons, ship-building, and the working of metals had survived from Roman times, or been brought over as part of the stock of knowledge of the invaders. Far the greater part of the population lived in villages, as they probably had done in Roman and in prehistoric times. The village with the surrounding farming lands, woods, and waste grounds made up what was known in later times as the "township."

The form of government in the earlier separate kingdoms, as in the united monarchy after its consolidation, gave limited though constantly increasing powers to the king. A body of nobles known as the "witan" joined with the king in most of the actions of government. The greater part of the small group of government functions which were undertaken in these barbarous times were fulfilled by local gatherings of the principal men. A district formed from a greater or less number of townships, with a meeting for the settlement of disputes, the punishment of crimes, the witnessing of agreements, and other purposes, was known as a "hundred" or a "wapentake." A "shire" was a grouping of hundreds, with a similar gathering of its principal men for judicial, military, and fiscal purposes. Above the shire came the whole kingdom.

The most important occurrences of the early Saxon period were the general adoption of Christianity and the organization of the church. Between A.D. 597 and 650 Christianity gained acceptance through the preaching and influence of missionaries, most of whom were sent from Rome, though some came from Christian Scotland and Ireland. The organization of the church followed closely. It was largely the work of Archbishop Theodore, and was practically complete before the close of the seventh century. By this organization England was divided into seventeen dioceses or church districts, religious affairs in each of these districts being under the supervision of a bishop. The bishop's church, called a "cathedral," was endowed by religious kings and nobles with extensive lands, so that the bishop was a wealthy landed proprietor, in addition to having control of the clergy of his diocese, and exercising a powerful influence over the consciences and actions of its lay population. The bishoprics were grouped into two "provinces," those of Canterbury and York, the bishops of these two dioceses having the higher title of archbishop, and having a certain sort of supervision over the other bishops of their province. Churches were gradually built in the villages, and each township usually became a parish with a regularly established priest. He was supported partly by the produce of the "glebe," or land belonging to the parish church, partly by tithe, a tax estimated at one-tenth of the income of each man's land, partly by the offerings of the people. The bishops, the parish priests, and others connected with the diocese, the cathedral, and the parish churches made up the ordinary or "secular" clergy. There were also many religious men and women who had taken vows to live under special "rules" in religious societies withdrawn from the ordinary life of the world, and were therefore known as "regular" clergy. These were the monks and nuns. In Anglo-Saxon England the regular clergy lived according to the rule of St.

Benedict, and were gathered into groups, some smaller, some larger, but always established in one building, or group of buildings. These monasteries, like the bishoprics, were endowed with lands which were increased from time to time by pious gifts of kings, nobles, and other laymen. Ecclesiastical bodies thus came in time to hold a very considerable share of the land of the country. The wealth and cultivation of the clergy and the desire to adorn and render more attractive their buildings and religious services fostered trade with foreign countries. The intercourse kept up with the church on the Continent also did something to lessen the isolation of England from the rest of the world. To these broadening influences must be added the effect which the Councils made up of churchmen from all England exerted in fostering the tardy growth of the unity of the country.

5. Danish and Late Saxon England. — At the end of the eighth century the Danes or Northmen, the barbarous and heathen inhabitants of the islands and coast-lands of Denmark, Norway, and Sweden, began to make rapid forays into the districts of England which lay near enough to the coasts or rivers to be at their mercy. Soon they became bolder or more numerous and established fortified camps along the English rivers, from which they ravaged the surrounding country. Still later, in the tenth and eleventh centuries, under their own kings as leaders, they became conquerors and permanent settlers of much of the country, and even for a time put a Danish dynasty on the throne to govern English and Danes alike. A succession of kings of the West Saxon line had struggled with varying success to drive the Danes from the country or to limit that portion of it which was under their control; but as a matter of fact the northern, eastern, and central portions of England were for more than a century and a half almost entirely under Danish rule. The constant immigration from Scandinavia during this time added an important element to the population — an element which soon, however, became completely absorbed in the mixed stock of the English people.

The marauding Danish invaders were early followed by fellow-countrymen who were tradesmen and merchants. The Scandinavian countries had developed an early and active trade with the other lands bordering on the Baltic and North seas, and England under Danish influence was drawn into the same lines of commerce. The Danes were also more inclined to town life than the English, so that advantageously situated villages now grew into trading towns, and the sites of some of the old Roman cities began again to be filled with a busy population. With trading came a greater development of handicrafts, so that the population of later Anglo-Saxon England had somewhat varied occupations and means of support, instead of being exclusively agricultural, as in earlier centuries.

During these later centuries of the Saxon period, from 800 to 1066, the most conspicuous and most influential ruler was King Alfred. When he became king, in 871, the Danish invaders were so completely triumphant as to force him to flee with a few followers to the forest as a temporary refuge. He soon emerged, however, with the nucleus of an army and, during his reign, which continued till 901, defeated the Danes repeatedly, obtained their acceptance of Christianity, forced upon them a treaty which restricted their rule to the northeastern shires, and transmitted to his son a military and naval organization which enabled him to win back much even of this part of England. He introduced greater order, prosperity, and piety into the church, and partly by his own writing, partly by his patronage of learned men, reawakened an interest in Anglo-Saxon literature and in learning which the ravages of the Danes and the demoralization of the country had gone far to destroy. Alfred, besides his actual work as king, impressed the recognition of his fine nature and strong character deeply on the men of his time and the memory of all subsequent times.

The power of the kingship in the Anglo-Saxon system of government was strengthened by the life and work of such kings as Alfred and some of his successors. There were other causes also which were tending to make the central government more of a reality. A national taxation, the Danegeld, was introduced for the purpose of ransoming the country from the Danes; the grant of lands by the king brought many persons through the country into closer relations with him; the royal judicial powers tended to increase with the development of law and civilization; the work of government was carried on by better-trained officials.

On the other hand, a custom grew up in the tenth and early eleventh century of placing whole groups of shires under the government of great earls or viceroys, whose subjection to the central government of the king was but scant. Church bodies and others who had received large grants of land from the king were also coming to exercise over their tenants judicial, fiscal, and probably even military powers, which would seem more properly to belong to government officials. The result was that although the central government as compared with the local government of shires and hundreds was growing more active, the king's power as compared with the personal power of the great nobles was becoming less strong. Violence was common, and there were but few signs of advancing prosperity or civilization, when an entirely new set of influences came into existence with the conquest by the duke of Normandy in the year 1066.

6. The Period following the Norman Conquest. — Normandy was a province of France lying along the shore of the English Channel. Its line of dukes and at least a considerable proportion of its people were of the same Scandinavian or Norse race which made up such a large element in the population of England. They had, however, learned more of the arts of life and of government from the more successfully preserved civilization of the Continent. The relations between England and Normandy began to be somewhat close in the early part of the eleventh century; the fugitive king of England, Ethelred, having taken refuge there, and marrying the sister of the duke. Edward the Confessor, their son, who was subsequently restored to the English throne, was brought up in Normandy, used the French language, and was accompanied on his return by Norman followers. Nine years after the accession of Edward, in 1051, William, the duke of Normandy, visited England and is said to have obtained a promise that he should receive the crown on the death of Edward, who had no direct heir. Accordingly, in 1065, when Edward died and Harold, a great English earl, was chosen king, William immediately asserted his claim and made strenuous military preparations for enforcing it. He took an army across the Channel in 1066, as Cæsar had done more than a thousand years before, and at the battle of Hastings or Senlac defeated the English army, King Harold himself being killed in the engagement. William then pressed on toward London, preventing any gathering of new forces, and obtained his recognition as king. He was crowned on Christmas Day, 1066. During the next five years he put down a series of rebellions on the part of the native English, after which he and his descendants were acknowledged as sole kings of England.

The Norman Conquest was not, however, a mere change of dynasty. It led to at least three other changes of the utmost importance. It added a new element to the population, it brought England into contact with the central and southern countries of the Continent, instead of merely with the northern as before, and it made the central government of the country vastly stronger. There is no satisfactory means of discovering how many Normans and others from across the Channel migrated into England with the Conqueror or in the wake of the Conquest, but there is no doubt that the number was large and their influence more than proportionate to their numbers. Within the lifetime of William, whose death occurred in 1087, of his two sons, William II and Henry I, and the nominal reign of Stephen extending to 1154, the whole body of the nobility, the bishops and abbots, and the government officials had come to be of Norman or other continental origin. Besides these the architects and artisans who built the castles and fortresses, and the cathedrals, abbeys, and parish churches, whose erection throughout the land was such a marked characteristic of the period, were immigrants from Normandy. Merchants from the Norman cities of Rouen and Caen came to settle in London and other English cities, and weavers from Flanders were settled in various towns and even rural districts. For a short time these newcomers remained a separate people, but before the twelfth century was over they had become for the most part indistinguishable from the great mass of the English people amongst whom they had come. They had nevertheless made that people stronger, more vigorous, more active-minded, and more varied in their occupations and interests.

King William and his successors retained their continental dominions and even extended them after their acquisition of the English kingdom, so that trade between the two sides of the Channel was more natural and easy than before. The strong government of the Norman kings gave protection and encouragement to this commerce, and by keeping down the violence of the nobles favored trade within the country. The English towns had been growing in number, size, and wealth in the years just before the Conquest. The contests of the years immediately following 1066 led to a short period of decay, but very soon increasing trade and handicraft led to still greater progress. London, especially, now made good its position as one of the great cities of Europe, and that preëminence among English towns which it has never since lost. The fishing and seaport towns along the southern and eastern coast also, and even a number of inland towns, came to hold a much more influential place in the nation than they had possessed in the Anglo-Saxon period.

The increased power of the monarchy arose partly from its military character as based upon a conquest of the country, partly from the personal character of William and his immediate successors, partly from the more effective machinery for administration of the affairs of government, which was either brought over from Normandy or developed in England. A body of trained, skilful government officials now existed, who were able to carry out the wishes of the king, collect his revenues, administer justice, gather armies, and in other ways make his rule effective to an extent unknown in the preceding period. The sheriffs, who had already existed as royal representatives in the shires in Anglo-Saxon times, now possessed far more extensive powers, and came up to Westminster to report and to present their financial accounts to the royal exchequer twice a year. Royal officials acting as judges not only settled an increasingly large number of cases that were brought before them at the king's court, but travelled through the country, trying suits and punishing criminals in the different shires. The king's income was vastly larger than that of the Anglo-Saxon monarchs had been. The old Danegeld was still collected from time to time, though under a different name, and the king's position as landlord of the men who had received the lands confiscated at the Conquest was utilized to obtain additional payments.

Perhaps the greatest proof of the power and efficiency of the government in the Norman period was the compilation of the great body of statistics known as "Domesday Book." In 1085 King William sent commissioners to every part of England to collect a variety of information about the financial conditions on which estates were held, their value, and fitness for further taxation. The information obtained from this investigation was drawn up in order and written in two large manuscript volumes which still exist in the Public Record Office at London. It is a much more extensive body of information than was collected for any other country of Europe until many centuries afterward. Yet its statements, though detailed and exact and of great interest from many points of view, are disappointing to the student of history. They were obtained for the financial purposes of government, and cannot be made to give the clear picture of the life of the people and of the relations of different classes to one another which would be so welcome, and which is so easily obtained from the great variety of more private documents which came into existence a century and a half later.

The church during this period was not relatively so conspicuous as during Saxon times, but the number of the clergy, both secular and regular, was very large, the bishops and abbots powerful, and the number of monasteries and nunneries increasing. The most important ecclesiastical change was the development of church courts. The bishops or their representatives began to hold courts for the trial of churchmen, the settlement of such suits as churchmen were parties to, and the decision of cases in certain fields of law. This gave the church a new influence, in addition to that which it held from its spiritual duties, from its position as landlord over such extensive tracts, and from the superior enlightenment and mental ability of its prominent officials, but it also gave greater occasion for conflict with the civil government and with private persons.

After the death of Henry I in 1135 a miserable period of confusion and violence ensued. Civil war broke out between two claimants for the crown, Stephen the grandson, and Matilda the granddaughter, of William the Conqueror. The organization of government was allowed to fall into disorder, and but little effort was made to collect the royal revenue, to fulfil the newly acquired judicial duties, or to insist upon order being preserved in the country. The nobles took opposite sides in the contest for the crown, and made use of the weakness of government to act as if they were themselves sovereigns over their estates and the country adjacent to their castles with no ruler above them. Private warfare, oppression of less powerful men, seizure of property, went on unchecked. Every baron's castle became an independent establishment carried on in accordance only with the unbridled will of its lord, as if there were no law and no central authority to which he must bow. The will of the lord was often one of reckless violence, and there was more disorder and suffering in England than at any time since the ravages of the Danes.

In Anglo-Saxon times, when a weak king appeared, the shire moots, or the rulers of groups of shires, exercised the authority which the central government had lost. In the twelfth century, when the power of the royal government was similarly diminished through the weakness of Stephen and the confusions of the civil war, it was a certain class of men, the great nobles, that fell heir to the lost strength of government. This was because of the development of feudalism during the intervening time. The greater landholders had come to exercise over those who held land from them certain powers which in modern times belong to the officers of government only. A landlord could call upon his tenants for military service to him, and for the contribution of money for his expenses; he held a court to decide suits between one tenant and another, and frequently to punish their crimes and misdemeanors; in case of the death of a tenant leaving a minor heir, his landlord became guardian and temporary holder of the land, and if there were no heirs, the land reverted to him, not to the national government. These relations which the great landholders held toward their tenants, the latter, who often themselves were landlords over whole townships or other great tracts of land with their population, held toward their tenants. Sometimes these subtenants granted land to others below them, and over these the last landlord also exercised feudal rights, and so on till the actual occupants and cultivators of the soil were reached. The great nobles had thus come to stand in a middle position. Above them was the king, below them these successive stages of tenants and subtenants. Their tenants owed to them the same financial and political services and duties as they owed to the king. From the time of the Norman Conquest, all land in England was looked upon as being held from the king directly by a comparatively few, and indirectly through them by all others who held land at all. Moreover, from a time at least soon after the Norman Conquest, the services and payments above mentioned came to be recognized as due from all tenants to their lords, and were gradually systematized and defined. Each person or ecclesiastical body that held land from the king owed him the military service of a certain number of knights or armed horse soldiers. The period for which this service was owed was generally estimated as forty days once a year. Subtenants similarly owed military service to their landlords, though in the lesser grades this was almost invariably commuted for money. "Wardship and marriage" was the expression applied to the right of the lord to the guardianship of the estate of a minor heir of his tenant, and to the choice of a husband or wife for the heir when he came of proper age. This right also was early turned into the form of a money consideration. There were a number of money payments pure and simple. "Relief" was a payment to the landlord, usually of a year's income of the estate, made by an heir on obtaining his inheritance. There were three generally acknowledged "aids" or payments of a set sum in proportion to the amount of land held. These were on the occasion of the knighting of the lord's son, of the marriage of his daughter, and for his ransom in case he was captured in war. Land could be confiscated if the tenant violated his duties to his landlord, and it "escheated" to the lord in case of failure of heirs. Every tenant was bound to attend his landlord to help form a court for judicial work, and to submit to the judgment of a court of his fellow-tenants for his own affairs.

In addition to the relations of landlord and tenant and to the power of jurisdiction, taxation, and military service which landlords exercised over their tenants, there was considered to be a close personal relationship between them. Every tenant on obtaining his land went through a ceremony known as "homage," by which he promised faithfulness and service to his lord, vowing on his knees to be his man. The lord in return promised faithfulness, protection, and justice to his tenant. It was this combination of landholding, political rights, and sworn personal fidelity that made up feudalism. It existed in this sense in England from the later Saxon period till late in the Middle Ages, and even in some of its characteristics to quite modern times. The conquest by William of Normandy through the wholesale confiscation and regrant of lands, and through his military arrangements, brought about an almost sudden development and spread of feudalism in England, and it was rapidly systematized and completed in the reigns of his two sons. By its very nature feudalism gives great powers to the higher ranks of the nobility, the great landholders. Under the early Norman kings, however, their strength was kept in tolerably complete check. The anarchy of the reign of Stephen was an indication of the natural tendencies of feudalism without a vigorous king. This time of confusion when, as the contemporary chronicle says, "every man did that which was good in his own eyes," was brought to an end by the accession to the throne of Henry II, a man whose personal abilities and previous training enabled him to bring the royal authority to greater strength than ever, and to put an end to the oppressions of the turbulent nobles.

7. The Period of the Early Angevin Kings, 1154–1338. — The two centuries which now followed saw either the completion or the initiation of most of the characteristics of the English race with which we are familiar in historic times.

The race, the language, the law, and the political organization have remained fundamentally the same as they became during the thirteenth and fourteenth centuries. No considerable new addition was made to the population, and the elements which it already contained became so thoroughly fused that it has always since been practically a homogeneous body. The Latin language remained through this whole period and till long afterward the principal language of records, documents, and the affairs of the church. French continued to be the language of the daily intercourse of the upper classes, of the pleadings in the law courts, and of certain documents and records. But English was taking its modern form, asserting itself as the real national language, and by the close of this period had come into general use for the vast majority of purposes. Within the twelfth and thirteenth centuries the Universities of Oxford and Cambridge grew up, and within the fourteenth took their later shape of self-governing groups of colleges. Successive orders of religious men and women were formed under rules intended to overcome the defects which had appeared in the early Benedictine rule. The organized church became more and more powerful, and disputes constantly arose as to the limits between its power and that of the ordinary government. The question was complicated from the fact that the English Church was but one branch of the general church of Western Christendom, whose centre and principal authority was vested in the Pope at Rome. One of the most serious of these conflicts was between King Henry II and Thomas, archbishop of Canterbury, principally on the question of how far clergymen should be subject to the same laws as laymen. The personal dispute ended in the murder of the archbishop, in 1170, but the controversy itself got no farther than a compromise. A contest broke out between King John and the Pope in 1205 as to the right of the king to dictate the selection of a new archbishop of Canterbury. By 1213 the various forms of influence which the church could bring to bear were successful in forcing the king to give way. He therefore made humble apologies and accepted the nominee of the Pope for the office. Later in the thirteenth century there was much popular opposition to papal taxation of England.

In the reign of Henry II, the conquest of Ireland was begun. In 1283 Edward I, great-grandson of Henry, completed the conquest of Wales, which had remained incompletely conquered from Roman times onward. In 1292 Edward began that interference in the affairs of Scotland which led on to long wars and a nominal conquest. For a while therefore it seemed that England was about to create a single monarchy out of the whole of the British Islands. Moreover, Henry II was already count of Anjou and Maine by inheritance from his father when he became duke of Normandy and king of England by inheritance from his mother. He also obtained control of almost all the remainder of the western and southern provinces of France by his marriage with Eleanor of Aquitaine. It seemed, therefore, that England might become the centre of a considerable empire composed partly of districts on the Continent, partly of the British Islands. As a matter of fact, Wales long remained separated from England in organization and feeling, little progress was made with the real conquest of Ireland till in the sixteenth century, and the absorption of Scotland failed entirely. King John, in 1204, lost most of the possessions of the English kings south of the Channel and they were not regained within this period. The unification of the English government and people really occurred during this period, but it was only within the boundaries which were then as now known as England.

Growth of the Nation

Henry II was a vigorous, clear-headed, far-sighted ruler. He not only put down the rebellious barons with a strong hand, and restored the old royal institutions, as already stated, but added new powers of great importance, especially in the organization of the courts of justice. He changed the occasional visits of royal officials to different parts of the country to regular periodical circuits, the kingdom being divided into districts in each of which a group of judges held court at least once in each year. In 1166, by the Assize of Clarendon, he made provision for a sworn body of men in each neighborhood to bring accusations against criminals, thus making the beginning of the grand jury system. He also provided that a group of men should be put upon their oath to give a decision in a dispute about the possession of land, if either one of the claimants asked for it, thus introducing the first form of the trial by jury. The decisions of the judges within this period came to be so consistent and so well recorded as to make the foundation of the Common Law the basis of modern law in all English-speaking countries.

Henry's successor was his son Richard I, whose government was quite unimportant except for the romantic personal adventures of the king when on a crusade, and in his continental dominions. Henry's second son John reigned from 1199 to 1216. Although of good natural abilities, he was extraordinarily indolent, mean, treacherous, and obstinate. By his inactivity during a long quarrel with the king of France he lost all his provinces on the Continent, except those in the far south. His contest with the Pope had ended in failure and humiliation. He had angered the barons by arbitrary taxation and by many individual acts of outrage or oppression. Finally he had alienated the affections of the mass of the population by introducing foreign mercenaries to support his tyranny and permitting to them unbridled excess and violence. As a result of this wide-spread unpopularity, a rebellion was organized, including almost the whole of the baronage of England, guided by the counsels of Stephen Langton, archbishop of Canterbury, and supported by the citizens of London. The indefiniteness of feudal relations was a constant temptation to kings and other lords to carry their exactions and demands upon their tenants to an unreasonable and oppressive length. Henry I, on his accession in 1100, in order to gain popularity, had voluntarily granted a charter reciting a number of these forms of oppression and promising to put an end to them. The rebellious barons now took this old charter as a basis, added to it many points which had become questions of dispute during the century since it had been granted, and others which were of special interest to townsmen and the middle and even lower classes. They then demanded the king's promise to issue a charter containing these points. John resisted for a while, but at last gave way and signed the document which has since been known as the "Great Charter," or Magna Carta. This has always been considered as, in a certain sense, the guarantee of English liberties and the foundation of the settled constitution of the kingdom. The fact that it was forced from a reluctant king by those who spoke for the whole nation, that it placed definite limitations on his power, and that it was confirmed again and again by later kings, has done more to give it this position than its temporary and in many cases insignificant provisions, accompanied only by a comparatively few statements of general principles.

The beginnings of the construction of the English parliamentary constitution fall within the next reign, that of John's son, Henry III, 1216–1272. He was a child at his accession, and when he became a man proved to have but few qualities which would enable him to exercise a real control over the course of events. Conflicts were constant between the king and confederations of the barons, for the greater part of the time under the leadership of Simon de Montfort, earl of Leicester. The special points of difference were the king's preference for foreign adventurers in his distribution of offices, his unrestrained munificence to them, their insolence and oppression relying on the king's support, the financial demands which were constantly being made, and the king's encouragement of the high claims and pecuniary exactions of the Pope. At first these conflicts took the form of disputes in the Great Council, but ultimately they led to another outbreak of civil war. The Great Council of the kingdom was a gathering of the nobles, bishops, and abbots summoned by the king from time to time for advice and participation in the more important work of government. It had always existed in one form or another, extending back continuously to the "witenagemot" of the Anglo-Saxons. During the reign of Henry the name "Parliament" was coming to be more regularly applied to it, its meetings were more frequent and its self-assertion more vigorous. But most important of all, a new class of members was added to it. In 1265, in addition to the nobles and great prelates, the sheriffs were ordered to see that two knights were selected from each of their shires, and two citizens from each of a long list of the larger towns, to attend and take part in the discussions of Parliament. This plan was not continued regularly at first, but Henry's successor, Edward I, who reigned from 1272 to 1307, adopted it deliberately, and from 1295 forward the "Commons," as they came to be called, were always included in Parliament. Within the next century a custom arose according to which the representatives of the shires and the towns sat in a separate body from the nobles and churchmen, so that Parliament took on its modern form of two houses, the House of Lords and the House of Commons.

Until this time and long afterward the personal character and abilities of the king were far the most important single factor in the growth of the nation. Edward I was one of the greatest of English kings, ranking with Alfred, William the Conqueror, and Henry II. His conquests of Wales and of Scotland have already been mentioned, and these with the preparation they involved and a war with France into which he was drawn necessarily occupied the greater part of his time and energy. But he found the time to introduce good order and control into the government in all its branches; to make a great investigation into the judicial and administrative system, the results of which, commonly known as the "Hundred Rolls," are comparable to Domesday Book in extent and character; to develop the organization of Parliament, and above all to enact through it a series of great reforming statutes. The most important of these were the First and Second Statutes of Westminster, in 1275 and 1285, which made provisions for good order in the country, for the protection of merchants, and for other objects; the Statute of Mortmain, passed in 1279, which put a partial stop to injurious gifts of land to the church, and the Statute *Quia Emptores*, passed in 1290, which was intended to prevent the excessive multiplication of subtenants. This was done by providing that whenever in the future any landholder should dispose of a piece of land it should be held from the same lord the grantor had held it from, not from the grantor himself. He also gave more liberal charters to the towns, privileges to foreign merchants, and constant encouragement to trade. The king's firm hand and prudent judgment were felt in a wide circle of regulations applying to taxes, markets and fairs, the purchase of royal supplies, the currency, the administration of local justice, and many other fields. Yet after all it was the organization of Parliament that was the most important work of Edward's reign. This completed the unification of the country. The English people were now one race, under one law, with one Parliament representing all parts of the country. It was possible now for the whole nation to act as a unit, and for laws to be passed which would apply to the whole country and draw its different sections continually more closely together. National growth was now possible in a sense in which it had not been before.

The reign of Edward II, like his own character, was insignificant compared with that of his father. He was deposed in 1327, and his son, Edward III, came to the throne as a boy of fourteen years. The first years of his reign were also relatively unimportant. By the time he reached his majority, however, other events were imminent which for the next century or more gave a new direction to the principal interests and energies of England. A description of these events will be given in a later chapter.

For the greater part of the long period which has now been sketched in outline it is almost solely the political and ecclesiastical events and certain personal experiences which have left their records in history. We can obtain but vague outlines of the actual life of the people. An important Anglo-Saxon document describes the organization of a great landed estate, and from Domesday Book and other early Norman records may be drawn certain inferences as to the degree of freedom of the masses of the people and certain facts as to agriculture and trade. From the increasing body of public records in the twelfth century can be gathered detached pieces of information as to actual social and economic conditions, but the knowledge that can be obtained is even yet slight and uncertain. With the thirteenth century, however, all this is changed. During the latter part of the period just described, that is to say the reigns of Henry III and the three Edwards, we have almost as full knowledge of economic as of political conditions, of the life of the mass of the people as of that of courtiers and ecclesiastics. From a time for which 1250 may be taken as an approximate date, written documents began to be so numerous, so varied, and so full of information as to the affairs of private life, that it becomes possible to obtain a comparatively full and clear knowledge of the methods of agriculture, handicraft, and commerce, of the classes of society, the prevailing customs and ideas, and in general of the mode of life and social organization of the mass of the people, this being the principal subject of economic and social history. The next three chapters will therefore be devoted respectively to a description of rural life, of town life, and of trading relations, as they were during the century from 1250 to 1350, while the succeeding chapters will trace the main lines of economic and social change during succeeding periods down to the present time.

CHAPTER II

RURAL LIFE AND ORGANIZATION

8. The Mediæval Village. — In the Middle Ages in the greater part of England all country life was village life. The farmhouses were not isolated or separated from one another by surrounding fields, as they are so generally in modern times, but were gathered into villages. Each village was surrounded by arable lands, meadows, pastures, and woods which spread away till they reached the confines of the similar fields of the next adjacent village. Such an agricultural village with its population and its surrounding lands is usually spoken of as a "vill." The word "manor" is also applied to it, though this word is also used in other senses, and has differed in meaning at different periods. The word "hamlet" means a smaller group of houses separated from but forming in some respects a part of a vill or manor.

The village consisted of a group of houses ranging in number from ten or twelve to as many as fifty or perhaps even more, grouped around what in later times would be called a "village green," or along two or three intersecting lanes. The houses were small, thatch-roofed, and one-roomed, and doubtless very miserable. Such buildings as existed for the protection of cattle or the preservation of crops were closely connected with the dwelling portions of the houses. In many cases they were under the same roof. Each vill possessed its church, which was generally, though by no means always, close to the houses of the village. There was usually a manor house, which varied in size from an actual castle to a building of a character scarcely distinguishable from the primitive houses of the villagers. This might be occupied regularly or occasionally by the lord of the manor, but might otherwise be inhabited by the steward or by a tenant, or perhaps only serve as the gathering place of the manor courts.

Connected with the manor house was an enclosure or courtyard commonly surrounded by buildings for general

THIRTEENTH CENTURY MANOR HOUSE, MILLICHOPE, SHROPSHIRE.
(Wright, *History of Domestic Manners and Sentiments*.)

farm purposes and for cooking or brewing. A garden o orchard was often attached.

The location of the vill was almost invariably such that a stream with its border meadows passed through or along its confines, the mill being often the only building that lay detached from the village group. A greater or less extent of woodland is also constantly mentioned.

The vill was thus made up of the group of houses of the villagers including the parish church and the manor house, all surrounded by a wide tract of arable land, meadow, pasture, and woods. Where the lands were extensive there might perhaps be a small group of houses forming a separate hamlet at some distance from the village, and occasionally a detached mill, grange, or other building. Its characteristic appearance, however, must have been that of a close group of buildings surrounded by an extensive tract of open land.

THIRTEENTH CENTURY MANOR HOUSE, BOOTHBY PAGNELL, LINCOLNSHIRE.

(Turner, *Domestic Architecture in England*.)

9. The Vill as an Agricultural System. — The support of the vill was in its agriculture. The plan by which the lands of the whole group of cultivators lay together in a large tract surrounding the village is spoken of as the " open field " system. The arable portions of this were ploughed in pieces equalling approximately acres, half-acres, or quarter-acres.

The mediæval English acre was a long narrow strip forty rods in length and four rods in width, a half-acre or quarter-acre being of the same length, but of two rods or one rod in width. The rod was of different lengths in different parts of the country, depending on local custom, but the most common length was that prescribed by statute, that is to say, sixteen and a half feet. The length of the acre, forty

VILLAGE WITH OPEN FIELDS, NÖRTERSHAUSEN, NEAR COBLENTZ, GERMANY.

(From a photograph taken in 1894.)

rods, has given rise to one of the familiar units of length, the furlong, that is, a "furrow-long," or the length of a furrow. A rood is a piece of land one rod wide and forty rods long, that is, the fourth of an acre. A series of such strips were ploughed up successively, being separated from each other either by leaving the width of a furrow or two unploughed, or by marking the division with stones, or perhaps by simply throwing the first furrow of the next strip in the opposite direction when it was ploughed. When an unploughed border was left covered with grass or stones, it was called a "balk." A number of such acres or fractions of acres with their slight dividing ridges thus lay alongside

VILLAGE WITH OPEN FIELDS, UDENHAUSEN, NEAR COBLENTZ, GERMANY.

(From a photograph taken in 1894.)

of one another in a group, the number being defined by the configuration of the ground, by a traditional division among a given number of tenants, or by some other cause. Other groups of strips lay at right angles or inclined to these, so that the whole arable land of the village when ploughed or under cultivation had, like many French, German, or Swiss landscapes at the present time, something of the appearance of a great irregular checker-board or patchwork quilt, each large square being divided in one direction by parallel lines. Usually the cultivated open fields belonging to a village were divided into three or more large tracts or fields and these were cultivated according to some established rotation of crops. The most common of these was the three-field system, by which in any one year all the strips in one tract or field would be planted with wheat, rye, or some other crop which is planted in the fall and harvested the next summer; a second great field would be planted with oats, barley, peas, or some such crop as is planted in the spring and harvested in the fall; the third field would be fallow, recuperating its fertility. The next year all the acres in the field which had lain fallow the year before might be planted with a fall crop, the wheat field of the previous year being planted with a spring crop, and the oats field in its turn now lying uncultivated for a year. The third year a further exchange would be made by which a fall crop would succeed the fallow of that year and the spring crop of the previous year, a spring crop would succeed the last year's fall crop and the field from which the spring crop was taken now it its turn would enjoy a fallow year. In the fourth year the rotation would begin over again.

Agriculture was extremely crude. But eight or nine bushels of wheat or rye were expected from an acre, where now in England the average is thirty. The plough regularly required eight draught animals, usually oxen, in breaking up the ground, though lighter ploughs were used in subsequent cultivation. The breed of all farm animals was small, carts were few and cumbrous, the harvesting of grain was done with a sickle, and the mowing of grass with a short, straight scythe. The distance of the outlying parts of the fields from the farm buildings of the village added its share to the laboriousness of agricultural life.

MODERN PLOUGHING WITH SIX OXEN IN SUSSEX.

(Hudson, W. H.: *Nature in Downland.* Published by Longmans, Green & Co.)

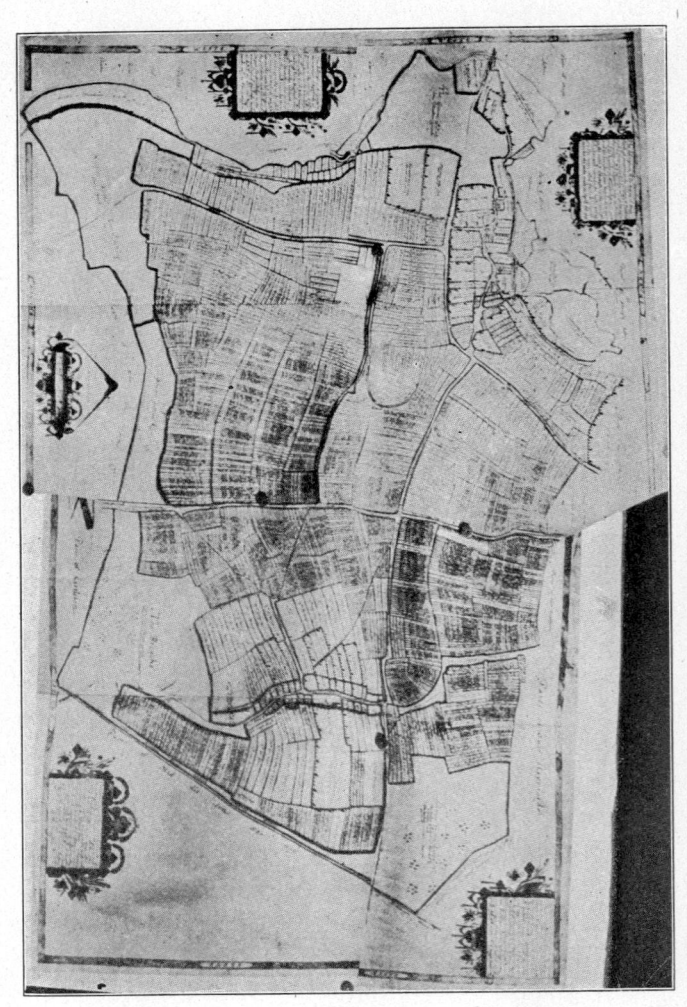

OPEN FIELDS OF HAYFORD BRIDGE, OXFORDSHIRE, 1607.

(Facsimile map published by the University of Oxford.)

The variety of food crops raised was small. Potatoes were of course unknown, and other root crops and fresh vegetables apparently were little cultivated. Wheat and rye of several varieties were raised as bread-stuff, barley and some other grains for the brewing of beer. Field peas and beans were raised, sometimes for food, but generally as forage for cattle. The main supply of winter forage for the farm animals had, however, to be secured in the form of hay, and for this reliance was placed entirely on the natural meadows, as no clover or grasses which could be artificially raised on dry ground were yet known. Meadow land was constantly estimated at twice the value of arable ground or more. To obtain a sufficient support for the oxen, horses, and breeding animals through the winter required, therefore, a constant struggle. Owing to this difficulty animals that were to be used for food purposes were regularly killed in the fall and salted down. Much of the unhealthiness of mediæval life is no doubt attributable to the use of salt meat as so large a part of what was at best a very monotonous diet.

Summer pasture for the horses, cattle, sheep, and swine of the village was found partly on the arable land after the grain crops had been taken off, or while it was lying fallow. Since all the acres in any one great field were planted with the same crop, this would be taken off from the whole expanse at practically the same time, and the animals of the whole village might then wander over it, feeding on the stubble, the grass of the balks, and such other growth as sprung up before the next ploughing, or before freezing weather. Pasturage was also found on the meadows after the hay had been cut. But the largest amount of all was on the "common pasture," the uncultivated land and woods which in the thirteenth century was still sufficiently abundant in most parts of England to be found in considerable extent on almost every manor. Pasturage in all these forms was for the most part common for all the animals of the vill, which were sent out under the care of shepherds or other guardians. There were, however, sometimes enclosed pieces of pasture land in the possession of the lord of the manor or of individual villagers.

The land of the vill was held and cultivated according to a system of scattered acres. That is to say, the land held by any one man was not all in one place, but scattered through various parts of the open fields of the vill. He would have an acre or two, or perhaps only a part of an acre, in one place, another strip not adjacent to it, but somewhere else in the fields, still another somewhere else, and so on for his whole holding, while the neighbor whose house was next to his in the village would have pieces of land similarly scattered through the fields, and in many cases probably have them adjacent to his. The result was that the various acres or other parts of any one man's holding were mingled apparently inextricably with those of other men, customary familiarity only distinguishing which pieces belonged to each villager.

In some manors there was total irregularity as to the number of acres in the occupation of any one man; in others there was a striking regularity. The typical holding, the group of scattered acres cultivated by one man or held by some two or three in common, was known as a "virgate," or by some equivalent term, and although of no universal equality, was more frequently of thirty acres than of any other number. Usually one finds on a given manor that ten or fifteen of the villagers have each a virgate of a given number of acres, several more have each a half virgate or a quarter. Occasionally, on the other hand, each of them has a different number of acres. In almost all cases, however, the agricultural holdings of the villagers were relatively small. For instance, on a certain manor in Norfolk there were thirty-six holdings, twenty of them below ten acres, eight between ten and twenty, six between twenty and thirty, and two between thirty and forty. On another, in Essex, there were nine holdings of five acres each, two of six, twelve of ten, three of twelve, one of eighteen, four of twenty, one of forty, and one of fifty. Sometimes larger holdings in the hands of individual tenants are to be found, rising to one hundred acres or more. Still these were quite exceptional and the mass of the villagers had very small groups of acres in their possession.

It is to be noted next that a large proportion of the cultivated strips were not held in virgates or otherwise by the villagers at all, but were in the direct possession and cultivation of the lord of the manor. This land held directly by the lord of the manor and cultivated for him was called the "demesne," and frequently included one-half or even a larger proportion of all the land of the vill. Much of the meadow and pasture land, and frequently all of the woods, was included in the demesne. Some of the demesne land was detached from the land of the villagers, enclosed and separately cultivated or pastured; but for the most part it lay scattered through the same open fields and was cultivated by the same methods and according to the same rotation as the land of the small tenants of the vill, though it was kept under separate management.

10. Classes of People on the Manor. — Every manor was in the hands of a lord. He might be a knight, esquire, or mere freeman, but in the great majority of cases the lord of the manor was a nobleman, a bishop, abbot, or other ecclesiastical official, or the king. But whether the manor was the whole estate of a man of the lesser gentry, or merely one part of the possessions of a great baron, an ecclesiastical corporation, or the crown, the relation between its possessor as lord of the manor and the other inhabitants as his tenants was the same. In the former case he was usually resident upon the manor; in the latter the individual or corporate lord was represented by a steward or other official who made occasional visits, and frequently, on large manors, by a resident bailiff. There was also almost universally a reeve, who was chosen from among the tenants and who had to carry on the demesne farm in the interests of the lord.

SEAL, WITH REPRESENTATION OF A MANOR HOUSE.

(Turner, *Domestic Architecture in England*.)

The tenants of the manor, ranging from holders of considerable amounts of land, perhaps as much as a hundred acres, through various gradations down to mere cotters, who held no more than a cottage with perhaps a half-acre or a rood of land, or even with no land at all, are usually grouped in the "extents" or contemporary descriptions of the manors and their inhabitants into several distinct classes. Some are described as free tenants, or tenants holding freely. Others, and usually the largest class, are called villains, or customary tenants. Some, holding only a half or a quarter virgate, are spoken of as half or quarter villains. Again, a numerous class are described by some name indicating that they hold only a dwelling-house, or at least that their holding of land is but slight. These are generally spoken of as cotters.

All these tenants hold land from the lord of the manor and make payments and perform services in return for their land. The free tenants most commonly make payments in money only. At special periods in the year they give a certain number of shillings or pence to the lord. Occasionally they are required to make some payment in kind, a cock or a hen, some eggs, or other articles of consumption. These money payments and payments of articles of money value are called "rents of assize," or established rents. Not unusually, however, the free tenant has to furnish *precariæ* or "boon-works" to the lord. That is, he must, either in his own person or through a man hired for the purpose, furnish one or more days' labor at the specially busy seasons of the year, at fall and spring ploughing, at mowing or harvest time. Free tenants were also frequently bound to pay relief and heriot. Relief was a sum of money paid to the lord by an heir on obtaining land by inheritance. Custom very generally established the amount to be paid as the equivalent of one year's ordinary payments. Heriot was a payment made in kind or in money from the property left by a deceased tenant, and very generally consisted by custom of the best animal which had been in the possession of the man, or its equivalent in value. On many manors heriot was not paid by free tenants, but only by those of lower rank.

The services and payments of the villains or customary tenants were of various descriptions. They had usually to make some money payments at regular periods of the year, like the free tenants, and, even more frequently than they, some regular payments in kind. But the fine paid on the inheritance of their land was less definitely restricted in amount, and heriot was more universally and more regularly collected. The greater part of their liability to the lord of the manor was, however, in the form of personal, corporal service. Almost universally the villain was required to work for a certain number of days in each week on the demesne of the lord. This "week-work" was most frequently for three days a week, sometimes for two, sometimes for four; sometimes for one number of days in the week during a part of the year, for another number during the remainder. In addition to this were usually the *precariæ* or boon-works already referred to. Sometimes as part of, sometimes in addition to, the week work and the boon-work, the villain was required to plough so many acres in the fall and spring; to mow, toss, and carry in the hay from so many acres; to haul and scatter so many loads of manure; carry grain to the barn or the market, build hedges, dig ditches, gather brush, weed grain, break clods, drive sheep or swine, or any other of the forms of agricultural labor as local custom on each manor had established his burdens. Combining the week-work, the regular boon-works, and the extra specified services, it will be seen that the labor required from the customary tenant was burdensome in the extreme. Taken on the average, much more than half of the ordinary villain's time must have been given in services to the lord of the manor.

The cotters made similar payments and performed similar labors, though less in amount. A wide-spread custom required them to work for the lord one day a week throughout the year, with certain regular payments, and certain additional special services.

Besides the possession of their land and rights of common pasture, however, there were some other compensations and alleviations of the burdens of the villains and cotters. At the boon-works and other special services performed by the tenants, it was a matter of custom that the lord of the manor provide food for one or two meals a day, and custom frequently defined the kind, amount, and value of the food for each separate meal; as where it is said in a statement of services: "It is to be known that all the above customary tenants ought to reap one day in autumn at one boon-work of wheat, and they shall have among them six bushels of wheat for their bread, baked in the manor, and broth and meat, that is to say, two men have one portion of beef and cheese, and beer for drinking. And the aforesaid customary tenants ought to work in autumn at two boon-works of oats. And they shall have six bushels of rye for their bread as described above, broth as before, and herrings, viz. six herrings for each man, and cheese as before, and water for drinking."

Thus the payments and services of the free tenants were principally of money, and apparently not burdensome; those of the villains were largely in corporal service and extremely heavy; while those of the cotters were smaller, in correspondence with their smaller holdings of land and in accordance with the necessity that they have their time in order to make their living by earning wages.

The villains and cotters were in bondage to the lord of the manor. This was a matter of legal status quite independent of the amount of land which the tenant held or of the services which he performed, though, generally speaking, the great body of the smaller tenants and of the laborers were of servile condition. In general usage the words *villanus*, *nativus*, *servus*, *custumarius*, and *rusticus* are synonymous, and the cotters belonged legally to the same servile class.

The distinction between free tenants and villains, using this word, as is customary, to include all those who were legally in servitude, was not a very clearly marked one.

Their economic position was often so similar that the classes shaded into one another. But the villain was, as has been seen, usually burdened with much heavier services. He was subject to special payments, such as "merchet," a payment made to the lord of the manor when a woman of villain rank was married, and "leyr," a payment made by women for breach of chastity. He could be "tallaged" or taxed to any extent the lord saw fit. He was bound to the soil. He could not leave the manor to seek for better conditions of life elsewhere. If he ran away, his lord could obtain an order from a court and have him brought back. When permission was obtained to remain away from the manor as an inhabitant of another vill or of a town, it was only upon payment of a periodical sum, frequently known as "chevage" or head money. He could not sell his cattle without paying the lord for permission. He had practically no standing in the courts of the country. In any suit against his lord the proof of his condition of villainage was sufficient to put him out of court, and his only recourse was the local court of the manor, where the lord himself or his representative presided. Finally, in the eyes of the law, the villain had no property of his own, all his possessions being, in the last resort, the property of his lord. This legal theory, however, apparently had but little application to real life; for in the ordinary course of events the customary tenant, if only by custom, not by law, yet held and bequeathed to his descendants his land and his chattels quite as if they were his own.

Serfdom, as it existed in England in the thirteenth century, can hardly be defined in strict legal terms. It can be described most correctly as a condition in which the villain tenant of the manor was bound to the locality and to his services and payments there by a legal bond, instead of merely by an economic bond, as was the case with the small free tenant.

There were commonly a few persons in the vill who were not in the general body of cultivators of the land and were not therefore in the classes so far described. Since the vill was generally a parish also, the village contained the parish priest, who, though he might usually hold some acres in the open fields, and might belong to the peasant class, was of course somewhat set apart from the villagers by his education and his ordination. The mill was a valued possession of the lord of the manor, for by an almost universal custom the tenants were bound to have their grain ground there, and this monopoly enabled the miller to pay a substantial rent to the lord while keeping enough profit for himself to become proverbially well-to-do.

There was often a blacksmith, whom we find sometimes exempted from other services on condition of keeping the demesne ploughs and other iron implements in order. A chance weaver or other craftsman is sometimes found, and when the vill was near sea or river or forest some who made their living by industries dependent on the locality. In the main, however, the whole life of the vill gathered around the arable, meadow, and pasture land, and the social position of the tenants, except for the cross division of serfdom, depended upon the respective amounts of land which they held.

11. The Manor Courts. — The manor was the sphere of operations of a manor court. On every manor the tenants gathered at frequent periods for a great amount of petty judicial and regulative work. The most usual period for the meeting of the manor court was once every three weeks, though in some manors no trace of a meeting is found more frequently than three times, or even twice, a year. In these cases, however, it is quite probable that less formal meetings occurred of which no regular record was kept. Different kinds of gatherings of the tenants are usually distinguished according to the authority under which they were held, or the class of tenants of which they were made up. If the court was held by the lord simply because of his feudal rights as a landholder, and was busied only with matters of the inheritance, transfer, or grant of lands, the fining of tenants for the breach of manorial custom, or failure to perform their duties to the lord of the manor, the election of tenants to petty offices on the manor, and such matters, it was described in legal language as a court baron. If a court so occupied was made up of villain tenants only, it was called a customary court. If, on the other hand, the court also punished general offences, petty crimes, breaches of contract, breaches of the assize, that is to say, the established standard of amount, price, or quality of bread or beer, the lord of the manor drawing his authority to hold such a court either actually or supposedly from a grant from the king, such a court was called a court leet. With the court leet was usually connected the so-called view of frank pledge. Frank pledge was an ancient system, according to which all men were obliged to be enrolled in groups, so that if any one committed an offence, the other members of the group would be obliged to produce him for trial. View of frank pledge was the right to punish by fine any who failed to so enroll themselves. In the court baron and the customary court it was said by lawyers that the body of attendants were the judges, and the steward, representing the lord of the manor, only a presiding official; while in the court leet the steward was the actual judge of the tenants. In practice, however, it is probable that not much was made of these distinctions, and that the periodic gatherings were made to do duty for all business of any kind that needed attention, while the procedure was that which had become customary on that special manor, irrespective of the particular form of authority for the court.

INTERIOR OF FOURTEENTH CENTURY MANOR HOUSE, SUTTON COURTENAY, BERKSHIRE.

(Domestic Architecture in the Fourteenth Century.)

The manor court was presided over by a steward or other officer representing the lord of the manor. Apparently all adult male tenants were expected to be present, and any inhabitant was liable to be summoned. A court was usually held in each manor, but sometimes a lord of several neighboring manors would hold the court for all of these in some one place. As most manors belonged to lords who had many manors in their possession, the steward or other official commonly proceeded from one manor or group of manors to another, holding the courts in each. Before the close of the thirteenth century the records of the manor courts, or at least of the more important of them, began to be kept with very great regularity and fulness, and it is to the mass of these manor court rolls which still remain that we owe most of our detailed knowledge of the condition of the body of the people in the later Middle Ages. The variety and the amount of business transacted at the court were alike considerable. When a tenant had died it was in the meeting of the manor court that his successor obtained a regrant of the land. The required relief was there assessed, and the heriot from the property of the deceased recorded. New grants of land were made, and transfers, leases, and abandonments by one tenant and assignments to another announced. For each of these processes of land transfer a fine was collected for the lord of the manor. Such entries as the following are constantly found : " John of Durham has come into court and taken one bond-land which Richard Avras formerly held but gave up because of his poverty ; to have and hold for his lifetime, paying and doing the accustomed services as Richard paid and did them. He gives for entrance 6*s*. 8*d*. ; " " Agnes Mabeley is given possession of a quarter virgate of land which her mother held, and gives the lord 33*s*. 4*d*. for entrance."

Disputes as to the right of possession of land and questions of dowry and inheritance were decided, a jury being granted in many cases by the lord at the petition of a claimant and on payment of a fee. Another class of cases consisted in the imposition of fines or amerciaments for the violation of the customs of the manor, of the rules of the lord, or of the requirements of the culprit's tenure; such as a villain marrying without leave, failure to perform boon-works or bad performance of work, failure to place the tenant's sheep in the lord's fold, cutting of wood or brush, making unlawful paths across the fields, the meadows, or the common, encroachment in ploughing upon other men's land or upon the common, or failure to send grain to the lord's mill for grinding. Sometimes the offence was of a more general nature, such as breach of assize, breach of contract, slander, assault, or injury to property. Still another part of the work of the court was the election of petty manorial officers; a reeve, a reaper, ale-tasters, and perhaps others. The duty of filling such offices when elected by the tenants and approved by the lord or his steward was, as has been said, one of the burdens of villainage. However, when a villain was fulfilling the office of reeve, it was customary for him to be relieved of at least a part of the payments and services to which he would otherwise be subject. Finally the manor court meetings were employed for the adoption of general regulations as to the use of the commons and other joint interests, and for the announcement of the orders of the steward in the keeping of the peace.

12. The Manor as an Estate of a Lord. — The manor was profitable to the lord in various ways. He received rents in money and kind. These included the rents of assize from free and villain land tenants, rent from the tenant of the mill, and frequently from other sources. Then came the profits derived from the cultivation of the demesne land. In this the lord of the manor was simply a large farmer, except that he had a supply of labor bound to remain at hand and to give service without wages almost up to his needs. Finally there were the profits of the manor courts. As has been seen, these consisted of a great variety of fees, fines, amerciaments, and collections made by the steward or other official. Such varied payments and profits combined to make up the total value of the manor to the landowner. Not only the slender income of the country squire or knight whose estate consisted of a single manor of some ten or twenty pounds yearly value, but the vast wealth of the great noble or of the rich monastery or powerful bishopric was principally made up of the sum of such payments from a considerable number of manors. An appreciable part of the income of the government even was derived from the manors still in the possession of the crown.

The mediæval manor was a little world in itself. The large number of scattered acres which made up the demesne farm cultivated in the interests of the lord of the manor, the small groups of scattered strips held by free holders or villain tenants who furnished most of the labor on the demesne farm, the little patches of ground held by mere laborers whose living was mainly gained by hired service on the land of the lord or of more prosperous tenants, the claims which all had to the use of the common pasture for their sheep and cattle and of the woods for their swine, all these together made up an agricultural system which secured a revenue for the lord, provided food and the raw material for primitive manufactures for the inhabitants of the vill, and furnished some small surplus which could be sold.

Life on the mediæval manor was hard. The greater part of the population was subject to the burdens of serfdom, and all, both free and serf, shared in the arduousness of labor, coarseness and lack of variety of food, unsanitary surroundings, and liability to the rigor of winter and the attacks of pestilence. Yet the average condition of comfort of the mass of the rural inhabitants of England was probably as high as at any subsequent time. Food in pro-

INTERIOR OF FOURTEENTH CENTURY MANOR HOUSE, GREAT MALVERN, WORCESTERSHIRE.

(*Domestic Architecture in the Fourteenth Century.*)

portion to wages was very cheap, and the almost universal possession of some land made it possible for the very poorest to avoid starvation. Moreover, the great extent to which custom governed all payments, services, and rights must have prevented much of the extreme depression which has occasionally existed in subsequent periods in which greater competition has distinguished more clearly the capable from the incompetent.

From the social rather than from the economic point of view the life of the mediæval manor was perhaps most clearly marked by this predominance of custom and by a second characteristic nearly related. This was the singularly close relationship in which all the inhabitants of the manor were bound to one another, and their correspondingly complete separation from the outside world. The common pasture, the intermingled strips of the holdings in the open fields, the necessary coöperation in the performance of their daily labor on the demesne land, the close contiguity of their dwellings, their universal membership in the same parish church, their common attendance and action in the manor courts, all must have combined to make the vill an organization of singular unity. This self-centred life, economically, judicially, and ecclesiastically so nearly independent of other bodies, put obstacles in the way of change. It prohibited intercourse beyond the manor, and opposed the growth of a feeling of common national life. The manorial life lay at the base of the stability which marked the mediæval period.

13. BIBLIOGRAPHY

General Works

Certain general works which refer to long periods of economic history will be mentioned here and not again referred to, excepting in special cases. It is to be understood that they contain valuable matter on the subject, not only of this, but of succeeding chapters. They should therefore be consulted in addition to the more specific works named under each chapter.

Cunningham, William : *Growth of English Industry and Commerce*, two volumes. The most extensive and valuable work that covers the whole field of English economic history.

Ashley, W. J. : *English Economic History*, two volumes. The first volume is a full and careful analysis of mediæval economic conditions, with detailed notes and references to the primary sources. The second volume is a work of original investigation, referring particularly to conditions in the fifteenth and sixteenth centuries, but it does not give such a clear analysis of the conditions of its period as the first volume.

Traill, H. D. : *Social England*, six volumes. A composite work including a great variety of subjects, but seldom having the most satisfactory account of any one of them.

Rogers, J. E. T. : *History of Agriculture and Prices; Six Centuries of Work and Wages; Economic Interpretation of History*. Professor Rogers' work is very extensive and detailed, and his books were largely pioneer studies. His statistical and other facts are useful, but his general statements are not very valuable, and his conclusions are not convincing.

Palgrave, R. H. I. : *Dictionary of Political Economy*. Many of the articles on subjects of economic history are the best and most recent studies on their respective subjects, and the bibliographies contained in them are especially valuable.

Four single-volume text-books have been published on this general subject : —

Cunningham, William, and McArthur, E. A. : *Outlines of English Industrial History*.

Gibbins, H. de B.: *Industry in England.*

Warner, George Townsend: *Landmarks in English Industrial History.*

Price, L. L.: *A Short History of English Commerce and Industry.*

Special Works

Seebohm, Frederic: *The English Village Community.* Although written for another purpose, — to suggest a certain view of the origin of the mediæval manor, — the first five chapters of this book furnish the clearest existing descriptive account of the fundamental facts of rural life in the thirteenth century. Its publication marked an era in the recognition of the main features of manorial organization. Green, for instance, the historian of the English people, seems to have had no clear conception of many of those characteristics of ordinary rural life which Mr. Seebohm has made familiar.

Vinogradoff, Paul: *Villainage in England.*

Pollock, Sir Frederick, and Maitland, F. W.: *History of English Law,* Vol. I.

These two works are of especial value for the organization of the manor courts and the legal condition of the population.

Sources

Much that can be explained only with great difficulty becomes clear to the student immediately when he reads the original documents. Concrete illustrations of general statements moreover make the work more interesting and real. It has therefore been found desirable by many teachers to bring their students into contact with at least a few typical illustrative documents. The sources for the subject generally are given in the works named above. An admirable bibliography has been recently published by

Gross, Charles: *The Sources and Literature of English History from the Earliest Times to about 1485.* References to abundant material for the illustration or further investigation of the subject of this chapter will be found in the following pamphlet: —

Davenport, Frances G.: *A Classified List of Printed Original Materials for English Manorial and Agrarian History.*

Sources for the mediæval period are almost all in Latin or French. Some of them, however, have been more accessible by being translated into English and reprinted in convenient form. A few of these are given in C. W. Colby: *Selections from the Sources of English History,* and G. C. Lee: *Source Book of English History.*

In the *Series of Translations and Reprints from the Original Sources of European History,* published by the Department of History of the University of Pennsylvania, several numbers include documents in this field. Vol. III, No. 5, is devoted entirely to manorial documents.

Discussions of the Origin of the Manor

The question of the origin of the mediæval manorial organization, whether it is principally of native English or of Roman origin, or hewn from still other materials, although not treated in this text-book, has been the subject of much interest and discussion. One view of the case is the thesis of Seebohm's book, referred to above. Other books treating of it are the following: —

Earle, John: *Land Charters and Saxonic Documents,* Introduction.

Gomme, G. L.: *The Village Community.*

Ashley, W. J.: A translation of Fustel de Coulanges, *Origin of Property in Land,* Introduction.

Andrews, Charles M.: *The Old English Manor,* Introduction.

Maitland, F. W.: *Domesday Book and Beyond.*

Meitzen, August: *Siedelung und Agrarwesen,* Vol. II, Chap. 7.

The writings of Kemble and of Sir Henry Maine belong rather to a past period of study and speculation, but their ideas still lie at the base of discussions on the subject.

CHAPTER III

TOWN LIFE AND ORGANIZATION

14. The Town Government. — In the middle of the thirteenth century there were some two hundred towns in England distinguishable by their size, form of government, and the occupations of their inhabitants, from the rural agricultural villages which have just been described. London probably had more than 25,000 inhabitants; York and Bristol may each have had as many as 10,000. The population of the others varied from as many as 6000 to less than 1000. Perhaps the most usual population of an English mediæval town lay between 1500 and 4000. They were mostly walled, though such protection was hardly necessary, and the military element in English towns was therefore but slightly developed. Those towns which contained cathedrals, and were therefore the seats of bishoprics, were called cities. All other organized towns were known as boroughs, though this distinction in the use of the terms city and borough was by no means always preserved. The towns differed widely in their form of government; but all had charters from the king or from some nobleman, abbey, or bishopric on whose lands they had grown up. Such a charter usually declared the right of the town to preserve the ancient customs which had come to be recognized among its inhabitants, and granted to it certain privileges, exemptions, and rights of self-government. The most universal and important of these privileges were the following: the town paid the tolls and dues owed to the king or other lord by its inhabitants in a lump sum, collecting the amount from its own citizens as the latter or their own authorities saw fit; the town courts had jurisdiction over most suits and offences, relieving the townsmen from answering at hundred and county court suits which concerned matters within their own limits; the townsmen, where the king granted the charter, were exempt from the

TOWN WALL OF SOUTHAMPTON, BUILT IN THE THIRTEENTH CENTURY.

(Turner: *Domestic Architecture in England*.)

payment of tolls of various kinds throughout his dominions; they could pass ordinances and regulations controlling the trade of the town, the administration of its property, and its internal affairs generally, and could elect officials to carry out such regulations. These officials also corresponded and negotiated in the name of the town with the authorities of other towns and with the government. From

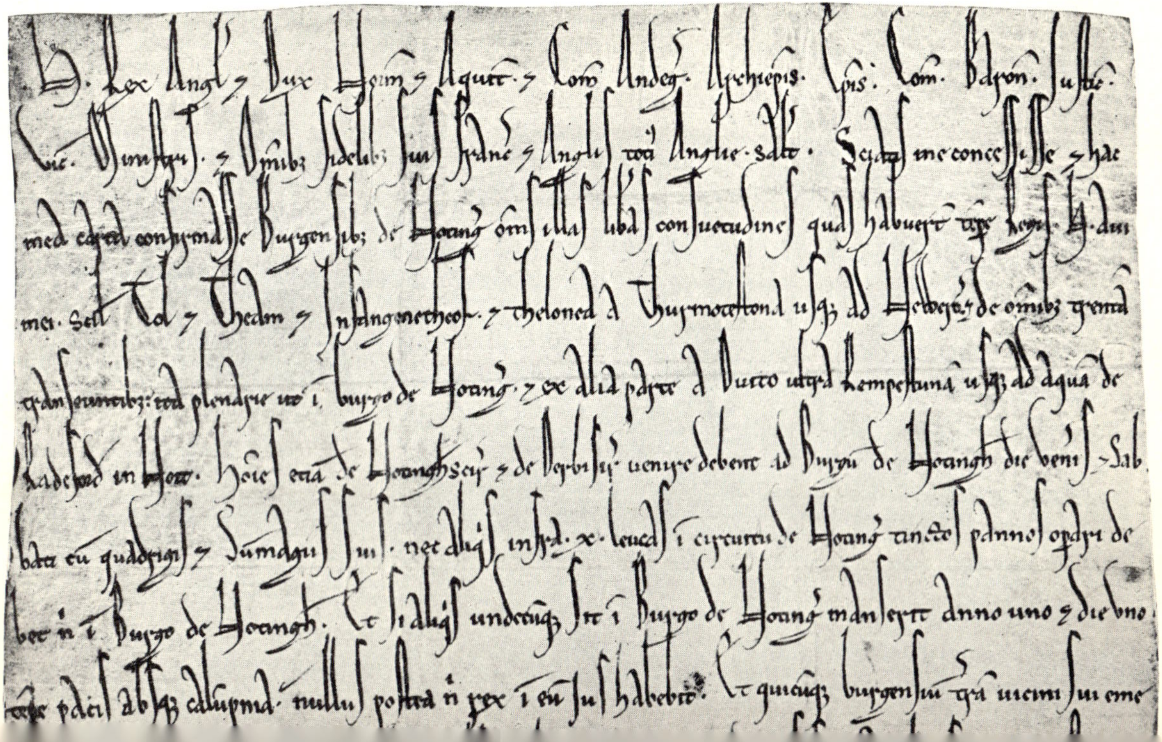

CHARTER OF HENRY II TO THE BOROUGH OF NOTTINGHAM.
(*Records of the Borough of Nottingham.* Published by the Corporation.)

the close of the thirteenth century all towns of any importance were represented in Parliament. These elements of independence were not all possessed by every town, and some had special privileges not enumerated in the above list. The first charter of a town was apt to be vague and inadequate, but from time to time a new charter was obtained giving additional privileges and defining the old rights more clearly. Nor had all those who dwelt within the town limits equal participation in its advantages. These were usually restricted to those who were known as citizens or burgesses; full citizenship depending primarily on the possession of a house and land within the town limits. In addition to the burgesses there were usually some inhabitants of the town — strangers, Jews, fugitive villains from the rural villages, or perhaps only poorer natives of the town — who did not share in these privileges. Those who did possess all civil rights of the townsmen were in many ways superior in condition to men in the country. In addition to the advantages of the municipal organization mentioned above, all burgesses were personally free, there was entire exemption from the vexatious petty payments of the rural manors, and burgage tenure was the nearest to actual land ownership existent during the Middle Ages.

15. The Gild Merchant. — The town was most clearly marked off from the country by the occupations by which its people earned their living. These were, in the first place, trading; secondly, manufacturing or handicrafts. Agriculture of course existed also, since most townsmen possessed some lands lying outside of the enclosed portions of the town. On these they raised crops and pastured their cattle. Of these varied occupations, however, it was trade which gave character and, indeed, existence itself to the town. Foreign goods were brought to the towns from abroad for sale, the surplus products of rural manors found their way there for marketing; the products of one part of the country which were needed in other parts were sought for and purchased in the towns. Men also sold the products

HALL OF MERCHANTS' COMPANY OF YORK.

(Lambert: *Two Thousand Years of Gild Life.* Published by A. Brown & Sons, Hull.)

of their own labor, not only food products, such as bread, meat, and fish, but also objects of manufacture, as cloth, arms, leather, and goods made of wood, leather, or metal. For the protection and regulation of this trade the organization known as the gild merchant had grown up in each town. The gild merchant seems to have included all of the population of the town who habitually engaged in the business of selling, whether commodities of their own manufacture or those they had previously purchased. Membership in the gild was not exactly coincident with burgess-ship; persons who lived outside of the town were sometimes admitted into that organization, and, on the other hand, some inhabitants of the town were not included among its members. Nevertheless, since practically all of the townsmen made their living by trade in some form or another, the group of burgesses and the group of gild members could not have been very different. The authority of the gild merchant within its field of trade regulation seems to have been as complete as that of the town community as a whole in its field of judicial, financial, and administrative jurisdiction. The gild might therefore be defined as that form of organization of the inhabitants of the town which controlled its trade and industry. The principal reason for the existence of the gild was to preserve to its own members the monopoly of trade. No one not in the gild merchant of the town could buy or sell there except under conditions imposed by the gild. Foreigners coming from other countries or traders from other English towns were prohibited from buying or selling in any way that might interfere with the interests of the gildsmen. They must buy and sell at such times and in such places and only such articles as were provided for by the gild regulations. They must in all cases pay the town tolls, from which members of the gild were exempt. At Southampton, for instance, we find the following provisions: "And no one in the city of Southampton shall buy anything to sell again in the same city unless he is of the gild merchant

62 *Industrial and Social History of England*

or of the franchise." Similarly at Leicester, in 1260, it was ordained that no gildsman should form a partnership with a stranger, allowing him to join in the profits of the sale of wool or other merchandise.

As against outsiders the gild merchant was a protective body, as regards its own members it was looked upon and

INTERIOR OF HALL OF MERCHANTS' COMPANY OF YORK.
(Lambert: *Two Thousand Years of Gild Life*. Published by A. Brown & Sons, Hull.)

constantly spoken of as a fraternity. Its members must all share in the common expenditures, they are called brethren of the society, their competition with one another is reduced to its lowest limits. For instance, we find the provision that "any one who is of the gild merchant may share in all merchandise which another gildsman shall buy."

EARLIEST MERCHANT GILD F

(Bateson: *Records of the Borough of Leic*

THE BOROUGH OF LEICESTER.

The presiding officer was usually known as the alderman, while the names given to other officials, such as stewards, deans, bailiffs, chaplains, skevins, and ushers, and the duties they performed, varied greatly from time to time.

Meetings were held at different periods, sometimes annually, in many cases more frequently. At these meetings new ordinances were passed, officers elected, and other business transacted. It was also a convivial occasion, a gild feast preceding or following the other labors of the meeting. In some gilds the meeting was regularly known as "the drinking." There were likewise frequent sittings of the officials of the fraternity, devoted to the decision of disputes between brethren, the admission of new members, the fining or expulsion of offenders against the gild ordinances, and other routine work. These meetings were known as "morrowspeches."

The greater part of the activity of the gild merchant consisted in the holding of its meetings with their accompanying feasts, and in the enforcement of its regulations upon its members and upon outsiders. It fulfilled, however, many fraternal duties for its members. It is provided in one set of statutes that, "If a gildsman be imprisoned in England in time of peace, the alderman, with the steward and with one of the skevins, shall go, at the cost of the gild, to procure the deliverance of the one who is in prison." In another, "If any of the brethren shall fall into poverty or misery, all the brethren are to assist him by common consent out of the chattels of the house or fraternity, or of their proper own." The funeral rites, especially, were attended by the man's gild brethren. "And when a gildsman dies, all those who are of the gild and are in the city shall attend the service for the dead, and gildsmen shall bear the body and bring it to the place of burial." The gild merchant also sometimes fulfilled various religious, philanthropic, and charitable duties, not only to its members, but to the public generally, and to the poor. The time of the fullest development of the gild merchant varied, of course, in different towns, but its widest expansion was probably in the early part of the period we are studying, that is, during the thirteenth century. Later it came to be in some towns indistinguishable from the municipal government in general, its members the same as the burgesses, its officers represented by the officers of the town. In some other towns the gild merchant gradually lost its control over trade, retaining only its fraternal, charitable, and religious features. In still other cases the expression gradually lost all definite significance and its meaning became a matter for antiquarian dispute.

16. The Craft Gilds. — By the fourteenth century the gild merchant of the town was a much less conspicuous institution than it had previously been. Its decay was largely the result of the growth of a group of organizations in each town which were spoken of as crafts, fraternities, gilds, misteries, or often merely by the name of their occupation, as "the spurriers," "the dyers," "the fishmongers." These organizations are usually described in later writings as craft gilds. It is not to be understood that the gild merchant and the craft gilds never existed contemporaneously in any town. The former began earlier and decayed before the craft gilds reached their height, but there was a considerable period when it must have been a common thing for a man to be a member both of the gild merchant of the town and of the separate organization of his own trade. The later gilds seem to have grown up in response to the needs of handicraft much as the gild merchant had grown up to regulate trade, though trading occupations also were eventually drawn into the craft gild form

OLD TOWNHALL OF LEICESTER, FORMERLY HALL OF CORPUS CHRISTI GILD.

(Drawing made in 1826.)

of organization. The weavers seem to have been the earliest occupation to be organized into a craft gild; but later almost every form of industry which gave employment to a handful of craftsmen in any town had its separate fraternity. Since even nearly allied trades, such as the glovers, girdlers, pocket makers, skinners, white tawyers, and other workers in leather; or the fletchers, the makers of arrows, the bowyers, the makers of bows, and the stringers, the makers of bowstrings, were organized into separate bodies, the number of craft gilds in any one town was often very large. At London there were by 1350 at least as many as forty, at York, some time later, more than fifty.

The craft gilds existed usually under the authority of the town government, though frequently they obtained authorization or even a charter from the crown. They were formed primarily to regulate and preserve the monopoly of their own occupations in their own town, just as the gild merchant existed to regulate the trade of the town in general. No one could carry on any trade without being subject to the organization which controlled that trade. Membership, however, was not intentionally restricted. Any man who was a capable workman and conformed to the rules of the craft was practically a member of the organization of that industry. It is a common requirement in the earliest gild statutes that every man who wishes to carry on that particular industry should have his ability testified to by some known members of the craft. But usually full membership and influence in the gild was reached as a matter of course by the artisans passing through the successive grades of apprentice, journeyman, and master. As an apprentice he was bound to a master for a number of years, living in his house and learning the trade in his shop. There was usually a signed contract entered into between the master and the parents of the apprentice, by which the former agreed to provide all necessary clothing, food, and lodging, and teach to the apprentice all he himself knew about his craft. The latter, on the other hand, was bound to keep secret his master's affairs, to obey all his commandments, and to behave himself properly in all things. After the expiration of the time agreed upon for his apprenticeship, which varied much in individual cases, but was apt to be about seven years, he became free of the trade as a journeyman, a full workman. The word "journeyman" may refer to the engagement being by the day, from the French word *journée*, or to the habit of making journeys from town to town in search of work, or it may be derived from some other origin. As a journeyman he served for wages in the employ of a master. In many cases he saved enough money for the small requirements of setting up an independent shop. Then as full master artisan or tradesman he might take part in all the meetings and general administration of the organized body of his craft, might hold office, and would himself probably have one or more journeymen in his employ and apprentices under his guardianship. As almost all industries were carried on in the dwelling-houses of the craftsmen, no establishments could be of very considerable size, and the difference of position between master, journeyman, and apprentice could not have been great. The craft gild was organized with its regular rules, its officers, and its meetings. The rules or ordinances of the fraternity were drawn up at some one time and added to or altered from time to time afterward. The approval of the city authorities was frequently sought for such new statutes as well as for the original ordinances, and in many towns appears to have been necessary. The rules provided for officers and their powers, the time and character of meetings, and for a considerable variety of functions. These varied of course in different trades and in different towns, but some characteristics were almost universal. Provisions were always either tacitly or formally included for the preservation of the monopoly of the crafts in the town. The hours of labor were regulated. Night work was very generally prohibited, apparently because of the difficulty of oversight at that time, as was work on

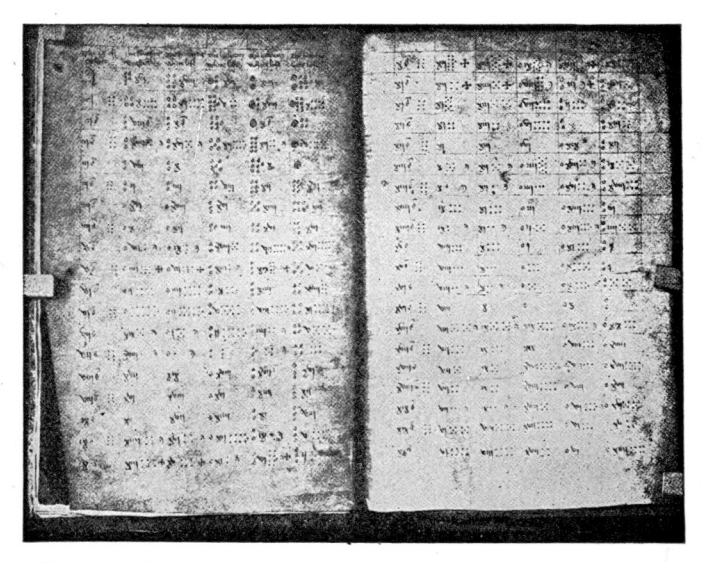

TABLE OF ASSIZE OF BREAD IN RECORD BOOK OF CITY OF HULL.
(Lambert: *Two Thousand Years of Gild Life.* Published by A. Brown & Sons, Hull.)

Saturday afternoons, Sundays, and other holy days. Provisions were made for the inspection of goods by the officers of the gild, all workshops and goods for sale being constantly subject to their examination, if they should wish it. In those occupations that involved buying and selling the necessities of life, such as those of the fishmongers and the bakers, the officers of the fraternity, like the town authorities, were engaged in a continual struggle with "regrators," "forestallers," and "engrossers," which were appellations as odious as they were common in the mediæval town. Regrating meant buying to sell again at a higher price without having made any addition to the value of the goods; forestalling was going to the place of production to buy, or in any other way trying to outwit fellow-dealers by purchasing things before they came into the open market where all had the same opportunity; engrossing was buying up the whole supply, or so much of it as not to allow other dealers to get what they needed, the modern "cornering of the market." These practices, which were regarded as so objectionable in the eyes of mediæval traders, were frequently nothing more than what would be considered commendable enterprise in a more competitive age. Another class of rules was for mutual assistance, for kindliness among members, and for the obedience and faithfulness of journeymen and apprentices. There were provisions for assistance to members of the craft when in need, or to their widows and orphans, for the visitation of those sick or in prison, for common attendance at the burial services of deceased members, and for other charitable and philanthropic objects. Thus the craft gild, like the gild merchant, combined close social relationship with a distinctly recognized and enforced regulation of the trade. This regulation provided for the protection of members of the organization from outside competition, and it also prevented any considerable amount of competition among members; it supported the interests of the full master members of the craft as against those in the journeyman stage, and enforced the custom of the trade in hours, materials, methods cf manufacture, and often in prices.

The officers were usually known as masters, wardens, or stewards. Their powers extended to the preservation of order among the master members of the craft at the meetings, and among the journeymen and apprentices of the craft at all times; to the supervision, either directly or through deputies, of the work of the members, seeing that it conformed to the rules and was not false in any way; to the settlement, if possible, of disputes among members of the craft; to the administration of its charitable work; and to the representation of the organized body of the craft before town or other authorities.

Common religious observances were held by the craftsmen not only at the funerals of members, but on the day of the saint to which the gild was especially dedicated. Most fraternities kept up a shrine or chapel in some parish church. Fines for the breach of gild rules were often ordered to be paid in wax that the candles about the body of dead brethren and in the gild chapel should never be wanting. All the brethren of the gild, dressed in common suits of livery, walked in procession from their hall or meeting room to the church, performed their devotions and joined in the services in commemoration of the dead. Members of the craft frequently bequeathed property for the partial support of a chaplain and payment of other expenses connected with their "obits," or masses for the repose of their souls and those of their relatives.

Closely connected with the religious observances was the convivial side of the gild's life. On the annual gild day, or more frequently, the members all gathered at their hall or some inn to a feast, which varied in luxuriousness according to the wealth of the fraternity, from bread, cheese, and ale to all the exuberance of which the Middle Ages were capable.

Somewhat later, we find the craft gilds taking entire charge of the series or cycles of "mystery plays," which were given in various towns. The words of the plays produced at York, Coventry, Chester, and Woodkirk have come down to us and are of extreme interest as embryonic forms of the drama and examples of purely vernacular language. It is quite certain that such groups of plays were given by the crafts in a number of other towns. They were generally given on Corpus Christi day, a feast which fell in the early summer time, when out-door pleasures were again enjoyable after the winter's confinement. A cycle consisted of a series of dialogues or short plays, each based upon some scene of biblical story, so arranged that the whole Bible narrative should be given consecutively from the Creation to the Second Advent. One of the crafts, starting early in the morning, would draw a pageant consisting of a platform on wheels, to a regularly appointed spot in a conspicuous part of the town, and on this platform, with some rude scenery, certain members of the gild or men employed by them would proceed to recite a dialogue in verse representative of some early part of the Bible story. After they had finished, their pageant would be dragged to another station, where they repeated their performance. In the meantime a second company had taken their former place, and recited a dialogue representative of a second scene. So the whole day would be occupied by the series of performances. The town and the craftsmen valued the celebration because it was an occasion for strangers visiting their city and thus increasing the volume of trade, as well as because it furnished an opportunity for the gratification of their social and dramatic instincts.

It was not only at the periodical business meetings, or on the feast days, or in the preparation for the dramatic shows, that the gildsmen were thrown together. Usually all the members of one craft lived on the same street or in the same part of the town, and were therefore members of the same parish church and constantly brought under one another's observation in all the daily concerns of life. All things combined to make the craft a natural and necessary centre for the interest of each of its members.

17. Non-industrial Gilds. — Besides the gilds merchant, which included persons of all industrial occupations, and the craft gilds, which were based upon separate organizations of each industry, there were gilds or fraternities in existence which had no industrial functions whatever. These are usually spoken of as "religious" or "social" gilds. It would perhaps be better to describe them simply as non-industrial gilds; for their religious and social functions they had in common, as has been seen, both with the gild merchant and the craft organizations. They only differed from these in not being based upon or interested in the monopoly or oversight of any kind of trade or handicraft. They differed also from the craft gilds in that all their members were on an equal basis, there being no such industrial grades as apprentice, journeyman, and master; and from both of the organizations already discussed in the fact that they existed in small towns and even in mere villages, as well as in industrial centres.

In these associations the religious, social, and charitable elements were naturally more prominent than in those fraternities which were organized primarily for some kind of economic regulation. They were generally named after some saint. The ordinances usually provided for one or more solemn services in the year, frequently with a procession in livery, and sometimes with a considerable amount of pantomime or symbolic show. For instance, the gild of St. Helen at Beverly, in their procession to the church of the Friars Minors on the day of their patron saint, were preceded by an old man carrying a cross; after him a fair young man dressed as St. Helen; then another old man carrying a shovel, these being intended to typify the finding of the cross. Next came the sisters two and two, after them the brethren of the gild, and finally the officers. There were always provisions for solemnities at the funerals of members, for burial at the expense of the gild if the member who had died left no means for a suitable ceremony, and for prayers for deceased members. What might be called the insurance feature was also much more nearly universal than in the case of the industrial fraternities. Help was given in case of theft, fire, sickness, or almost any kind of loss which was not chargeable to the member's own misdoing. Finally it was very customary for such gilds to provide for the support of a certain number of dependents, aged men or women, cripples, or lepers, for charity's sake; and occasionally educational facilities were also provided by them from their regular income or from bequests made for the purpose. The social-religious gilds were extremely numerous, and seem frequently to have existed within the limits of a craft, including some of its members and not others, or within a certain parish, including some of the parishioners, but not all.

Thus if there were men in the mediæval town who were not members of some trading or craft body, they would in all probability be members of some society based merely on religious or social feeling. The whole tendency of mediæval society was toward organization, combination, close union with one's fellows. It might be said that all town life involved membership in some organization, and usually in that one into which a man was drawn by the occupation in which he made his living. These gilds or the town government itself controlled even the affairs of private economic life in the city, just as the customary agriculture of the country prevented much freedom of action there. Methods of trading, or manufacture, the kind and amount of material to be used, hours of labor, conditions of employment, even prices of work, were regulated by the gild ordinances. The individual gildsman had as little opportunity to emancipate himself from the controlling force of the association as the individual tenant on the rural manor had to free himself from the customary agriculture and the customary services. Whether we study rural or urban society, whether we look at the purely economic or at the broader social side of existence, life in the thirteenth and fourteenth centuries was corporate rather than individual.

18. BIBLIOGRAPHY

Gross, Charles: *The Gild Merchant*, two volumes. The first volume consists of a full account and discussion of the character and functions of the gild merchant, with a number of appendices on cognate subjects. The second volume contains the documents on which the first is based.

Seligman, E. R. A.: *Two Chapters on Mediæval Gilds*.

Brentano, L.: *The History and Development of English Gilds*. An essay prefixed to a volume of ordinances of English Gilds, edited by T. Smith. Brentano's essay is only referred to because of the paucity of works on the subject, as it is fanciful and unsatisfactory. No thorough and scholarly description of the craft gilds exists. On the other hand, a considerable body of original materials is easily accessible in English, as in the following works: —

Riley: *Memorials of London and London Life*.

Smith, Toulmin: *English Gilds*.

Various documents illustrative of town and gild history will also be found in Vol. II, No. 1, of the *Translations and*

Reprints, published by the Department of History of the University of Pennsylvania.

Better descriptions exist for the position of the gilds in special towns than for their general character, especially in London by Herbert, in Hull by Lambert, in Shrewsbury by Hibbert, and in Coventry by Miss Harris.

CHAPTER IV

MEDIÆVAL TRADE AND COMMERCE

19. Markets and Fairs. — Within the towns, in addition to the ordinary trading described in the last chapter, much buying and selling was done at the weekly or semi-weekly markets. The existence of a market in a town was the result of a special grant from the king, sometimes to the burgesses themselves, sometimes to a neighboring nobleman or abbey. In the latter case the tolls paid by outsiders who bought or sold cattle or victuals in the market did not go to the town or gild authorities, but to the person who was said to "own" the market. Many places which differed in scarcely any other way from agricultural villages possessed markets, so that "market towns" became a descriptive term for small towns midway in size between the larger boroughs or cities and mere villages. The sales at markets were usually of the products of the surrounding country, especially of articles of food consumption, so that the fact of the existence of a market on one or more days of the week in a large town was of comparatively little importance from the point of view of more general trade.

Far more important was the similar institution of periodical fairs. Fairs, like markets, existed only by grant from the king. They differed from markets, however, in being held only once a year or at most semi-annually or quarterly, in being invariably in the possession of private persons, never of town governments, and in the fact that during their continuance as a rule all buying and selling except at the fairs was suspended within a considerable circuit. Several hundred grants of fairs are recorded on the rolls of royal charters, most of them to abbeys, bishoprics, and noblemen; but comparatively few of them were of sufficient size or importance to play any considerable part in the trade and commerce of the country. Moreover, the development of the towns with their continuous trade tended to draw custom away from all the fairs except those which had obtained some especial importance and an international reputation. Of these, however, there was still a considerable number whose influence was very great. The best known were those of Winchester, of Stourbridge near Cambridge, of St. Ives belonging to the abbot of Ramsay, and of Boston. In early times fairs were frequently held in the churchyards, but this came to be looked upon as a scandal, and was prohibited by a law of 1285. The fairs were in many cases held just beyond the limits of a town in an open field or on a smooth hillside. Each year, some time before the opening day of the fair, this ground was formally occupied by the servants of the owner of the fair, wooden booths were erected or ground set apart for those who should put up their own tents or prefer to sell in the open. Then as merchants appeared from foreign or English towns they chose or were assigned places which they were bound to retain during the continuance of the fair. By the time of the opening of the fair those who expected to sell were arranged in long rows or groups, according to the places they came from, or the kind of goods in which they dealt. After the opening had been proclaimed no merchant of the nearby town could buy or sell, except within the borders of the fair. The town authorities resigned their functions into the hands of the

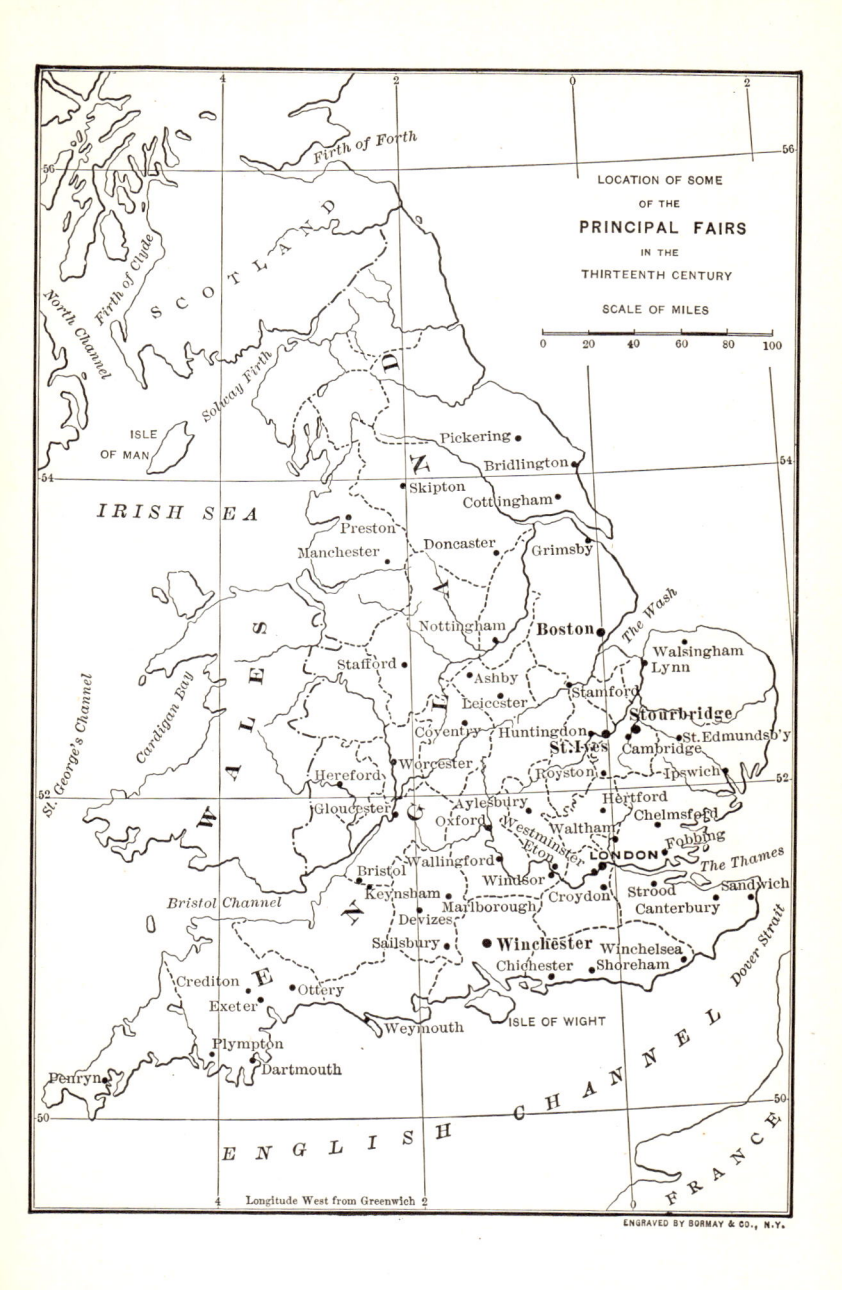

LOCATION OF SOME
OF THE
PRINCIPAL FAIRS
IN THE
THIRTEENTH CENTURY

SCALE OF MILES

officials whom the lord of the fair had placed in charge of it, and for the time for which the fair was held, usually from six to twelve days, everything within the enclosure of the fair, within the town, and in the surrounding neighborhood was under their control.

Tolls were collected for the advantage of the lord of the fair from all goods as they were brought into or taken out from the bounds of the fair, or at the time of their sale; stallage was paid for the rent of booths, fees were charged for the use of space, and for using the lord's weights and scales. Good order was preserved and fair dealing enforced by the officials of the lord. To prevent offences and settle disputes arising in the midst of the busy trading the officials of the lord formed a court which sat continually and followed a summary procedure. This was known as a court of "pie-powder," that is *pied poudré*, or *dusty foot*, so called, no doubt, from its readiness to hear the suits of merchants and wayfarers, as they were, without formality or delay. At this court a great variety of cases came up, such as disputes as to debts, failure to perform contracts of sale or purchase, false measurements, theft, assault, defamation, and misdemeanors of all kinds. Sometimes the court decided offhand, sometimes compurgation was allowed immediately or on the next day, sometimes juries were formed and gave decisions. The law which the court of pie-powder administered was often referred to as the "law merchant," a somewhat less rigid system than the common law, and one whose rules were generally defined, in these courts and in the king's courts, by juries chosen from among the merchants themselves.

At these fairs, even more than in the towns, merchants from a distance gathered to buy the products peculiar to the part of England where the fair was held, and to sell their own articles of importation or production. The large fairs furnished by far the best markets of the time. We find mention made in the records of one court of pie-powder of men from a dozen or twenty English towns, from Bordeaux, and from Rouen. The men who came from any one town, whether of England or the Continent, acted and were treated as common members of the gild merchant of that town, as forming a sort of community, and being to a certain extent responsible for one another. They did their buying and selling, it is true, separately, but if disputes arose, the whole group were held responsible for each member. For example, the following entry was made in the roll of the fair of St. Ives in the year 1275 : " William of Fleetbridge and Anne his wife complain of Thomas Coventry of Leicester for unjustly withholding from them 55*s*. 2½*d*. for a sack of wool. . . . Elias is ordered to attach the community of Leicester to answer . . . and of the said community Allan Parker, Adam Nose and Robert Howell are attached by three bundles of ox-hides, three hundred bundles of sheep skins and six sacks of wool."

20. Trade Relations between Towns.—The fairs were only temporary selling places. When the time for which the fair was held had expired the booths were removed, the merchants returned to their native cities or travelled away to some other fair, and the officials were withdrawn. The place was deserted until the next quarter or year. But in the towns, as has been already stated, more or less continuous trade went on ; not only petty retail trade and that of the weekly or semi-weekly markets between townsmen or countrymen coming from the immediate vicinity, but a wholesale trade between the merchants of that town and those from other towns in England or on the Continent.

It was of this trade above all that the gild merchant of

each town possessed the regulation. Merchants from another town were treated much the same, whether that town was English or foreign. In fact, "foreigner" or "alien," as used in the town records, of Bristol, for instance, may apply to citizens of London or Oxford just as well as to those of Paris or Cologne. Such "foreign" merchants could deal when they came to a town only with members of the gild, and only on the conditions required by the gild. Usually they could buy or sell only at wholesale, and tolls were collected from them upon their sales or purchases. They were prohibited from dealing in some kinds of articles altogether, and frequently the duration of their stay in the town was limited to a prescribed period. Under such circumstances the authorities of various towns entered into trade agreements with those of other towns providing for mutual concessions and advantages. Correspondence was also constantly going on between the officials of various towns for the settlement of individual points of dispute, for the return of fugitive apprentices, asking that justice might be done to aggrieved citizens, and on occasion threatening reprisal. Southampton had formal agreements with more than seventy towns or other trading bodies. During a period of twenty years the city authorities of London sent more than 300 letters on such matters to the officials of some 90 other towns in England and towns on the Continent. The merchants from any one town did not therefore trade or act entirely as separate individuals, but depended on the prestige of their town, or the support of the home authorities, or the privileges already agreed upon by treaty. The non-payment of a debt by a merchant of one town usually made any fellow-townsman liable to seizure where the debt was owed, until the debtor could be made to pay. In 1285, by a law of Edward I, this was prohibited as far as England was concerned, but a merchant from a French town might still have his person and property seized for a debt of which he may have had no previous knowledge. External trade was thus not so much individual, between some Englishmen and others; or international, between Englishmen and Frenchmen, Flemings, Spaniards, or Germans, as it was intermunicipal, as it has been well described. Citizens of various towns, London, Bristol, Venice, Ghent, Arras, or Lubeck, for instance, carried on their trade under the protection their city had obtained for them.

21. Foreign Trading Relations. — The regulations and restrictions of fairs and town markets and gilds merchant must have tended largely to the discouragement of foreign trade. Indeed, the feeling of the body of English town merchants was one of strong dislike to foreigners and a desire to restrict their trade within the narrowest limits. In addition to the burdens and limitations placed upon all traders not of their own town, it was very common in the case of merchants from abroad to require that they should only remain within the town for the purpose of selling for forty days, and that they should board not at an inn but in the household of some town merchant, who could thus keep oversight of their movements, and who would be held responsible if his guest violated the law in any way. This was called the custom of "hostage."

The king, on the other hand, and the classes most influential in the national government, the nobility and the churchmen, favored foreign trade. A series of privileges, guarantees, and concessions were consequently issued by the government to individual foreign merchants, to foreign towns, and even to foreigners generally, the object of which was to encourage their coming to England to trade. The most remarkable instance of this was the so-called *Carta*

Mercatoria issued by Edward I in 1303. It was given, according to its own terms, for the peace and security of merchants coming to England from Germany, France, Spain, Portugal, Navarre, Lombardy, Tuscany, Provence, Catalonia, Aquitaine, Toulouse, Quercy, Flanders, Brabant, and all other foreign lands. It allowed such merchants to bring in and sell almost all kinds of goods, and freed them from the payment of many tolls and payments habitually exacted by the towns; it gave them permission to sell to strangers as well as to townsmen, and to retail as well as sell by wholesale. It freed them from the necessity of dwelling with native merchants, and of bringing their stay to a close within a restricted time. Town and market authorities were required by it to give prompt justice to foreigners according to the law merchant, and it was promised that a royal judge would be specially appointed to listen to appeals. It is quite evident that if this charter had been enforced some of the most familiar and valued customs of the merchants of the various English towns would have been abrogated. In consequence of vigorous protests and bitter resistance on the part of the townsmen its provisions were partly withdrawn, partly ignored, and the position of foreign merchants in England continued to depend on the tolerably consistent support of the crown. Even this was modified by the steady policy of hostility, limitation, and control on the part of the native merchants.

With the exception of some intercourse between the northern towns and the Scandinavian countries, the foreign trade of England was carried on almost entirely by foreigners. English merchants, until after the fourteenth century, seem to have had neither the ability, the enterprise, nor the capital to go to continental cities in any numbers to sell the products of their own country or to buy goods which would be in demand when imported into England. Foreigners were more enterprising. From Flemish, French, German, Italian, and even Spanish cities merchants came over as traders. The product of England which was most in demand was wool. Certain parts of England were famous throughout all Europe for the quality and quantity of the wool raised there. The relative good order of England and its exemption from civil war made it possible to raise sheep more extensively than in countries where foraging parties from rival bodies of troops passed frequently to and fro. Many of the monasteries, especially in the north and west, had large outlying wastes of land which were regularly used for the raising of sheep. The product of these northern and western pastures as well as the surplus product of the demesnes and larger holdings of the ordinary manors was brought to the fairs and towns for sale and bought up readily by foreign merchants. Sheepskins, hides, and tanned leather were also exported, as were certain coarse woven fabrics. Tin and lead were well-known products, at that time almost peculiar to England, and in years of plentiful production, grain, salt meat, and dairy products were exported. England was far behind most of the Continent in industrial matters, so that there was much that could be brought into the country that would be in demand, both of the natural productions of foreign countries and of their manufactured articles.

Trade relations existed between England and the Scandinavian countries, northern Germany, southern Germany, the Netherlands, northeastern, northwestern, and southern France, Spain and Portugal, and various parts of Italy. Of these lines of trade the most important were the trade with the Hanse cities of northern Germany, with the Flemish cities, and with those in Italy, especially Venice.

22. The Italian and Eastern Trade. — The merchandise which Venice had to offer was of an especially varied nature. Her prosperity had begun with a coastwise trade along the shores of the Adriatic. Later, especially during the period of the Crusades, her training had been extended to the eastern Mediterranean, where she obtained trading concessions from the Greek Emperor and formed a half commercial, half political empire of her own among the island cities and coast districts of the Ionian Sea, along the Dardanelles and the Sea of Marmora, and finally in the Black Sea. From these regions she brought the productions peculiar to the eastern Mediterranean: wines, sugar, dried fruits and nuts, cotton, drugs, dyestuffs, and certain kinds of leather and other manufactured articles.

Eventually Venice became the special possessor of a still more distant trade, that of the far East. The products of Arabia and Persia, India and the East Indian Islands, and even of China, all through the Middle Ages, as in antiquity, made their way by long and difficult routes to the western countries of Europe. Silk and cotton, both raw and manufactured into fine goods, indigo and other dyestuffs, aromatic woods and gums, narcotics and other drugs, pearls, rubies, diamonds, sapphires, turquoises, and other precious stones, gold and silver, and above all the edible spices, pepper, ginger, cinnamon, cloves, and allspice, could be obtained only in Asia. There were three principal routes by which these goods were brought into Europe: first, along the Red Sea and overland across Egypt; second, up the Persian Gulf to its head, and then either along the Euphrates to a certain point whence the caravan route turned westward to the Syrian coast, or along the Tigris to its upper waters, and then across to the Black Sea at Trebizond; third, by caravan routes across Asia, then across the Caspian Sea, and

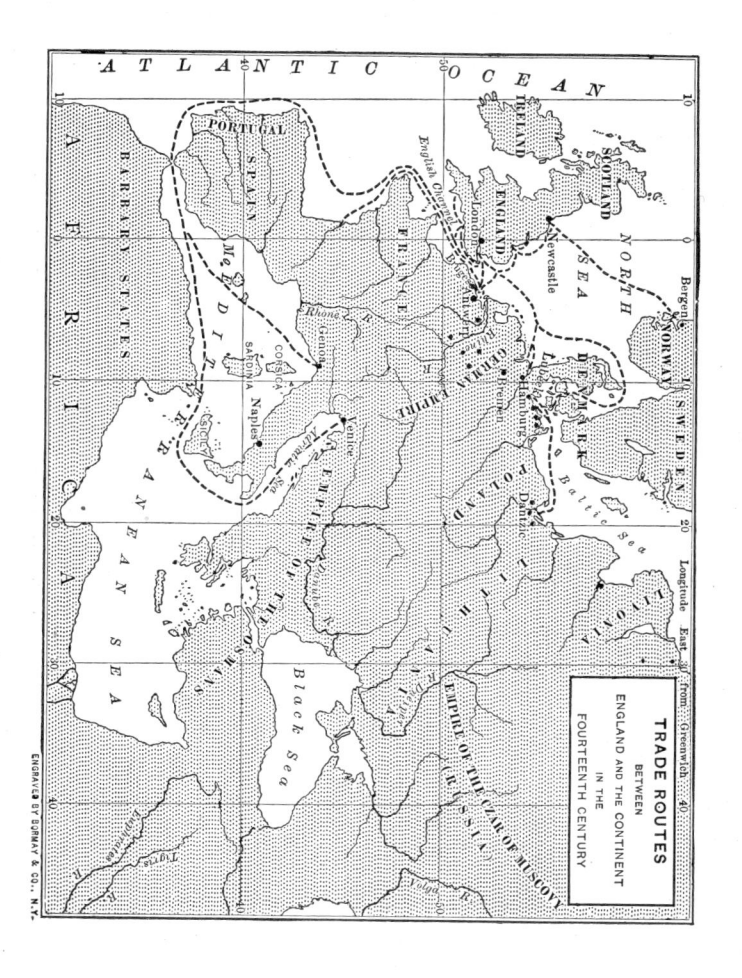

TRADE ROUTES
BETWEEN
ENGLAND AND THE CONTINENT
IN THE
FOURTEENTH CENTURY

overland again, either to the Black Sea or through Russia to the Baltic. A large part of this trade was gathered up by the Italian cities, especially Venice, at its various outlets upon the Mediterranean or adjacent waters. She had for exportation therefore, in addition to her own manufactures, merchandise which had been gathered from all parts of the then known world. The Venetian laws regulated commerce with the greatest minuteness. All goods purchased by Venetian traders must as a rule be brought first to the city and unloaded and stored in the city warehouses. A certain amount of freedom of export by land or water was then allowed, but by far the greater proportion of the goods remained under the partial control of the government. When conditions were considered favorable, the Senate voted a certain number of government galleys for a given voyage. There were several objective points for these voyages, but one was regularly England and Flanders, and the group of vessels sent to those countries was known as the "Flanders Fleet." Such an expedition was usually ordered about once a year, and consisted of two to five galleys. These were put under the charge of an admiral and provided with sailing masters, crews of rowers, and armed men to protect them, all at the expense of the merchants who should send goods in the vessels. Stringent regulations were also imposed upon them by the government, defining the length of their stay and appointing a series of stopping places, usually as follows: Capo d' Istria, Corfu, Otranto, Syracuse, Messina, Naples, Majorca, certain Spanish ports, Lisbon; then across the Bay of Biscay to the south coast of England, where usually the fleet divided, part going to Sluys, Middleburg, or Antwerp, in the Netherlands; the remainder going to Southampton, Sandwich, London, or elsewhere in England. At one or other of the southern ports of England the fleet would reassemble on its return, the whole outward and return voyage usually taking about a year.

The merchants who had come with the fleet thereupon proceeded to dispose of their goods in the southern towns and fairs of England and to buy wool or other goods which might be taken back to Venice or disposed of on the way. A somewhat similar trade was kept up with other Italian cities, especially with Genoa and Florence, though these lines of trade were more extensive in the fifteenth century than in the fourteenth.

23. The Flanders Trade and the Staple. — A trade of greater bulk and greater importance, though it did not include articles from such a distance as that of Italy, was the trade with the Flemish cities. This was more closely connected with English wool production than was that with any other country. Ghent, Bruges, Ypres, Courtrai, Arras, and a number of other cities in Flanders and the adjacent provinces of the Netherlands and France had become populous and rich, principally from their weaving industry. For their manufacture of fine fabrics they needed the English wool, and in turn their fine woven goods were in constant demand for the use of the wealthier classes in England. English skill was not yet sufficient to produce anything more than the crudest and roughest of textile fabrics. The fine cloths, linens, cambrics, cloth of gold and silver, tapestries and hangings, were the product of the looms of the Flemish cities. Other fine manufactured goods, such as armor and weapons, glass and furniture, and articles which had been brought in the way of trade to the Netherlands, were all exported thence and sold in England.

The Flemish dealers who habitually engaged in the English trade were organized among themselves in a company or league known as the "Flemish Hanse of London." A considerable number of towns held such membership in the organization that their citizens could take part in the trade and share in the benefits and privileges of the society, and no citizen of these towns could trade in England without paying the dues and submitting himself to the rules of the Hanse. The export trade from England to the Netherlands was controlled from the English side by the system known as the "Staple." From early times it had been customary to gather English standard products in certain towns in England or abroad for sale. These towns were known as "staples" or "staple towns," and wool, woolfells, leather, tin, and lead, the goods most extensively exported, were known as "staple goods." Subsequently the government took control of the matter, and appointed a certain town in the Netherlands to which staple goods must be sent in the first place when they were exported from England. Later certain towns in England were appointed as staple towns, where all goods of the kinds mentioned above should be taken to be registered, weighed, and taxed before exportation. Just at the close of the period under discussion, in 1354, a careful organization was given to the system of staple towns in England, by which in each of the ten or twelve towns to which staple goods must be brought for exportation, a Mayor of the Staple and two Constables were elected by the "merchants of the staple," native and foreign. These officials had a number of duties, some of them more particularly in the interest of the king and treasury, others in the interest of the foreign merchants, still others merely for the preservation of good order and the enforcement of justice. The law merchant was made the basis of judgment, and every effort made to grant protection to foreigners and at the same time secure the financial interests of the government. But the policy of the government was by no means consistent. Both before and after this date, the whole system of staples was repeatedly abolished for a time and the whole trade in these articles thrown open. Again, the location of the staple towns was shifted from England to the continent and again back to England. Eventually, in 1363, the staple came to be established at Calais, and all "staplers," or exporters of staple goods from England, were forced to give bonds that their cargoes would be taken direct to Calais to be sold.

24. The Hanse Trade. — The trade with Germany was at this time almost all with the group of citizens which made up the German Hanse or League. This was a union of a large number of towns of northern Germany, such as Lubeck, Hamburg, Bremen, Dantzig, Brunswick, and perhaps sixty or eighty others. By a series of treaties and agreements among themselves, these towns had formed a close confederation which acted as a single whole in obtaining favorable trading concessions and privileges in various countries. There had been a considerable trade between the merchants of these towns and England from an early time. They brought the products of the Baltic lands, such as lumber, tar, salt, iron, silver, salted and smoked fish, furs, amber, certain coarse manufactures, and goods obtained by Hanseatic merchants through their more distant trade connections, such as fine woven goods, armor and other metal goods, and even spices and other Eastern goods, obtained from the great Russian fairs. The Hanse cities had entered into treaties with the English government, and possessed valuable concessions and privileges, and imported and exported quite extensively. The term "sterling," as applied to standard English money, is derived from the word

"Easterling," which was used as synonymous with "German," "Hansard," "Dutch," and several other names descriptive of these traders.

The trade with the cities of northwestern France was similar to that with the neighboring towns of Flanders. That with northwestern France consisted especially of salt, sail-cloth, and wine. The trade with Poitou, Gascony, and Guienne was more extensive, as was natural from their long political connection with England. The chief part of the export from southern France was wine, though a variety of other articles, including fruits and some manufactured articles, were sent to England. A trade of quite a varied character also existed between England and the various countries of the Spanish Peninsula, including Portugal. Foreign trade with all of these countries was destined to increase largely during the later fourteenth and the fifteenth century, but its foundations were well laid within the first half of the fourteenth. Vessels from all these countries appeared from time to time in the harbors of England, and their merchants traded under government patronage and support in many English towns and fairs.

25. Foreigners settled in England. — The fact that almost all of the foreign trade of England was in the hands of aliens necessarily involved their presence in the country temporarily or permanently in considerable numbers. The closely related fact that the English were distinctly behind the people of the Continent in economic knowledge, skill, and wealth also led foreigners to seek England as a field for profitable exercise of their abilities in finance, in trade, and manufactures. The most conspicuous of these foreigners at the close of the thirteenth century and during the early part of the fourteenth were the Italian bankers. Florence was not only a great trading and manufacturing city, but a money centre, a capitalist city. The Bardi, Peruzzi, Alberti, Frescobaldi, and other banking companies received deposits from citizens of Florence and other Italian cities, and loaned the money, as well as their own capital, to governments, great nobles, and ecclesiastical corporations in other countries. When the Jews were expelled from England in 1290, there being no considerable amount of money among native Englishmen, the Italian bankers were the only source from which the government could secure ready money. When a tax had been authorized by Parliament, but the product of it could be obtained only after a year or more spent in its collection, the Florentines were at hand to offer the money at once, receiving security for repayment when the receipts from the tax should come in. Government monopolies like the Cornwall tin mines were leased to them for a lump sum; arrangements were made by which the bankers furnished a certain amount of money each day during a campaign or a royal progress. The immediate needs of an impecunious king were regularly satisfied with money borrowed to be repaid some months afterward. The equipment for all of the early expeditions of the Hundred Years' War was obtained with money borrowed from the Florentines. Payments abroad were also made by means of bills of exchange negotiated by the same money-lenders. Direct payment of interest was forbidden by law, but they seem to have been rewarded by valuable government concessions, by the profits on exchange, and no doubt by the indirect payment of interest, notwithstanding its illegality.

The Italian bankers evidently loaned to others besides the king, for in 1327 the Knights Hospitallers in England repaid to the Society of the Bardi £848 5*d*., and to the Peruzzi £551 12*s*. 11*d*. They continued to loan freely to the king, till in 1348 he was indebted to one company alone to the extent of more than £50,000, a sum equal in modern value to about $3,000,000. The king now failed to repay what he had promised, and the banking companies fell into great straits. Defalcations having occurred in other countries also, some of them failed, and after the middle of the century they never held so conspicuous a place, though some Italians continued to act as bankers and financiers through

THE STEELYARD IN THE SEVENTEENTH CENTURY.
(Herbert: *History of London Livery Companies.*)

the remainder of the fourteenth and fifteenth century. Many Italian merchants who were not bankers, especially Venetians and Genoese, were settled in England, but their occupation did not make them so conspicuous as the financiers of the same nation.

The German or Hanse merchants had a settlement of their own in London, known as the "Steelyard," "Gildhall of the Dutch," or the "Easterling's House." They had similar establishments on a smaller scale in Boston and

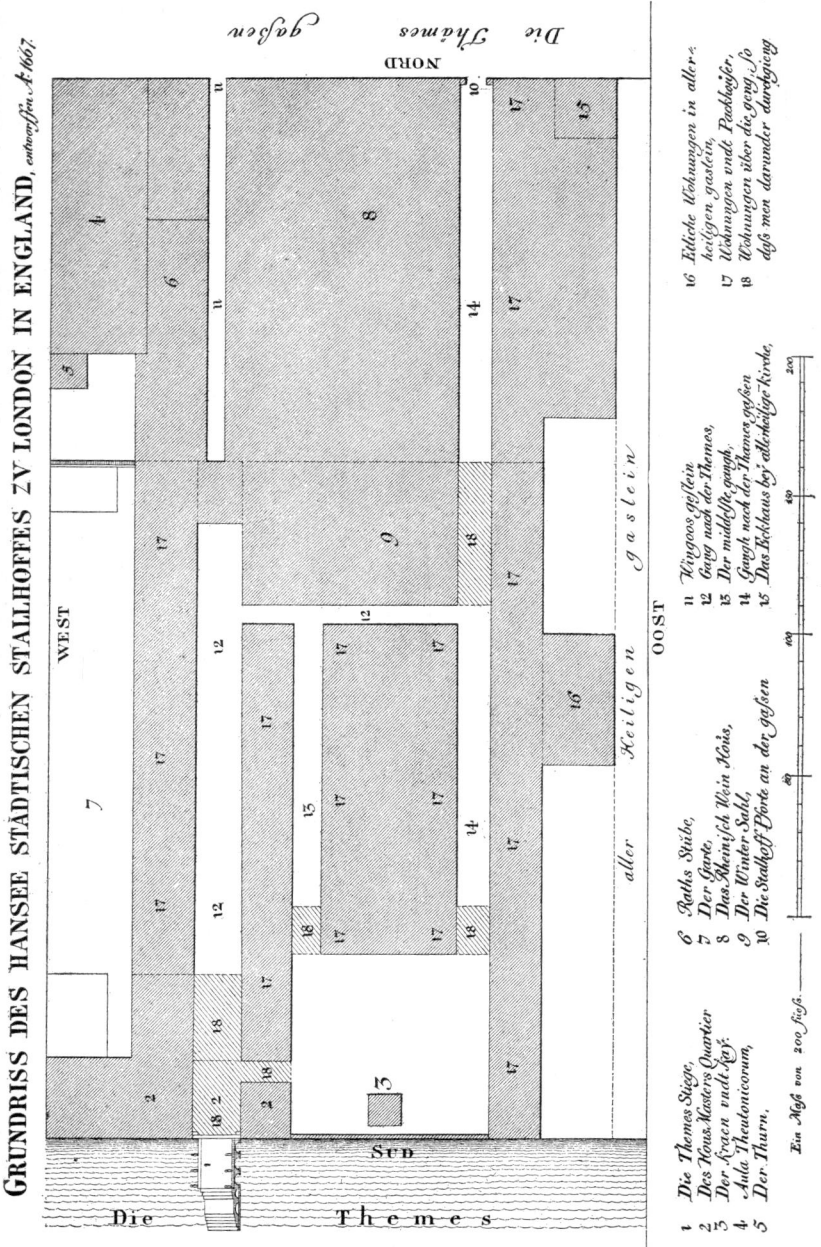

GRUNDRISS DES HANSEE STÄDTISCHEN STALLHOFFES ZV LONDON IN ENGLAND, *entworffen A° 1667.*

1. Die Themes Stiege,
2. Des Haus Masters Quartier
3. Der Kraen vndt Kay,
4. Aula Theutonicorum,
5. Der Thurn,
6. Raths Stube,
7. Der Garten,
8. Das Rheinisch Wein Hans,
9. Der Winter Sahl,
10. Die Stalhoff Porte an der gaßen
11. Wingoos gäßlein
12. Gang nach der Thames,
13. Der middelste gangh,
14. Gangh nach der Thames gehen
15. Das Kothaus bey altenheilige Kirche,
16. Etliche Wohnungen in aller-heiligen gaslein,
17. Wohnungen vndt Packleger,
18. Wohnungen über die gengl, so daß men darunder durchgieng

Ein Maß von 200 fueß.

GROUND PLAN OF THE STEELYARD IN THE SEVENTEENTH CENTURY

Lynn, and perhaps in other towns. Their permission to own property and to live in their own house instead of in the houses of native merchants, as was the usual custom, was derived, like most privileges of foreigners, from the gift of the king. Little by little they had purchased property surrounding their original grants until they had a great group of buildings, including a meeting and dining hall, tower, kitchen, storage house, offices and other warehouses, and a considerable number of dwelling-houses, all enclosed by a wall and fences. It was located immediately on the Thames just above London Bridge so that their vessels unloaded at their own wharf. The merchants or their agents lived under strict rules, the gates being invariably closed at nine o'clock, and all discords among their own nation were punished by their own officers. Their trade was profitable to the king through payment of customs, and after the failure of the Italian bankers the merchants of the Steelyard made considerable loans to the English government either directly or acting for citizens at home. In 1343, when the king had been granted a tax of 40*s.* a sack on all wool exported, he immediately borrowed the value of it from Tiedemann van Limberg and Johann van Wolde, Easterlings. Similarly in 1346 the Easterlings loaned the king money for three years, holding his second crown as security. Like the Florentines, at one time they took the Cornwall tin mines at farm. They had many privileges not accorded generally to foreigners, but were exceedingly unpopular alike with the population and the authorities of the city of London. There were some other Germans domiciled in England, but nowhere else were they so conspicuous or influential as at the Steelyard.

The trade with Flanders brought Flemish merchants into England temporarily, but they do not seem to have formed any settlement or located permanently in any one place. Flemish artisans, on the other hand, had migrated to England from early times and were scattered here and there in several towns and villages. In the early part of the fourteenth century Edward III made it a matter of deliberate policy to encourage the immigration of Flemish weavers and other handicraftsmen, with the expectation that they would teach their art to the more backward native English. In 1332 he issued a charter of protection and privilege to a Fleming named John Kempe, a weaver of woollen cloth, offering the same privilege and protection to all other weavers, dyers, and fullers who should care to come to England to live. In 1337 a similar charter was given to a body of weavers coming from Zealand to England. It is believed that a considerable number of immigrants from the Netherlands came in at this period, settled largely in the smaller towns and rural villages, and taking English apprentices brought about a great improvement in the character of English manufactures. Flemings are also met with in local records in various occupations, even in agriculture.

There were other foreigners resident in England, especially Gascons from the south of France, and Spaniards; but the main elements of alien population in the thirteenth and fourteenth centuries were those which have just been described, Italians, Germans from the Hanse towns, and Flemings. These were mainly occupied as bankers, merchants, and handicraftsmen.

26. BIBLIOGRAPHY

Dr. Cunningham's *Growth of English Industry and Commerce* is particularly full and valuable on this subject. He has given further details on one branch of it in his *Alien Immigrants in England*.

Schanz, Georg: *Englische Handelspolitik gegen Ende des Mittelalters.* This work refers to a later period than that included in this chapter, but the summaries which the author gives of earlier conditions are in many cases the best accounts that we have.

Ashley, W. J.: *Early History of the Woolen Industry in England.*

Pauli, R.: *Pictures from Old England.* Contains an interesting account of the Steelyard.

Pirenne, Henri: *La Hanse flamande de Londres.*

Von Ochenkowski, W.: *England's Wirthsschaftliche Entwickelung im Ausgange des Mittelalters.*

CHAPTER V

THE BLACK DEATH AND THE PEASANTS' REBELLION

Economic Changes of the Later Fourteenth and Early Fifteenth Centuries

27. National Affairs from 1338 to 1461. — For the last century or more England had been standing with her back to the Continent. Deprived of most of their French possessions, engaged in the struggle to bring Wales, Scotland, and Ireland under the English crown, occupied with repeated conflicts with their barons or with the development of the internal organization of the country, John, Henry III, and the two Edwards had had less time and inclination to interest themselves in continental affairs than had Henry II and Richard. But after 1337 a new influence brought England for the next century into close connection with the rest of Europe. This was the "Hundred Years' War" between England and France. Several causes had for years combined to make this war unavoidable: the interference of France in the dispute with Scotland, the conflicts between the rising fishing and trading towns on the English and the French side of the Channel, the desire of the French king to drive the English kings from their remaining provinces in the south of France, and the reluctance of the English kings to accept their dependent position in France. Edward III commenced the war in 1338 with the invasion of France, and it was continued with comparatively short intervals of peace until 1452. During its progress the English won three of the most brilliant military victories in their history, at Crecy, Poitiers, and Agincourt, in 1346, 1356, and 1415. But most of the campaigns were characterized by brutality, destructive ravaging, and the reduction of cities by famine. The whole contest indeed often degenerated into desultory, objectless warfare. A permanent settlement was attempted at Bretigny in 1360. The English required the dismemberment of France by the surrender of almost one-third of the country and the payment by the French of a large ransom for their king, who had been captured by the English. In return King Edward withdrew any other claims he might have to territory, or the French crown. These terms were, however, so humiliating to the French that they did not adhere to them, the war soon broke out again, and finally terminated in the driving out of the English from all of France except the city of Calais, in the middle years of the next century.

The many alliances, embassies, exchanges of visits, and other international intercourse which the prosecution of the Hundred Years' War involved brought England into a closer participation in the general life of Europe than ever before, and caused the ebb and flow of a tide of influences between England and the Continent which deeply affected economic, political, and religious life on both sides of the Channel.

The Universities continued to flourish during almost the whole of this period. It was from Oxford as a centre, under the influence of John Wycliffe, a lecturer there, that a great revival and reforming movement in the church emanated. From about 1370 Wycliffe and others began to agitate for a more earnest religious life. They translated the Bible into English, wrote devotional and polemic tracts, preached throughout the country, spoke and wrote against the evils in the church at the time, then against its accepted form of organization, and finally against its official teachings. They thus became heretics. Thousands were influenced by their teachings, and a wave of religious revival and ecclesiastical rebellion spread over the country. The powers of the church and the civil government were ultimately brought to bear to crush out the "Lollards," as those who held heretical beliefs at that time were called. New and stringent laws were passed in 1401 and 1415, several persons were burned at the stake, and a large number forced to recant, or frightened into keeping their opinions secret. This religious movement gradually died out, and by the middle of the fifteenth century nothing more is heard of Lollardry.

Wycliffe had been not only a religious innovator, but a writer of much excellent English. Contemporary with him or slightly later were a number of writers who used the native language and created permanent works of literature. *The Vision of Piers Plowman* is the longest and best of a number of poems written by otherwise unknown men. Geoffrey Chaucer, one of England's greatest poets, wrote at first in French, then in English; his *Canterbury Tales* showing a perfected English form, borrowed originally, like so much of what was best in England at the time, from Italy or France, but assimilated, improved, and reconstructed until it seemed a purely English production. During the reign of Edward III English became the official language of the courts and the usual language of conversation, even among the higher classes.

Edward III lived until 1377. Through his long reign of half a century, during which he was entirely dependent on the grants of Parliament for the funds needed to carry on the war against France, this body obtained the powers, privileges, and organization which made it thereafter such an influential part of the government. His successor, Richard II, after a period of moderate government tried to rule with a high hand, but in 1399 was deposed through the influence of his cousin, Henry of Lancaster, who was crowned as Henry IV. Henry's title to the throne, according to hereditary principles, was defective, for the son of an older brother was living. He was, however, a mere child, and there was no considerable opposition to Henry's accession. Under the Lancastrian line, as Henry IV, Henry V, and Henry VI, who now reigned successively, are called, Parliament reached the highest position which it had yet attained, a position higher in fact than it held for several centuries afterward. Henry VI was a child at the death of his father in 1422. On coming to be a man he proved too mild in temper to control the great nobles who, by the chances of inheritance, had become almost as powerful as the great feudal barons of early Norman times. The descendants of the older branch of the royal family were now represented by a vigorous and capable man, the duke of York. An effort was therefore made about 1450 by one party of the nobles to depose Henry VI in favor of the duke of York. A number of other nobles took the side of the king, and civil war broke out. After a series of miserable contests known as the "Wars of the Roses" the former party was successful, at least temporarily, and the duke of York became king in 1461 as Edward IV.

28. The Black Death and its Effects. — During the earlier mediæval centuries the most marked characteristic of society was its stability. Institutions continued with but slight changes during a long period. With the middle of the fourteenth century changes become more prominent. Some of the most conspicuous of these gather around a series of attacks of epidemic disease during the latter half of the century.

DISTRIBUTION OF POPULATION

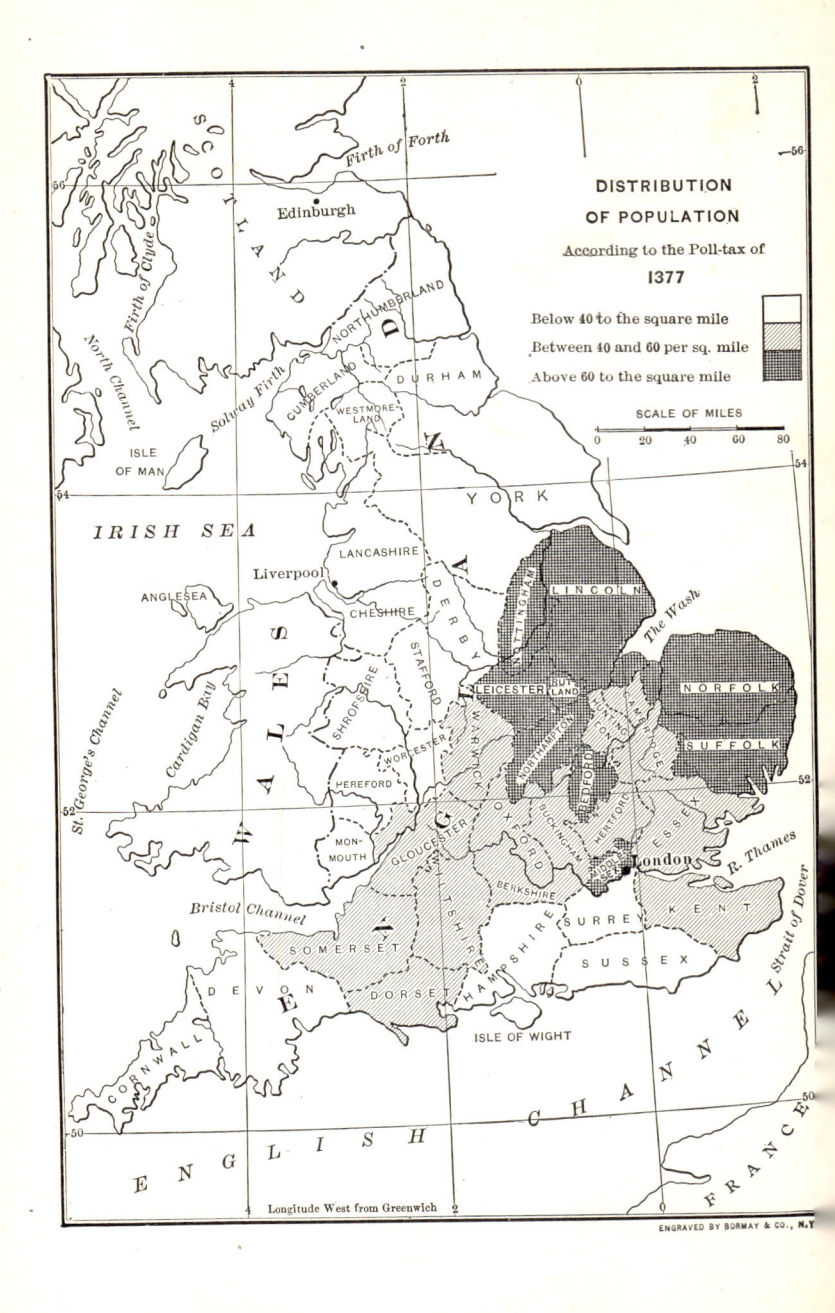

According to the Poll-tax of 1377

- ☐ Below 40 to the square mile
- ▨ Between 40 and 60 per sq. mile
- ▩ Above 60 to the square mile

From the autumn of 1348 to the spring of 1350 a wave of pestilence was spreading over England from the southwest northward and eastward, progressively attacking every part of the country. The disease was new to Europe. Its course in the individual case, like its progress through the community, was very rapid. The person attacked either died within two or three days or even less, or showed signs of recovery within the same period. The proportion of cases which resulted fatally was extremely large; the infectious character of the disease quite remarkable. It was, in fact, an extremely violent epidemic attack, the most violent in history, of the bubonic plague, with which we have unfortunately become again familiar within recent years.

From much careful examination of several kinds of contemporary evidence it seems almost certain that as each locality was successively attacked in 1348 and 1349 something like a half of the population died. In other words, whereas in an ordinary year at that time perhaps one-twentieth of the people died, in the plague year one-half died. Such entries as the following are frequent in the contemporary records. At the abbey of Newenham, "in the time of this mortality or pestilence there died in this house twenty monks and three lay brothers, whose names are entered in other books. And Walter, the abbot, and two monks were left alive there after the sickness." At Leicester, "in the little parish of St. Leonard there died more than 380, in the parish of Holy Cross more than 400, in that of St. Margaret more than 700; and so in every parish great numbers." The close arrangement of houses in the villages, the crowding of dwellings along narrow streets in the towns, the promiscuous life in the monasteries and in the inns, the uncleanly habits of living universally prevalent, all helped to make possible this sweeping away of perhaps a majority of the population by an attack of epidemic disease. It had devastated several of the countries of Europe before appearing in England, having been introduced into Europe apparently along the great trade routes from the far East. Within a few months the attack in each successive district subsided, the disease in the southwestern counties of England having run its course between August, 1348, and May, 1349, in and about London between November, 1348, and July, 1349, in the eastern counties in the summer of 1349, and in the more northern counties through the last months of that year or within the spring of 1350. Pestilence was frequent throughout the Middle Ages, but this attack was not only vastly more destructive and general than any which had preceded it, but the disease when once introduced became a frequent scourge in subsequent times, especially during the remainder of the fourteenth century. In 1361, 1368, and 1396 attacks are noticed as occurring more or less widely through the country, but none were so extensive as that which is usually spoken of as the "Black Death" of 1348–1349. The term "Black Death" was not used contemporaneously, nor until comparatively modern times. The occurrence of the pestilence, however, made an extremely strong impression on men's minds, and as "the great mortality," "the great pestilence," or "the great death," it appears widely in the records and the literature of the time.

Such an extensive and sudden destruction of life could not take place without leaving its mark in many directions. Monasteries were depopulated, and the value of their property and the strictness of their discipline diminished. The need for priests led to the ordination of those who were less carefully prepared and selected. The number of students at Oxford and Cambridge was depleted; the building and adornment of many churches suspended.

The war between England and France, though promptly renewed, involved greater difficulty in obtaining equipment, and ultimately required new devices to meet its expense. Many of the towns lost numbers and property that were never regained, and the distribution of population throughout England was appreciably changed.

But the most evident and far-reaching results of the series of pestilences occurring through the last half of the fourteenth century were those connected with rural life and the arrangement of classes described in Chapter II.

The lords of manors might seem at first thought to have reaped advantage from the unusually high death rate. The heriots collected on the death of tenants were more numerous; reliefs paid by their successors on obtaining the land were repeated far more frequently than usual; much land escheated to the lord on the extinction of the families of free tenants, or fell into his hands for redisposal on the failure of descendants of villains or cotters. But these were only temporary and casual results. In other ways the diminution of population was distinctly disadvantageous to the lords of manors. They obtained much lower rents for mills and other such monopolies, because there were fewer people to have their grain ground and the tenants of the mills could therefore not make as much profit. The rents of assize or regular periodical payments in money and in kind made by free and villain tenants were less in amount, since the tenants were fewer and much land was unoccupied. The profits of the manor courts were less, for there were not so many suitors to attend, to pay fees, and to be fined. The manor court rolls for these years give long lists of vacancies of holdings, often naming the days of the deaths of the tenants. Their successors are often children, and in many cases whole families were swept away and the land taken into the hands of the lord of the manor. Juries appointed at one meeting of the manor court are sometimes all dead by the time of the next meeting. There are constant complaints by the stewards that certain land "is of no value because the tenants are all dead;" in one place that a water-mill is worthless because "all the tenants who used it are dead," in another that the rents are £7 14s. less than in the previous year because fourteen holdings, consisting of 102 acres of land, are in the hands of the lord, in still another that the rents of assize which used to be £20 are now only £2 and the court fees have fallen from 40 to 5 shillings "because the tenants there are dead." There was also less required service performed on the demesne lands, for many of the villain holdings from which it was owed were now vacant. Last, and most seriously of all, the lords of manors suffered as employers of labor. It had always been necessary to hire additional labor for the cultivation of the demesne farm and for the personal service of the manor, and through recent decades somewhat more had come to be hired because of a gradual increase of the practice of commutation of services. That is, villain tenants were allowed to pay the value of their required days' work in money instead of in actual service. The bailiff or reeve then hired men as they were wanted, so that quite an appreciable part of the work of the manor had come to be done by laborers hired for wages.

After the Black Death the same demesne lands were to be cultivated, and in most cases the larger holdings remained or descended or were regranted to those who would expect to continue their cultivation. Thus the demand for laborers remained approximately as great as it had been before. The number of laborers, on the other hand, was vastly diminished. They were therefore eagerly sought for by employers. Naturally they took advantage of their position to demand higher wages, and in many cases combined to refuse to work at the old accustomed rates. A royal ordinance of 1349 states that, " because a great part of the people, especially of workmen and servants, have lately died in the pestilence, many, seeing the necessity of masters and great scarcity of servants, will not serve unless they may receive excessive wages." A contemporary chronicler says that "laborers were so elated and contentious that they did not pay any attention to the command of the king, and if anybody wanted to hire them he was bound to pay them what they asked, and so he had his choice either to lose his harvest and crops or give in to the proud and covetous desires of the workmen." Thus, because of this rise in wages, at the very time that many of the usual sources of income of the lords of manors were less remunerative, the expenses of carrying on their farming operations were largely increased. On closer examination, therefore, it becomes evident that the income of the lords of manors, whether individuals or corporations, was not increased, but considerably diminished, and that their position was less favorable than it had been before the pestilence.

The freeholders of land below lords of manors were disadvantageously affected in as far as they had to hire laborers, but in other ways were in a more favorable position. The rent which they had to pay was often reduced. Land was everywhere to be had in plenty, and a threat to give up their holdings and go to where more favorable terms could be secured was generally effective in obtaining better terms where they were.

The villain holders legally of course did not have this opportunity, but practically they secured many of its advantages. It is probable that many took up additional land, perhaps on an improved tenure. Their payments and their labor, whether done in the form of required "week-work," or, if this were commuted, done for hire, were much valued, and concessions made to them accordingly. They might, as they frequently did, take to flight, giving up their land and either obtaining a new grant somewhere else or becoming laborers without lands of their own.

This last-named class, made up of those who depended entirely on agricultural labor on the land of others for their support, was a class which had been increasing in numbers, and which was the most distinctly favored by the demand for laborers and the rise of wages. They were the representatives of the old cotter class, recruited from those who either inherited no land or found it more advantageous to work for wages than to take up small holdings with their burdens.

But the most important social result of the Black Death and the period of pestilence which followed it was the general shock it gave to the old settled life and established relations of men to one another. It introduced many immediate changes, and still more causes of ultimate change; but above all it altered the old stability, so that change in future would be easy.

29. The Statutes of Laborers. — The change which showed itself most promptly, the rise in the prevailing rate of wages, was met by the strenuous opposition of the law. In the summer of 1349, while the pestilence was still raging in the north of England, the king, acting on the advice of his Council, issued a proclamation to all the sheriffs and the officials of the larger towns, declaring that the laborers were taking advantage of the needs of their lords to demand excessive wages, and prohibiting them from asking more than had been due and accustomed in the year before the outbreak of the pestilence or for the preceding five or six years. Every laborer when offered service at these wages must accept it; the lords of manors having the first right to the labor of those living on their manors, provided they did not insist on retaining an unreasonable number. If any laborers, men or women, bond or free, should refuse to accept such an offer of work, they were to be imprisoned till they should give bail to serve as required. Commissioners were then appointed by the king in each county to inquire into and punish violations of this ordinance.

When Parliament next met, in February, 1351, the Commons sent a petition to the king stating that his ordinance had not been obeyed and that laborers were claiming double and treble what they had received in the years before the pestilence. In response to the petition what is usually called the "First Statute of Laborers" was enacted. It repeated the requirement that men must accept work when it was offered to them, established definite rates of wages for various classes of laborers, and required all such persons to swear twice a year before the stewards, bailiffs, or other officials that they would obey this law. If they refused to swear or disobeyed the law, they were to be put in the stocks for three days or more and then sent to the nearest jail till they should agree to serve as required. It was ordered that stocks should be built in each village for this purpose, and that the judges should visit each county twice a year to inquire into the enforcement of the law. In 1357 the law was reënacted, with some changes of the destination of the fines collected for its breach. In 1361 there was a further reënactment of the law with additional penalties. If laborers will not work unless they are given higher wages than those established by law, they can be taken and imprisoned by lords of manors for as much as fifteen days, and then be sent to the next jail to await the coming of the justices. If any one after accepting service leaves it, he is to be arrested and sued before the justices. If he cannot be found, he is to be outlawed and a writ sent to every sheriff in England ordering that he should be arrested, sent back, and imprisoned till he pays his fine and makes amends

THE STOCKS AT SHALFORD, NEAR GUILDFORD.

Present State.

(Jusserand: *English Wayfaring Life in the Fourteenth Century.* Published by G. P. Putnam's Sons.)

to the party injured; "and besides for the falsity he shall be burnt in the forehead with an iron made and formed to this letter F in token of Falsity, if the party aggrieved shall ask for it." This last provision, however, was probably intended as a threat rather than an actual punishment, for its application was suspended for some months, and even then it was to be inflicted only on the advice of the judges, and the iron was to remain in the custody of the sheriff. The statute was reënacted with slight variations thirteen times within the century after its original introduction; namely, in addition to the dates already mentioned, in 1362, 1368, 1378, 1388, 1402, 1406, 1414, 1423, 1427, 1429, and 1444.

LABORERS REAPING.

From a Fourteenth Century Manuscript.

(Jusserand: *English Wayfaring Life in the Fourteenth Century.* Published by G. P. Putnam's Sons.)

The necessity for these repeated reissues of the statutes of laborers indicates that the general rise of wages was not prevented. Forty years after the pestilence the law of 1388 is said to be passed, "because that servants and laborers are not, nor by a long time have been willing to serve and labor without outrageous and excessive hire." Direct testimony also indicates that the prevailing rate of wages was much higher, probably half as much again, as it had been before the pestilence. Nevertheless, the enforcement of the law in individual cases must have been a very great hardship. The fines which were collected from breakers of the law were of sufficient amount to be estimated at one time as part payment of a tax, at another as a valuable source of income to the lords of manors. Their enforcement was intrusted at different times to the local justices of the peace, the royal judges on circuit, and special commissioners.

The inducement to the passage of the laws prohibiting a rise in wages was no doubt partly the self-interest of the employing classes who were alone represented in Parliament, but partly also the feeling that the laboring class were taking advantage of an abnormal condition of affairs to change the well established customary rates of remuneration of labor. The most significant fact indicated by the laws, however, was the existence of a distinct class of laborers. In earlier times when almost all rural dwellers held some land this can hardly have been the case; it is quite evident that there was now an increasing class who made their living simply by working for wages. Another fact frequently referred to in the laws is the frequent passage of laborers from one district to another; it is evident that the population was becoming somewhat less stationary. Therefore while the years following the great pestilence were a period of difficulty for the lords of manors and the employing classes, for the lower classes the same period was one of increasing opportunity and a breaking down of old restrictions. Whether or not the statutes had any real effect in keeping the rate of wages lower than it would have otherwise become is hard to determine, but there is no doubt that the efforts to enforce the law and the frequent punishment of individuals for its violation embittered the minds of the laborers and helped to throw them into opposition to the government and to the upper classes generally. The statutes of laborers thus became one of the principal causes of the growth of that hostility which culminated in the Peasants' Rebellion.

30. The Peasants' Rebellion of 1381. — From the scanty contemporary records still remaining we can obtain glimpses of a widespread restlessness among the masses of the English people during the latter half of the fourteenth century. According to a petition submitted to Parliament in 1377 the villains were refusing to pay their customary services to their lords and to acknowledge the requirements of their serfdom. They were also gathering together in great bodies to resist the efforts of the lords to collect from them their dues and to force them to submit to the decisions of the manor courts. The ready reception given to the religious revival preached by the Lollards throughout the country indicates an attitude of independence and of self-assertion on the part of the people of which there had been no sign during earlier times. The writer who represents most nearly popular feeling, the author of the *Vision of Piers Plowman*, reflects a certain restless and questioning mysticism which has no particular plan of reform to propose, but is nevertheless thoroughly dissatisfied with the world as it is. Lastly, a series of vague appeals to revolt, written in the vernacular, partly in prose, partly in doggerel rhyme, have been preserved and seem to testify to a deliberate propaganda of lawlessness. Some of the general causes of this rising tide of discontent are quite apparent. The efforts to enforce the statutes of laborers, as has been said, kept continual friction between the employing and the employed class. Parliament, which kept petitioning for reënactments of these laws, the magistrates and special commissioners who enforced them, and the land-owners who appealed to them for relief, were alike engaged in creating class antagonism and multiplying individual grievances. Secondly, the very improvement in the economic position of the lower classes, which was undoubtedly in progress, made them doubly impatient of the many burdens which still pressed upon them. Another cause for the prevalent

ADAM AND EVE.

From a Fourteenth Century Manuscript.

(Jusserand: *English Wayfaring Life in the Fourteenth Century.* Published by G. P. Putnam's Sons.)

unrest may have lain in the character of much of the teaching of the time. Undisguised communism was preached by a wandering priest, John Ball, and the injustice of the claims of the property-holding classes was a very natural inference from much of the teachings of Wycliffe and his "poor priests." Again, the corruption of the court, the

Black Death and Peasants' Rebellion 113

incapacity of the ministers, and the failure of the war in France were all reasons for popular anger, if the masses of the people can be supposed to have had any knowledge of such distant matters.

But the most definite and widespread cause of discontent was probably the introduction of a new form of taxation, the general poll tax. Until this time taxes had either been direct taxes laid upon land and personal property, or indirect taxes laid upon various objects of export and import. In 1377, however, Parliament agreed to the imposition of a tax of four pence a head on all laymen, and Convocation soon afterward taxed all the clergy, regular and secular, the same amount. Notwithstanding this grant and increased taxes of the old forms, the government still needed more money for the expenses of the war with France, and in April, 1379, a graduated poll tax was laid on all persons above sixteen years of age. This was regulated according to the rank of the payer from mere laborers, who were to pay four pence, up to earls, who must pay £4. But this only produced some £20,000, while more than £100,000 were needed; therefore in November of 1380 a third poll tax was laid in the following manner. The tax was to be collected at the rate of three groats or one shilling for each person over fifteen years of age. But although the total amount payable from any town or manor was to be as many shillings as there were inhabitants over fourteen years of age, it was to be assessed in each manor upon individuals in proportion to their means, the more well-to-do paying more, the poorer paying less; but with the limits that no one should have to pay more than £1 for himself and his wife, and no one less than four pence for himself and his wife.

The poll tax was extremely unpopular. In the first place, it was a new tax, and to all appearances an additional weight

I

given to the burden of contributing to the never ending expenses of the government of which the people were already weary. Moreover, it fell upon everybody, even upon those who from their lack of property had probably never before paid any tax. The inhabitants of every cottage were made to realize, by the payment of what amounted to two or three days' wages, that they had public and political as well as private and economic burdens. Lastly, the method of assessing the tax gave scope for much unfairness and favoritism.

In addition to this general unpopularity of the poll tax there was a special reason for opposition in the circumstances of that imposed in 1380. As the returns began to come in they were extremely disappointing to the government. Therefore in March, 1381, the king, suspecting negligence on the part of the collectors, appointed groups of commissioners for a number of different districts who were directed to go from place to place investigating the former collection and enforcing payment from any who had evaded it before. This no doubt seemed to many of the ignorant people the imposition of a second tax. The first rumors of disorder came in May from some of the villages of Essex, where the tax-collectors and the commissioners who followed them were driven away violently by the people. Finally, during the second week in June, rioting began in several parts of England almost simultaneously. In Essex those who had refused to pay the poll tax and driven out the collectors now went from village to village persuading or compelling the people to join them. In Kent the villagers seized pilgrims on their way to Canterbury and forced them to take an oath to resist any tax except the old taxes, to be faithful to "King Richard and the Commons," to join their party when summoned, and never to allow John of Gaunt to become king.

A riot broke out at Dartford in Kent, then Canterbury was overrun and the sheriff was forced to give up the tax rolls to be destroyed. They proceeded to break into Maidstone jail and release the prisoners there, and subsequently entered Rochester. These Kentish insurgents then set out toward London, wishing no doubt to obtain access to the young king, who was known to be there, but also directed by an instinctive desire to strike at the capital of the kingdom. By Wednesday, the 12th of June, they had formed a rendezvous at Blackheath some five miles below the city. Some of the Essex men had crossed the river and joined them, others had also taken their way toward London, marching along the northern side of the Thames. At the same time, or by the next day, another band was approaching London from Hertfordshire on the north. The body of insurgents gathered at Blackheath, who were stated by contemporary chroniclers, no doubt with the usual exaggeration, to have numbered 60,000, succeeded in communicating with King Richard, a boy of fourteen years, who was residing at the Tower of London with his mother and principal ministers and several great nobles, asking him to come to meet them. On the next day, Corpus Christi day, June 12th, he was rowed with a group of nobles to the other bank of the river, where the insurgents were crowding to the water side. The confusion and danger were so great that the king did not land, and the conference amounted to nothing. During the same day, however, the rebels pressed on to the city, and a part of the populace of London having left the drawbridge open for them, they made their way in. The evening of the same day the men from Essex entered through one of the city gates which had also been opened for them by connivance from within. There had already been much destruction of property and of life. As the rebels passed along the roads, the villagers joined them and many of the lower classes of the town population as well. In several cases they burned the houses of the gentry and of the great ecclesiastics, destroyed tax and court rolls and other documents, and put to death persons connected with the law. When they had made their way into London they burned and pillaged the Savoy palace, the city house of the duke of Lancaster, and the houses of the Knights Hospitallers at Clerkenwell and at Temple Bar. By this time leaders had arisen among the rebels. Wat Tyler, John Ball, and Jack Straw were successful in keeping their followers from stealing and in giving some semblance of a regular plan to their proceedings. On the morning of Friday, the 14th, the king left the Tower, and while he was absent the rebels made their way in, ransacked the rooms, seized and carried out to Tower Hill Simon Sudbury, archbishop of Canterbury, who was Lord Chancellor, Robert Hales, Grand Master of the Hospitallers, who was then Lord Treasurer, and some lower officials. These were all put through the hasty forms of an irregular trial and then beheaded. There were also many murders throughout the city. Foreigners especially were put to death, probably by Londoners themselves or by the rural insurgents at their instigation. A considerable number of Flemings were assassinated, some being drawn from one of the churches where they had taken refuge. The German merchants of the Steelyard were attacked and driven through the streets, but took refuge in their well-defended buildings.

During the same three days, insurrection had broken out in several other parts of England. Disorders are mentioned in Kent, Essex, Hertfordshire, Middlesex, Suffolk, Norfolk, Cambridge, Huntingdon, Hampshire, Sussex, Somerset, Leicester, Lincoln, York, Bedford, Northampton, Surrey, and Wiltshire. There are also indications of risings in nine other counties. In Suffolk the leadership was taken by a man named John Wrawe, a priest like John Ball. On June 12th, the same day that the rendezvous was held on Blackheath, a great body of peasants under Wrawe attacked and pillaged a manor house belonging to Richard Lyons, an unpopular minister of the last days of Edward III. The next day they looted a parish church where were stored the valuables of Sir John Cavendish, Chief Justice of the Court of King's Bench and Chancellor of the town of Cambridge. On the 14th they occupied Bury, where they sacked the houses of unpopular men and finally captured and put to death Cavendish himself, John of Cambridge, prior of the St. Edmund's Abbey, and John of Lakenheath, an officer of the king. The rioters also forced the monks of the abbey to hand over to them all the documents giving to the monastery power over the townsmen. There were also a large number of detached attacks on persons and on manor houses, where manor court rolls and other documents were destroyed and property carried off. There was more theft here than in London; but much of the plundering was primarily intended to settle old disputes rather than for its own sake. In Norfolk the insurrection broke out a day or two later than in Suffolk, and is notable as having among its patrons a considerable number of the lesser gentry and other well-to-do persons. The principal leader, however, was a certain Geoffrey Lister. This man had issued a proclamation calling in all the people to meet on the 17th of June on Mushold Heath, just outside the city of Norwich. A great multitude gathered, and they summoned Sir Robert Salle, who was in the military service of the king, but was living at Norwich, and who had risen from peasant rank to knighthood, to come out for a conference. When he declined their request to become their leader they assassinated him, and subsequently made their way into the city, of which they kept control for several days. Throughout Norfolk and Cambridgeshire we hear of the same murders of men who had obtained the hatred of the lower classes in general, or that of individuals who were temporarily influential with the insurgents. There were also numerous instances of the destruction of court rolls found at the manor houses of lay lords of manors or obtained from the muniment rooms of the monasteries. It seems almost certain that there was some agreement beforehand among the leaders of the revolt in the eastern districts of England, and probably also with the leaders in Essex and Kent.

Another locality where we have full knowledge of the occurrences during the rebellion is the town and monastery of St. Albans, just north of London. The rising here was either instigated by, or, at least, drew its encouragement from, the leaders who gathered at London. The townsmen and villains from surrounding manors invaded the great abbey, opened the prison, demanded and obtained all the charters bearing on existing disputes, and reclaimed a number of millstones which were kept by the abbey as a testimony to the monopoly of all grinding by the abbey mill. In many other places disorders were in progress. For a few days in the middle of June a considerable part of England was at the mercy of the revolted peasants and artisans, under the leadership partly of men who had arisen among their own class, partly of certain persons of higher position who had sufficient reason for throwing in their lot with them.

The culmination of the revolt was at the time of the execution of the great ministers of government on Tower Hill on the morning of the 14th. At that very time the young

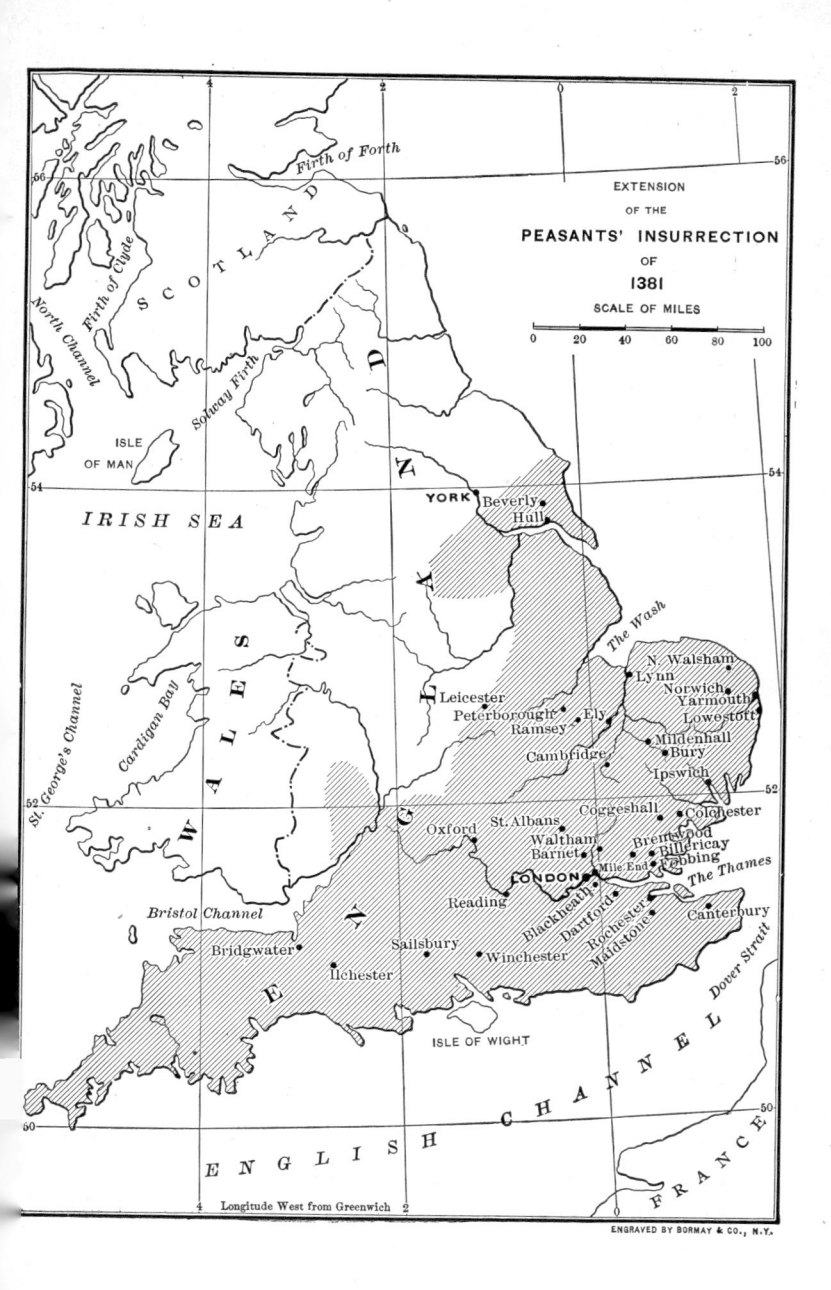

EXTENSION
OF THE
PEASANTS' INSURRECTION
OF
1381
SCALE OF MILES

king had met a body of the rebels, mostly made up of men from Essex and Hertfordshire at Mile End, just outside of one of the gates of London. In a discussion in which they stated their grievances, the king apparently in good faith, but as it afterward proved in bad, promised to give them what they demanded, begged them to disperse and go to their homes, only leaving representatives from each village to take back the charters of emancipation which he proceeded to have prepared and issued to them. There had been no intentional antagonism to the king himself, and a great part of the insurgents took him at his word and scattered to their homes. The charters which they took with them were of the following form: —

"Richard, by the grace of God, King of England and France, and Lord of Ireland, to all his bailiffs and faithful ones, to whom these present letters shall come, greeting. Know that of our special grace, we have manumitted all of our lieges and each of our subjects and others of the County of Hertford; and them and each of them have made free from all bondage, and by these presents make them quit. And moreover we pardon our same lieges and subjects for all kinds of felonies, treasons, transgressions, and extortions, however done or perpetrated by them or any of them, and also outlawry, if any shall have been promulgated on this account against them or any of them; and our most complete peace to them and each of them we concede in these matters. In testimony of which things we have caused these our letters to be made patent. Witness, myself, at London, on the fifteenth day of June, in the fourth year of our reign."

The most prominent leaders remained behind, and a large body of rioters spent the rest of Friday and the following night in London. The king, after the interview at

Mile End, had returned to the Tower, then to the Queen's Wardrobe, a little palace at the other side of London, where he spent the night with his mother. In the morning he mounted his horse, and with a small group of attendants rode toward the Tower. As he passed through the open square of Smithfield he met Wat Tyler, also on horseback, accompanied by the great body of rebels. Tyler rode forward to confer with the king, but an altercation having broken out between him and some of the king's attendants, the mayor of London, Sir William Walworth, suddenly dashed forward, struck him from his horse with the blow of a sword, and while on the ground he was stabbed to death by the other attendants of the king. There was a moment of extreme danger of an attack by the leaderless rebels on the king and his companions, but the ready promises of the king, his natural gifts of pretence, and the strange attachment which the peasants showed to him through all the troubles, tided over a little time until they had been led outside of the city gates, and the armed forces which many gentlemen had in their houses in the city had at last been gathered together and brought to where they had the disorganized body of rebels at their mercy. These were then disarmed, bidden to go to their homes, and a proclamation issued that if any stranger remained in London over Sunday he would pay for it with his life.

The downfall of Tyler and the dispersion of the insurgents at London turned the tide of the whole revolt. In the various districts where disorders were in progress the news of that failure came as a blow to all their own hopes of success. The revolt had been already disintegrating rather than gaining in strength and unity; and now its leaders lost heart, and local bodies of gentry proportionately took courage to suppress revolt in their own localities. The most conspicuous and influential of such efforts was that of Henry de Spencer, bishop of Norwich. This warlike prelate was in Rutlandshire when the news of the revolt came. He hastened toward Norwich ; on his way met an embassy from the rioters to the king ; seized and beheaded two of its peasant members, and still pushing on met the great body of the rebels near Walsham, where after a short conflict and some parleying the latter were dispersed, and their leaders captured and hung without any ceremony other than the last rites of religion. As a matter of fact the rising had no cohesion sufficient to withstand attack from any constituted authority or from representatives of the dominant classes.

The king's government acted promptly. On the 17th of June, two days after the death of Tyler, a proclamation was issued forbidding unauthorized gatherings of people ; on the 23d a second, requiring all tenants, villains, and freemen alike to perform their usual services to their lords ; and on the 2d of July a third, withdrawing the charters of pardon and manumission which had been granted on the 15th of June. Special sessions of the courts were organized in the rebellious districts, and the leaders of the revolt were searched out and executed by hanging or decapitation.

On the 3d of November Parliament met. The king's treasurer explained that he had issued the charters under constraint, and recognizing their illegality, with the expectation of withdrawing them as soon as possible, which he had done. The suggestion of the king that the villains should be regularly enfranchised by a statute was declined in vigorous terms by Parliament. Laws were passed relieving all those who had made grants under compulsion from carrying them out, enabling those whose charters had been destroyed to obtain new ones under the great seal, granting exemption from prosecution to all who had exercised illegal violence in putting down the late insurrection, and finally granting a general pardon, though with many exceptions, to the late insurgents.

Thus the rising of June, 1381, had become a matter of the past by the close of the year. The general conditions which brought about a popular uprising have already been discussed. The specific objects which the rioters had in view in each part of the country are a much more obscure and complicated question.

There is no reason to believe that there was any general political object, other than opposition to the new and burdensome taxation, and disgust with the existing ministry. Nor was there any religious object in view. No doubt a large part of the disorder had no general purpose whatever, but consisted in an attempt, at a period of confusion and relaxation of the law, to settle by violence purely local or personal disputes and grievances.

Apart from these considerations the objects of the rioters were of an economic nature. There was a general effort to destroy the rolls of the manor courts. These rolls, kept either in manor houses, or in the castles of great lords, or in the monasteries, were the record of the burdens and payments and disabilities of the villagers. Previous payments of heriot, relief, merchet, and fines, acknowledgments of serfdom, the obtaining of their land on burdensome conditions, were all recorded on the rolls and could be produced to prove the custom of the manor to the disadvantage of the tenant. It is true that these same rolls showed who held each piece of ground and defined the succession to it, and that they were long afterward to be recognized in the national courts as giving to the customary holder the right of retaining and of inheriting the land, so that it might seem an injury to themselves to destroy the manor court records. But in that period when tenants were in such demand their hold on their land had been in no danger of being disturbed. If these records were destroyed, the villains might well expect that they could claim to be practically owners of the houses and little groups of acres which they and their ancestors had held from time immemorial; and this without the necessity for payments and reservations to which the rolls testified.

Again, lawyers and all connected with the law were the objects of special hostility on the part of insurgents. This must have been largely from the same general cause as that just mentioned. It was lawyers who acted as stewards for the great lords, it was through lawyers that the legal claims of lords of manors were enforced in the king's courts. It was also the judges and lawyers who put in force the statutes of laborers, and who so generally acted as collectors of the poll tax.

More satisfactory relations with their lords were demanded by insurgents who were freeholders, as well as by those who were villains. Protests are recorded against the tolls on sales and purchases, and against attendance at the manorial courts, and a maximum limit to the rent of land is asked for. Finally, the removal of the burdens of serfdom was evidently one of the general objects of the rebels, though much of the initiative of the revolt was taken by men from Kent, where serfdom did not exist. The servitude of the peasantry is the burden of the sermon of John Ball at Blackheath, its abolition was demanded in several places by the insurgents, and the charters of emancipation as given by the king professed to make them " free from all bondage."

These objects were in few if any cases obtained. It is extremely difficult to trace any direct results from the rising other than those involved in its failure, the punishment of the leaders, and the effort to restore everything to its former condition. There was indeed a conservative reaction in several directions. The authorities of London forbade the admission of any former villain to citizenship, and the Commons in Parliament petitioned the king to reduce the rights of villains still further. On the whole, the revolt is rather an illustration of the general fact that great national crises have left but a slight impress on society, while the important changes have taken place slowly and by an almost imperceptible development. The results of the rising are rather to be looked for in giving increased rapidity and definite direction to changes already in progress, than in starting any new movement or in obtaining the results which the insurgents may have wished.

31. Commutation of Services. — One of these changes, already in progress long before the outbreak of the revolt, has already been referred to. A silent transformation was going on inside of the manorial life in the form of a gradual substitution of money payments by the villain tenants for the old labor for two, three, or four days a week, and at special times during the year. This was often described as " selling to the tenants their services." They " bought " their exemption from furnishing actual work by paying the value of it in money to the official representing the lord of the manor.

This was a mutually advantageous arrangement. The villain's time would be worth more to himself than to his lord; for if he had sufficient land in his possession he could occupy himself profitably on it, or if he had not so much land he could choose his time for hiring himself out to the best advantage. The lord, on the other hand, obtained money which could be spent in paying men whose services would be more willing and interested, and who could be engaged at more available times. It is not, therefore, a matter of surprise that the practice of allowing tenants to pay for their services arose early. Commutation is noticeable as early as the thirteenth century and not very unusual in the first half of the fourteenth. After the pestilence, however, there was a very rapid substitution of money payments for labor payments. The process continued through the remainder of the fourteenth century and the early fifteenth, and by the middle of that century the enforcement of regular labor services had become almost unknown. The boon-works continued to be claimed after the week-work had disappeared, since labor was not so easy to obtain at the specially busy seasons of the year, and the required few days' services at ploughing or mowing or harvesting were correspondingly valuable. But even these were extremely unusual after the middle of the fifteenth century.

This change was dependent on at least two conditions, an increased amount of money in circulation and an increased number of free laborers available for hire. These conditions were being more and more completely fulfilled. Trade at fairs and markets and in the towns was increasing through the whole fourteenth century. The increase of weaving and other handicrafts produced more wealth and trade. Money coming from abroad and from the royal mints made its way into circulation and came into the hands of the villain tenants, through the sale of surplus products or as payment for their labor. The sudden destruction of one-half of the population by the Black Death while the amount of money in the country remained the same, doubled the circulation *per capita*. Tenants were thus able to offer regular money payments to their lords in lieu of their personal services.

During the same period the number of free laborers who could be hired to perform the necessary work on the demesne was increasing. Even before the pestilence there were men and women on every manor who held little or no land and who could be secured by the lord for voluntary labor if the compulsory labor of the villains was given up. Some of these laborers were fugitive villains who had fled from one manor to another to secure freedom, and this class became much more numerous under the circumstance of disorganization after the Black Death. Thus the second condition requisite for the extensive commutation was present also.

It might be supposed that after the pestilence, when wages were high and labor was so hard to procure, lords of manors would be unwilling to allow further commutation, and would even try to insist on the performance of actual labor in cases where commutation had been previously allowed. Indeed, it has been very generally stated that there was such a reaction. The contrary, however, was the case. Commutation was never more rapid than in the generation immediately after the first attack of the pestilence. The laborers seem to have been in so favorable a position, that the dread of their flight was a controlling inducement to the lords to allow the commutation of their services if they desired it. The interest of the lords in their labor services was also, as will be seen, becoming less.

When a villain's labor services had been commuted into money, his position must have risen appreciably. One of the main characteristics of his position as a villain tenant had been the uncertainty of his services, the fact that during the days in which he must work for his lord he could be put to any kind of labor, and that the number of days he must serve was itself only restricted by the custom of the manor

His services once commuted into a definite sum of money, all uncertainty ceased. Moreover, his money payments to the lord, although rising from an entirely different source, were almost indistinguishable from the money rents paid by the freeholder. Therefore, serf though he might still be in legal status, his position was much more like that of a freeman.

32. The Abandonment of Demesne Farming. — A still more important change than the commutation of services was in progress during the fourteenth and fifteenth centuries. This was the gradual withdrawal of the lords of manors from the cultivation of the demesne farms. From very early times it had been customary for lords of manors to grant out small portions of the demesne, or of previously uncultivated land, to tenants at a money rent. The great demesne farm, however, had been still kept up as the centre of the agricultural system of the vill. But now even this was on many manors rented out to a tenant or group of tenants. The earliest known instances are just at the beginning of the fourteenth century, but the labor troubles of the latter half of the century made the process more usual, and within the next hundred years the demesne lands seem to have been practically all rented out to tenants. In other words, whereas, during the earlier Middle Ages lords of manors had usually carried on the cultivation of the demesne lands themselves, under the administration of their bailiffs and with the labor of the villains, making their profit by obtaining a food supply for their own households or by selling the surplus products, now they gave up their cultivation and rented them out to some one else, making their profit by receiving a money payment as rent. They became therefore landlords of the modern type. A typical instance of this change is where the demesne land of the manor of Wilburton in Cambridgeshire, consisting of 246 acres of arable land and 42 acres of meadow, was rented in 1426 to one of the villain tenants of the manor for a sum of £8 a year. The person who took the land was usually either a free or a villain tenant of the same or a neighboring manor. The land was let only for a certain number of years, but afterward was usually relet either to the same or to another tenant. The word *farmer* originally meant one of these tenants who took the demesne or some other piece of land, paying for it a "farm" or *firma*, that is, a settled established sum, in place of the various forms of profit that might have been secured from it by the lord of the manor. The free and villain holdings which came into the hands of the lord by failure of heirs in those times of frequent extinction of families were also granted out very generally at a money rent, so that a large number of the cultivators of the soil came to be tenants at a money rent, that is, lease-holders or "farmers." These free renting farmers, along with the smaller freeholders, made up the "yeomen" of England.

33. The Decay of Serfdom. — It is in the changes discussed in the last two paragraphs that is to be found the key to the disappearance of serfdom in England. Men had been freed from villainage in individual cases by various means. Manumission of serfs had occurred from time to time through all the mediæval centuries. It was customary in such cases either to give a formal charter granting freedom to the man himself and to his descendants, or to have entered on the manor court roll the fact of his obtaining his enfranchisement. Occasionally men were manumitted in order that they might be ordained as clergymen. In the period following the pestilences of the fourteenth century the difficulty in recruiting the ranks of the priesthood made the practice more frequent. The charters of manumission issued by the king to the insurgents of 1381 would have granted freedom on a large scale had they not been disowned and subsequently withdrawn. Still other villains had obtained freedom by flight from the manors where they had been born. When a villain who had fled was discovered he could be reclaimed by the lord of the manor by obtaining a writ from the court, but many obstacles might be placed in the way of obtaining this writ, and it must always have involved so much difficulty as to make it doubtful whether it was worth while. So long as a villain was anywhere else than on the manor to which he belonged, he was practically a free man, but few of the disabilities of villainage existing except as between him and his own lord. Therefore, if a villain was willing to sacrifice his little holding and make the necessary break with his usual surroundings, he might frequently escape into a veritable freedom.

The attitude of the common law was favorable to liberty as against servitude, and in cases of doubt the decisions of the royal courts were almost invariably favorable to the freedom of the villain.

But all these possibilities of liberty were only for individual cases. Villainage as an institution continued to exist and to characterize the position of the mass of the peasantry. The number of freemen through the country was larger, but the serfdom of the great majority can scarcely have been much influenced by these individual cases. The commutation of services, however, and still more the abandonment of demesne farming by the lords of manors, were general causes conducive to freedom. The former custom indicated that the lords valued the money that could be paid by the villains more than they did their compulsory services. That is, villains whose services were paid for in money were practically renters of land from the lords, no longer serfs on the land of the lords. The lord of the manor could still of course enforce his claim to the various payments and restrictions arising from the villainage of his tenants, but their position as payers of money was much less servile than as performers of forced labor. The willingness of the lords to accept money instead of service showed as before stated that there were other persons who could be hired to do the work. The villains were valued more as tenants now that there were others to serve as laborers. The occupants of customary holdings were a higher class and a class more worth the lord's consideration and favor than the mere laborers. The villains were thus raised into partial freedom by having a free class still below them.

The effect of the relinquishment of the old demesne farms by the lords of the manors was still more influential in destroying serfdom. The lords had valued serfdom above all because it furnished an adequate and absolutely certain supply of labor. The villains had to stay on the manor and provide the labor necessary for the cultivation of the demesne. But if the demesne was rented out to a farmer or divided among several holders, the interest of the lord in the labor supply on the manor was very much diminished. Even if he agreed in his lease of the demesne to the new farmer that the villains should perform their customary services in as far as these had not been commuted, yet the farmer could not enforce this of himself, and the lord of the manor was probably languid or careless or dilatory in doing so. The other payments and burdens of serfdom were not so lucrative, and as the ranks of the old villain class were depleted by the extinction of families, and fewer inhabitants were bound to attend the manor courts, they became less so. It became, therefore, gradually more common, then quite universal, for the lords of manors to cease to enforce the requirements of serfdom. A legal relation of which neither party is reminded is apt to become obsolete; and that is what practically happened to serfdom in England. It is true that many persons were still legally serfs, and occasionally the fact of their serfdom was asserted in the courts or inferred by granting them manumission. These occasional enfranchisements continued down into the second half of

AN OLD STREET IN WORCESTER.

(Britton: *Picturesque Antiquities of English Cities.*)

the sixteenth century, and the claim that a certain man was a villain was pleaded in the courts as late as 1618. But long before this time serfdom had ceased to have much practical importance. It may be said that by the middle of the fifteenth century the mass of the English rural population were free men and no longer serfs. With their labor services commuted to money and the other conditions of their villainage no longer enforced, they became an indistinguishable part either of the yeomanry or of the body of agricultural laborers.

34. Changes in Town Life and Foreign Trade. — The changes discussed in the last three sections apply in the

TOWN HOUSES IN THE FIFTEENTH CENTURY.

(Wright, T.: *History of Domestic Manners and Sentiments.*)

main to rural life. The economic and social history of the towns during the same period, except in as far as it was part of the general national experience, consisted in a still more complete adoption of those characteristics which have already been described in Chapter III. Their wealth and prosperity became greater, they were still more independent of the rural districts and of the central government, the intermunicipal character of their dealings, the closeness of connection between their industrial interests and their government, the completeness with which all occupations were organized under the "gild system," were all of them still more marked in 1450 than they had been in 1350. It is true that far-reaching changes were beginning, but they were only beginning, and did not reach an important development until a time later than that included in this chapter. The same thing is true in the field of foreign trade. The latter part of the fourteenth and the early fifteenth century saw a considerable increase and development of the trade of England, but it was still on the same lines and carried on by the same methods as before. The great proportion of it was in the hands of foreigners, and there was the same inconsistency in the policy of the central government on the occasions when it did intervene or take any action on the subject. The important changes in trade and in town life which have their beginning in this period will be discussed in connection with those of the next period in Chapter VI.

35. BIBLIOGRAPHY

Jessop, Augustus : *The Coming of the Friars and other Essays*. Two interesting essays in this volume are on *The Black Death in East Anglia*.

Gasquet, F. A. : *The Great Pestilence of 1349*.

Creighton, C. : *History of Epidemics in Britain*, two volumes. This gives especial attention to the nature of the disease.

Trevelyan, G. M.: *England in the Age of Wycliffe.* This book, published in 1899, gives by far the fullest account of the Peasant Rising which has so far appeared in English.

Petit-Dutaillis, C., et Reville, A.: *Le Soulèvement des Travailleurs d'Angleterre en 1381.* The best account of the Rebellion.

Powell, Edgar: *The Peasant Rising in East Anglia in 1381.* Especially valuable for its accounts of the poll tax.

Powell, Edgar, and Trevelyan, G. M.: *Documents Illustrating the Peasants' Rising and the Lollards.*

Page, Thomas Walker: *The End of Villainage in England.* This monograph, published in 1900, is particularly valuable for the new facts which it gives concerning the rural changes of the fourteenth century.

CHAPTER VI

THE BREAKING UP OF THE MEDIÆVAL SYSTEM

Economic Changes of the Later Fifteenth and the Sixteenth Centuries

36. National Affairs from 1461 to 1603. — The close of the fifteenth and the opening of the sixteenth century has been by universal consent settled upon as the passage from one era to another, from the Middle Ages to modern times. This period of transition was marked in England by at least three great movements: a new type of intellectual life, a new ideal of government, and the Reformation. The greatest changes in English literature and intellectual interests are traceable to foreign influence. In the fifteenth century the paramount foreign influence was that of Italy. From the middle of the fifteenth century an increasing number of young Englishmen went to Italy to study, and brought back with them an interest in the study of Greek and of other subjects to which this led. Somewhat later the social intercourse of Englishmen with Italy exercised a corresponding influence on more courtly literature. In 1491 the teaching of Greek was begun at Oxford by Grocyn, and after this time the passion for classical learning became deep, widespread, and enthusiastic. But not only were the subjects of intellectual interest different, but the attitude of mind in the study of these subjects was much more critical than it had been in the Middle Ages. The discoveries of new routes to the far East and of America, as well as the new speculations in natural science which came at this time, reacted on the minds of men and broadened their whole mental outlook. The production of works of pure literature had suffered a decline after the time of Wycliffe and Chaucer, from which there was no considerable revival till the early part of the sixteenth century. Sir Thomas More's *Utopia*, written in Latin in 1514, was a philosophical work thrown into the form of a literary dialogue and description of an imaginary commonwealth. But writing became constantly more abundant and more varied through the reigns of Henry VIII, 1509–1547, Edward VI, 1547–1553, and Mary, 1553–1558, until it finally blossomed out into the splendid Elizabethan literature, just at the close of our period.

A stronger royal government had begun with Edward IV. The conclusion of the war with France made the king's need for money less, and at the same time new sources of income appeared. Edward, therefore, from 1461, neglected to call Parliament annually, as had been usual, and frequently allowed three or more years to go by without any consultation with it. He also exercised very freely what was called the dispensing power, that is, the power to suspend the law in certain cases, and in other ways asserted the royal prerogative as no previous king had done for two hundred years. But the true founder of the almost absolute monarchy of this period was Henry VII, who reigned from 1485 to 1509. He was not the nearest heir to the throne, but acted as the representative of the Lancastrian line, and by his marriage with the lady who represented the claim of the York family joined the two contending factions. He was the first of the Tudor line, his successors being his son, Henry VIII, and the three children of Henry VIII, Edward VI, Mary, and Elizabeth. Henry VII was an able, shrewd, far-sighted, and masterful man. During his reign he put an end to the disorders of the nobility; made Parliament relatively insignificant by calling it even less frequently than Edward IV had done, and by initiating its legislation when it did meet. He also increased and regulated the income of the crown, and rendered its expenditures subject to control. He was able to keep ambassadors regularly abroad, for the first time, and in many other ways to support a more expensive administration, though often by unpopular and illegal means of extortion from the people. He formed foreign political and commercial treaties in all directions, and encouraged the voyages of the Cabots to America. He brought a great deal of business constantly before the Royal Council, but chose its members for their ability rather than for their high rank. In these various ways he created a strong personal government, which left but little room for Parliament or people to do anything except carry out his will. In these respects Henry's immediate successors and their ministers followed the same policy. In fact, the Reformation in the reign of Henry VIII, and new internal and foreign difficulties in the reign of Elizabeth, brought the royal power into a still higher and more independent position.

The need for a general reformation of the church had long been recognized. More than one effort had been made by the ecclesiastical authorities to insist on higher intellectual and moral standards for the clergy and to rid the church of various evil customs and abuses. Again, there had been repeated efforts to clothe the king, who was at the head of all civil government, with extensive control and oversight of church affairs also. Men holding different views on questions of church government and religious belief from those held by the general Christian church in the Middle Ages, had written and taught and found many to agree with them. Thus efforts to bring about changes in the established church had not been wanting, but they had produced no permanent result. In the early years of the sixteenth century, however, several causes combined to bring about a movement of this nature extending over a number of years and profoundly affecting all subsequent history. This is known as the Reformation. The first steps of the Reformation in England were taken as the result of a dispute between King Henry VIII and the Pope. In the first place, several laws were passed through Parliament, beginning with the year 1529, abolishing a number of petty evils and abusive practices in the church courts. The Pope's income from England was then cut off, and his jurisdiction and all other forms of authority in England brought to an end. Finally, the supremacy of the king over the church and clergy and over all ecclesiastical affairs was declared and enforced. By the year 1535 the ancient connection between the church in England and the Pope was severed. Thus in England, as in many continental countries at about the same time, a national church arose independent of Rome. Next, changes began to be made in the doctrine and practices of the church. The organization under bishops was retained, though they were now appointed by the king. Pilgrimages and the worship of saints were forbidden, the Bible translated into English, and other changes gradually introduced. The monastic life came under the condemnation of the reformers. The monasteries were therefore dissolved and their property confiscated and sold, between the years 1536 and 1542. In the reign of Edward VI, 1547–1553, the Reformation was carried much further. An English prayer-book was issued which was to be used in all religious worship, the adornments of the churches were removed, the services made more simple, and doctrines introduced which assimilated the church of England to the contemporary Protestant churches on the Continent.

Queen Mary, who had been brought up in the Roman faith, tried to make England again a Roman Catholic country, and in the later years of her reign encouraged severe persecutions, causing many to be burned at the stake, in the hope of thus crushing out heresy. After her death, however, in 1558, Queen Elizabeth adopted a more moderate position, and the church of England was established by law in much the form it had possessed at the death of Henry VIII.

In the meantime, however, there had been growing up a far more spontaneous religious movement than the official Reformation which has just been described. Many thousands of persons had become deeply interested in religion and enthusiastic in their faith, and had come to hold different views on church government, doctrines, and practices from those approved of either by the Roman Catholic church or by the government of England. Those who held such views were known as Puritans, and throughout the reign of Elizabeth were increasing in numbers and making strenuous though unsuccessful efforts to introduce changes in the established church.

The reign of Elizabeth was marked not only by the continuance of royal despotism, by brilliant literary production, and by the struggle of the established church against the Catholics on the one side and the Puritans on the other, but by difficult and dangerous foreign relations.

More than once invasion by the continental powers was imminent. Elizabeth was threatened with deposition by the English adherents of Mary, Queen of Scots, supported by France and Spain. The English government pursued a policy of interference in the internal conflicts of other countries that brought it frequently to the verge of war with

SIXTEENTH CENTURY FARMHOUSE, THURCASTON, LEICESTERSHIRE.

(Drawing made in 1826.)

their governments and sometimes beyond. Hostility bordering on open warfare was therefore the most frequent condition of English foreign relations. Especially was this true of the relations with Spain. The most serious contest with that country was the war which culminated in the battle of the Armada in 1588. Spain had organized an immense fleet which was intended to go to the Netherlands and convoy an army to be taken thence for the invasion of England. While passing through the English Channel, a storm broke upon them, they were attacked and harried by the English and later by the Dutch, and the whole fleet was eventually scattered and destroyed. The danger of invasion was greatly reduced after this time and until the end of Elizabeth's reign in 1603.

37. Enclosures. — The century and a half which extends from the middle years of the fifteenth century to the close of the sixteenth was, as has been shown, a period remarkable for the extent and variety of its changes in almost every aspect of society. In the political, intellectual, and religious world the sixteenth century seemed far removed from the fifteenth. It is not therefore a matter of surprise that economic changes were numerous and fundamental, and that social organization in town and country alike was completely transformed.

During the period last discussed, the fourteenth and the early fifteenth century, the manorial system had changed very considerably from its mediæval form. The demesne lands had been quite generally leased to renting farmers, and a new class of tenants was consequently becoming numerous; serfdom had fallen into decay; the old manorial officers, the steward, the bailiff, and the reeve had fallen into unimportance; the manor courts were not so active, so regular, or so numerously attended. These changes were gradual and were still uncompleted at the middle of the fifteenth century; but there was already showing itself a new series of changes, affecting still other parts of manorial life, which became steadily more extensive during the remainder of the fifteenth and through much of the sixteenth century. These changes are usually grouped under the name "enclosures."

The enclosure of land previously open was closely connected with the increase of sheep-raising. The older form of agriculture, grain-raising, labored under many difficulties. The price of labor was high, there had been no improvement in the old crude methods of culture, nor, in the open fields and under the customary rules, was there opportunity to introduce any. On the other hand, the inducements to sheep-raising were numerous. There was a steady demand at good prices for wool, both for export, as of old, and for the manufactures within England, which were now increasing. Sheep-raising required fewer hands and therefore high wages were less an obstacle, and it gave opportunity for the investment of capital and for comparative freedom from the restrictions of local custom. Therefore, instead of raising sheep simply as a part of ordinary farming, lords of manors, freeholders, farming tenants, and even customary tenants began here and there to raise sheep for wool as their principal or sole production. Instances are mentioned of five thousand, ten thousand, twenty thousand, and even twenty-four thousand sheep in the possession of a single person. This custom spread more and more widely, and so attracted the attention of observers as to be frequently mentioned in the laws and literature of the time.

But sheep could not be raised to any considerable extent on land divided according to the old open field system. In a vill whose fields all lay open, sheep must either be fed

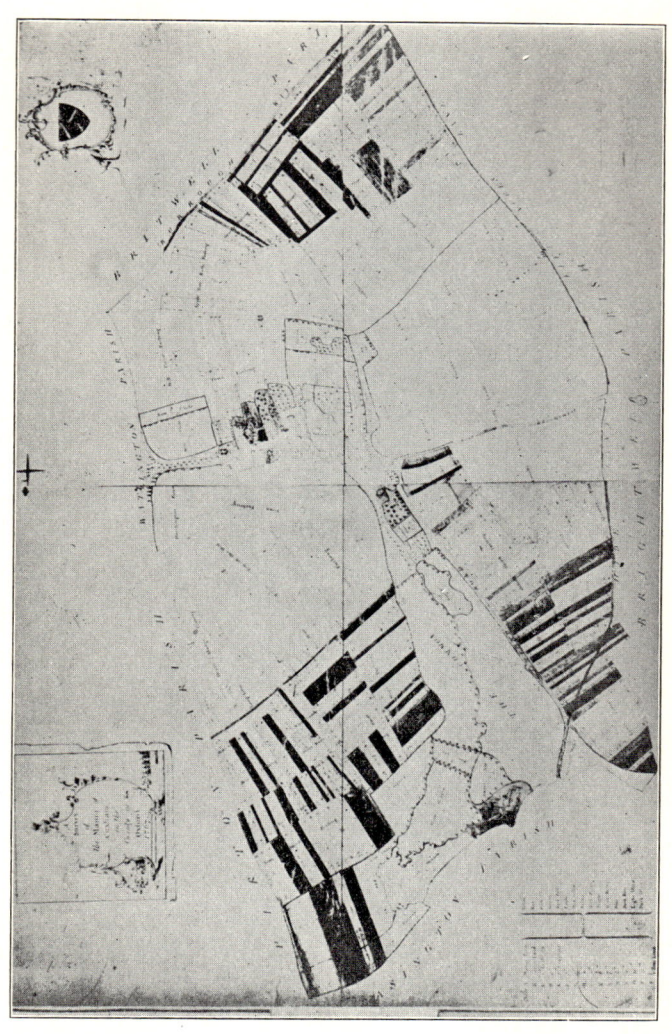

PARTIALLY ENCLOSED FIELDS OF CUXHAM, OXFORDSHIRE, 1767.
(Facsimile map, published by the University of Oxford.)

with those of other men on the common pasture, or must be kept in small groups by shepherds within the confines of the various acres or other small strips of the sheep-raiser's holding. No large number could of course be kept in this way, so the first thing to be done by the sheep-raiser was to get enough strips together in one place to make it worth while to put a hedge or other fence around them, or else to separate off in the same way a part or the whole of the open pastures or meadows. This was the process known as enclosing. Separate enclosed fields, which had existed only occasionally in mediæval farming, became numerous in this time, as they have become practically universal in modern farming in English-speaking countries.

But it was ordinarily impracticable to obtain groups of adjacent acres or sufficiently extensive rights on the common pasture for enclosing without getting rid of some of the other tenants. In this way enclosing led to evictions. Either the lord of the manor or some one or more of the tenants enclosed the lands which they had formerly held and also those which were formerly occupied by some other holders, who were evicted from their land for this purpose.

Some of the tenants must have been protected in their holdings by the law. As early as 1468 Chief Justice Bryan had declared that " tenant by the custom is as well inheritor to have his land according to the custom as he which hath a freehold at the common law." Again, in 1484, another chief justice declared that a tenant by custom who continued to pay his service could not be ejected by the lord of the manor. Such tenants came to be known as copy-holders, because the proof of their customary tenure was found in the manor court rolls, from which a copy was taken to serve as a title. Subsequently copyhold became one of the most generally recognized forms of land tenure in England, and gave practically as secure title as did a freehold. At this time, however, notwithstanding the statements just given, the law was probably not very definite or not very well understood, and customary tenants may have had but little practical protection of the law against eviction. Moreover, the great body of the small tenants were probably no longer genuine customary tenants. The great proportion of small farms had probably not been inherited by a long line of tenants, but had repeatedly gone back into the hands of the lords of the manors and been subsequently rented out again, with or without a lease, to farmers or rent-paying tenants. These were in most cases probably the tenants who were now evicted to make room for the new enclosed sheep farms.

By these enclosures and evictions in some cases the open lands of whole vills were enclosed, the old agriculture came to an end, and as the enclosers were often non-residents, the whole farming population disappeared from the village. Since sheep-raising required such a small number of laborers, the farm laborers also had to leave to seek work elsewhere, and the whole village, therefore, was deserted, the houses fell into ruin, and the township lost its population entirely. This was commonly spoken of at the time as "the decaying of towns," and those who were responsible for it were denounced as enemies of their country. In most cases, however, the enclosures and depopulation were only partial. A number of causes combined to carry this movement forward. England was not yet a wealthy country, but such capital as existed, especially in the towns, was utilized and made remunerative by investment in the newly enclosed farms and in carrying on the expenses of enclosure. The dissolution of the monasteries between 1536 and

1542 brought the lands which they had formerly held into the possession of a class of men who were anxious to make them as remunerative as possible, and who had no feeling against enclosures.

Nevertheless, the changes were much disapproved. Sir Thomas More condemns them in the *Utopia*, as do many other writers of the same period and of the reign of Elizabeth. The landlords, the enclosers, the city merchants who took up country lands, were preached against and inveighed against by such preachers as Latimer, Lever, and Becon, and in a dozen or more pamphlets still extant. The government also put itself into opposition to the changes which were in progress. It was believed that there was danger of a reduction of the population and thus of a lack of soldiers; it was feared that not enough grain would be raised to provide food for the people; the dangerous masses of wandering beggars were partly at least recruited from the evicted tenants; there was a great deal of discontent in the country due to the high rents, lack of occupation, and general dislike of change. A series of laws were therefore carried through Parliament and other measures taken, the object of which was to put a stop to the increase of sheep-farming and its results. In 1488 a statute was enacted prohibiting the turning of tillage land into pasture. In 1514 a new law was passed reënacting this and requiring the repair by their owners of any houses which had fallen into decay because of the substitution of pasture for tillage, and their reoccupation with tenants. In 1517 a commission of investigation into enclosures was appointed by the government. In 1518 the Lord Chancellor, Cardinal Wolsey, issued a proclamation requiring all those who had enclosed lands since 1509 to throw them open again, or else give proof that their enclosure was for the public advantage.

In 1534 the earlier laws were reënacted and a further provision made that no person holding rented lands should keep more than twenty-four hundred sheep. In 1548 a new commission on enclosures was appointed which made extensive investigations, instituted prosecutions, and recommended new legislation. A law for more careful enforcement was passed in 1552, and the old laws were reënacted in 1554 and 1562. This last law was repealed in 1593, but in 1598 others were enacted and later extended. In 1624, however, all the laws on the subject were repealed. As a matter of fact, the laws seem to have been generally ineffective. The nobility and gentry were in the main in favor of the enclosures, as they increased their rents even when they were not themselves the enclosers; and it was through these classes that legislation had to be enforced at this time if it was to be effective.

Besides the official opposition of the government, there were occasional instances of rioting or violent destruction of hedges and other enclosures by the people who felt themselves aggrieved by them. Three times these riots rose to the height of an insurrection. In 1536 the so-called " Pilgrimage of Grace" was a rising of the people partly in opposition to the introduction of the Reformation, partly in opposition to enclosures. In 1549 a series of risings occurred, the most serious of which was the " camp " under Kett in Norfolk, and in 1552 again there was an insurrection in Buckinghamshire. These risings were harshly repressed by the government. The rural changes, therefore, progressed steadily, notwithstanding the opposition of the law, of certain forms of public opinion, and of the violence of mobs. Probably enclosures more or less complete were made during this period in as many as half the manors of England. They were at their height in the early years of

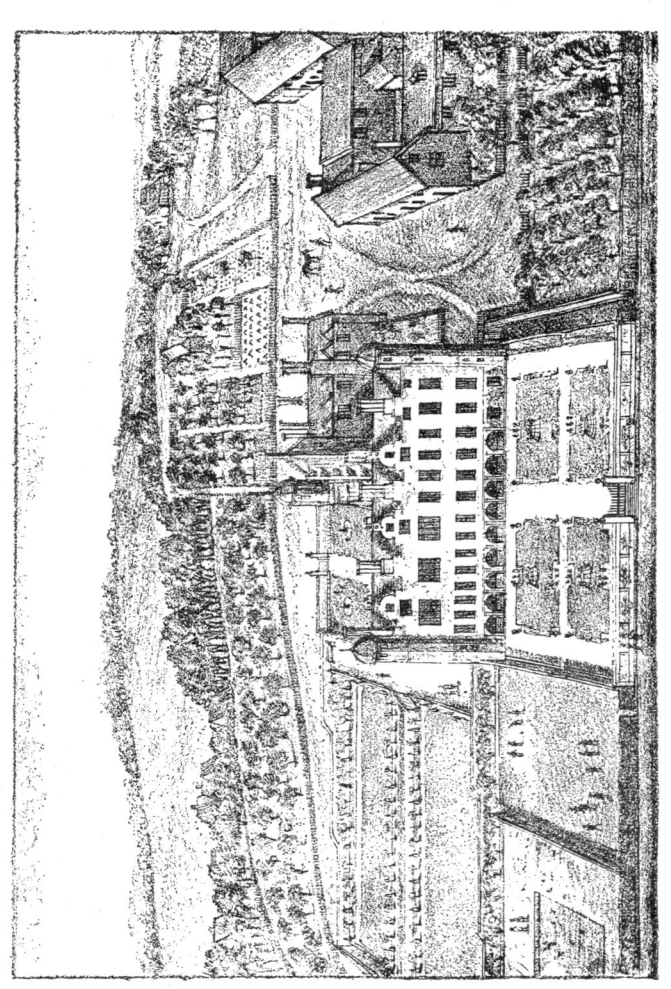

SIXTEENTH CENTURY MANOR HOUSE AND VILLAGE, MADDINGLEY, CAMBRIDGESHIRE.

Nichols: *Progresses of Queen Elizabeth.*

the sixteenth century, during its latter half they were not so numerous, and by its close the enclosing movement had about run its course, at least for the time.

38. Internal Divisions in the Craft Gilds.— Changes in town life occurred during this period corresponding quite closely to the enclosures and their results in the country. These consisted in the decay of the gilds, the dispersion of certain town industries through the rural districts, and the loss of prosperity of many of the old towns. In the earlier craft gilds each man had normally been successively an apprentice, a journeyman, and a full master craftsman, with a little establishment of his own and full participation in the administration of the fraternity. There was coming now to be a class of artisans who remained permanently employed and never attained to the position of master craftsmen. This was sometimes the result of a deliberate process of exclusion on the part of those who were already masters. In 1480, for instance, a new set of ordinances given to the Mercers' Gild of Shrewsbury declares that the fines assessed on apprentices at their entry to be masters had been excessive and should be reduced. Similarly, the Oxford Town Council in 1531 restricts the payment required from any person who should come to be a full brother of any craft in that town to twenty shillings, a sum which would equal perhaps fifty dollars in modern value. In the same year Parliament forbade the collection of more than two shillings and sixpence from any apprentice at the time of his apprenticeship, and of more than three shillings and fourpence when he enters the trade fully at the expiration of his time. This indicates that the fines previously charged must have been almost prohibitive. In some trades the masters required apprentices at the time of indenture to take an oath that they would not set up independent establishments when they had fulfilled the years of their apprenticeship, a custom which was forbidden by Parliament in 1536. In other cases it was no doubt the lack of sufficient capital and enterprise which kept a large number of artisans from ever rising above the class of journeymen.

Under these circumstances the journeymen evidently ceased to feel that they enjoyed any benefits from the organized crafts, for they began to form among themselves what are generally described as "yeomen gilds" or "journeymen gilds." At first the masters opposed such bodies and the city officials supported the old companies by prohibiting the journeymen from holding assemblies, wearing a special livery, or otherwise acting as separate bodies. Ultimately, however, they seem to have made good their position, and existed in a number of different crafts in more or less subordination to the organizations of the masters. The first mention of such bodies is soon after the Peasants' Rebellion, but in most cases the earliest rise of a journeyman gild in any industry was in the latter part of the fifteenth or in the sixteenth century. They were organizations quite similar to the older bodies from which they were a split, except that they had of course no general control over the industry. They had, however, meetings, officers, feasts, and charitable funds. In addition to these functions there is reason to believe that they made use of their organization to influence the rate of wages and to coerce other journeymen. Their relations to the masters' companies were frequently defined by regular written agreements between the two parties. Journeymen gilds existed among the saddlers, cordwainers, tailors, blacksmiths, carpenters, drapers, ironmongers, founders, fishmongers, cloth-workers, and armorers in London, among the weavers in Coventry, the tailors in Exeter and in Bristol, the shoemakers in Oxford, and no doubt in some other trades in these and other towns.

Among the masters also changes were taking place in the same direction. Instead of all master artisans or tradesmen in any one industry holding an equal position and taking an equal part in the administration of affairs of the craft, there came, at least in some of the larger companies, to be quite distinct groups usually described as those " of the livery " and those " not of the livery." The expression no doubt arose from the former class being the more well-to-do and active masters who had sufficient means to purchase the suits of livery worn on state occasions, and who in other ways were the leading and controlling members of the organization. This came, before the close of the fifteenth century, in many crafts to be a recognized distinction of class or station in the company. A statement of the members in one of the London fraternities made in 1493 gives a good instance of this distinction of classes, as well as of the subordinate body last described. There were said to be at that date in the Drapers' Company of the craft of drapers in the clothing, including the masters and four wardens, one hundred and fourteen, of the brotherhood out of the clothing one hundred and fifteen, of the bachelors' company sixty. It was from this prominence of the liveried gildsmen, that the term " Livery Companies " came to be applied to the greater London gilds. It was the wealthy merchants and the craftsmen of the livery of the various fraternities who rode in procession to welcome kings or ambassadors at their entrance into the city, to add lustre to royal wedding ceremonies, or give dignity to other state occasions. In 1483 four hundred and six members of livery companies riding in mulberry colored coats attended the coronation procession of Richard III. The mayors and sheriffs and aldermen of London were almost always livery men in one or another of the companies. A substantial fee had usually to be paid when a member was chosen into the livery, which again indicates that they were the wealthier members. Those of the livery controlled the policy of the gild to the exclusion of the less conspicuous members, even though these were also independent masters with journeymen and apprentices of their own.

But the practical administration of the affairs of the wealthier companies came in many cases to be in the hands of a still smaller group of members. This group was often known as the "Court of Assistants," and consisted of some twelve, twenty, or more members who possessed higher rights than the others, and, with the wardens or other officials, decided disputes, negotiated with the government or other authorities, disposed of the funds, and in other ways governed the organized craft or trade. At a general meeting of the members of the Mercers of London, for instance, on July 23, 1463, the following resolution was passed: " It is accorded that for the holding of many courts and congregations of the fellowship, it is odious and grievous to the body of the fellowship and specially for matters of no great effect, that hereafter yearly shall be chosen and associated to the wardens for the time being twelve other sufficient persons to be assistants to the said wardens, and all matters by them finished to be holden firm and stable, and the fellowship to abide by them." Sixteen years later these assistants with the wardens were given the right to elect their successors.

Thus before the close of the sixteenth century the craft and trading organizations had gone through a very considerable internal change. In the fourteenth century they had been bodies of masters of approximately equal position, in which the journeymen participated in some of the elements of membership, and would for the most part in due time become masters and full members. Now the journeymen had become for the most part a separate class, without prospect of mastership. Among the masters themselves a distinct division between the more and the less wealthy had taken place, and an aristocratic form of government had grown up which put the practical control of each of the companies in the hands of a comparatively small, self-perpetuating ruling body. These developments were all more marked, possibly some of them were only true, in the case of the London companies. London, also, so far as known, is the only English town in which the companies were divided into two classes, the twelve "Greater Companies," and the fifty or more "Lesser Companies"; the former having practical control of the government of the city, the latter having no such influence.

39. Change of Location of Industries. — The changes described above were, as has been said, the result of development from within the craft and trading organizations themselves, resulting probably in the main from increasing wealth. There were other contemporary changes in these companies which were rather the result of external influences. One of these external factors was the old difficulty which arose from artisans and traders who were not members of the organized companies. There had always been men who had carried on work surreptitiously outside of the limits of the authorized organizations of their respective industries. They had done this from inability or unwillingness to conform to the requirements of gild membership, or from a desire to obtain more employment by underbidding in price, or additional profit by using unapproved materials or methods. Most of the bodies of ordinances mention such workmen and traders, men who have not gone through a regular apprenticeship, "foreigners" who have come in from some other locality and are not freemen of the city where they wish to work, irresponsible men who will not conform to the established rules of the trade. This class of persons was becoming more numerous through the fifteenth and sixteenth centuries, notwithstanding the efforts of the gilds, supported by municipal and national authority. The prohibition of any workers setting up business in a town unless they had previously obtained the approval of the officials of their trade was more and more vigorous in the later ordinances; the fines imposed upon masters who engaged journeymen who had not paid the dues, newcomers into the town, were higher. The complaints of the intrusion of outsiders were more loud and frequent. There was evidently more unsupervised, unregulated labor.

But the increase in the number of these unorganized laborers, these craftsmen and traders not under the control of the gilds, was most marked in the rural districts, that is to say, in market towns and in villages entirely outside of the old manufacturing and trading centres. Even in the fourteenth century there were a number of weavers, and probably of other craftsmen, who worked in the villages in the vicinity of the larger towns, such as London, Norwich, and York, and took their products to be sold on fair or market days in these towns. But toward the end of the fifteenth century this rural labor received a new kind of encouragement and a corresponding extension far beyond anything before existing. The English clothmaking industry at this period was increasing rapidly. Whereas during the earlier periods, as we have seen, wool was the greatest of English exports, now it was coming to be manufactured within the country. In connection with this manufacture a new kind of industrial organization began to show itself which, when it was completed, became known as the "domestic system." A class of merchants or manufacturers arose who are spoken of as "clothiers," or "merchant clothiers," who bought the wool or other raw material, and gave it out to carders or combers, spinners, weavers, fullers, and other craftsmen, paying them for their respective parts in the process of manufacture, and themselves disposing of the product at home or for export. The clothiers were in this way a new class of employers, putting the master weavers or other craftsmen to work for wages. The latter still had their journeymen and apprentices, but the initiative in their industry was taken by the merchants, who provided the raw material and much of the money capital, and took charge of the sale of the completed goods. The craftsmen who were employed in this form of industry did not usually dwell in the old populous and wealthy towns. It is probable that the restrictions of the gild ordinances were disadvantageous both to the clothiers and to the small master craftsmen, and that the latter, as well as journeymen who had no chance to obtain an independent position, now that the town craft organizations were under the control of the more wealthy members, were very ready to migrate to rural villages. Thus, in as far as the weaving industry was growing up under the management of the employing clothiers, it was slipping out from under the control of the town gilds by its location in the country. The same thing occurred in other cases, even without the intermediation of a new employing class. We hear of mattress makers, of rope makers, of tile makers, and other artisans establishing themselves in the country villages outside of the towns, where, as a law of 1495 says, "the wardens have no power or authority to make search." In certain parts of England, in the southwest, the west, and the northwest, independent weavers now set up for themselves in rural districts as those of the eastern counties had long done, buying their own raw materials, bringing their manufactures to completion, and then taking them to the neighboring towns and markets to sell, or hawking them through the rural districts.

These changes, along with others occurring simultaneously, led to a considerable diminution of the prosperity of many of the large towns. . They were not able to pay their usual share of taxation, the population of some of them declined, whole streets or quarters, when destroyed by fire or other catastrophe, were left unbuilt and in ruins. Many of the largest and oldest towns of England are mentioned in the statutes of the reign of Henry VIII as being more or less depleted in population. The laws and literature of the time are ringing with complaints of the "decay of the towns," where the reference is to cities, as well as where it is to rural villages. Certain new towns, it is true, were rising into greater importance, and certain rural districts were becoming populous with this body of artisans whose living was made partly by their handicraft, partly by small farming. Nevertheless the old city craft organizations were permanently weakened and impoverished by thus losing control of such a large proportion of their various industries. The occupations which were carried on in the country were pursued without supervision by the gilds. They retained control only of that part of industry which was still carried on in the towns.

40. The Influence of the Government on the Gilds. — Internal divisions and external changes in the distribution of industry were therefore alike tending to weaken the gild organization. It had to suffer also from the hostility or intrusion of the national government. Much of the policy of the government tended, it is true, as in the case of the enclosures, to check the changes in progress, and thus to protect the gild system. It has been seen that laws were passed to prohibit the exclusion of apprentices and journeymen from full membership in the crafts. As early as 1464 a law was passed to regulate the growing system of employment of craftsmen by clothiers. This was carried further in a law of 1511, and further still in 1551 and 1555. The manufacture of rope in the country parts of Dorsetshire was prohibited and restricted to the town of Bridport in 1529; the cloth manufacture which was growing up through the "hamlets, thorps, and villages" in Worcestershire was forbidden in 1553 to be carried on except in the five old towns of Worcester, Evesham, Droitwich, Kidderminster, and Bromsgrove; in 1543 it was enacted that coverlets were not to be manufactured in Yorkshire outside of the city of York, and there was still further legislation in the same direction. Numerous acts were also passed for the purpose of restoring the populousness of the towns. There is, however, little reason to believe that these laws had much more effect in preventing the narrowing of the control of the gilds and the scattering of industries from the towns to the country than the various laws against enclosures had, and the latter object was practically surrendered by the numerous exceptions to it in laws passed in 1557, 1558, and 1575. All the laws favoring the older towns were finally repealed in 1623.

Another class of laws may seem to have favored the craft organizations. These were the laws regulating the carrying on of various industries, in some of which the enforcement of the laws was intrusted to the gild authorities. The statute book during the sixteenth century is filled with laws "for the true making of pins," "for the making of friezes and cottons in Wales," "for the true currying of leather," "for the making of iron gads," "for setting prices on wines," for the regulation of the coopers, the tanners, the makers of woollen cloth, the dyers, the tallow chandlers, the saddlers and girdlers, and dozens of other occupations. But although in many of these laws the wardens of the appropriate crafts are given authority to carry out the requirements of the statute, either of themselves or along with the town officials or the justices of the peace ; yet, after all, it is the rules established by government that they are to carry out, not their own rules, and in many of the statutes the craft authorities are entirely ignored. This is especially true of the "Statute of Apprentices," passed in the fifth year of the reign of Queen Elizabeth, 1563. This great industrial code, which remained on the statute book for two hundred and fifty years, being repealed only in 1813, was primarily a reënactment of the statutes of laborers, which had been continued from time to time ever since their introduction in 1349. It made labor compulsory and imposed on the justices of the peace the duty of meeting in each locality once a year to establish wages for each kind of industry. It required a seven years' apprenticeship for every person who should engage in any trade ; established a working day of twelve hours in summer and during daylight in winter ; and enacted that all engagements, except those for piece work, should be by the year, with six months' notice of a close of the contract by either employer or employee. By this statute all the relations between master and journeyman and the rules of apprenticeship were regulated by the government instead of by the individual craft gilds. It is evident that the old trade organizations were being superseded in much of their work by the national government. Freedom of action was also restricted by the same power in other respects also. As early as 1436 a law had been passed, declaring that the ordinances made by the gilds were in many cases unreasonable and injurious, requiring them to submit their existing ordinances to the justices at Westminster, and prohibiting them from issuing any new

RESIDENCE OF CHANTRY PRIESTS OF ALTAR OF ST. NICHOLAS,
NEAR LINCOLN CATHEDRAL.

(*Domestic Architecture in the Fourteenth Century.*)

ones until they had received the approval of these officials. There is no indication of the enforcement of this law. In 1504, however, it was reënacted with the modification that approval might be sought from the justices on circuit. In

1530 the same requirement was again included in the law already referred to prohibiting excessive entrance fees. As the independent legislation of the gilds for their industries was already much restricted by the town governments, their remaining power to make rules for themselves must now have been very slight. Their power of jurisdiction was likewise limited by a law passed in 1504, prohibiting the companies from making any rule forbidding their members to appeal to the ordinary national courts in trade disputes.

But the heaviest blow to the gilds on the part of the government came in 1547, as a result of the Reformation. Both the organizations formed for the control of the various industries, the craft gilds, and those which have been described in Chapter III as non-industrial, social, or religious gilds, had property in their possession which had been bequeathed or given to them by members on condition that the gild would always support or help to support a priest, should see that mass was celebrated for the soul of the donor and his family, should keep a light always burning before a certain shrine, or for other religious objects. These objects were generally looked upon as superstitious by the reformers who became influential under Edward VI, and in the first year of his reign a statute was passed which confiscated to the crown, to be used for educational or other purposes, all the property of every kind of the purely religious and social gilds, and that part of the property of the craft gilds which was employed by them for religious purposes. One of the oldest forms of voluntary organization in England therefore came to an end altogether, and one of the strongest bonds which had held the members of the craft gilds together as social bodies was removed. After this time the companies had no religious functions, and were besides deprived of a considerable proportion of their

MONASTERY TURNED INTO A FARMHOUSE, DARTFORD PRIORY, KENT.
Nichols: *Progresses of Queen Elizabeth.*

wealth. This blow fell, moreover, just at a time when all the economic influences were tending toward their weakening or actual disintegration.

The trade and craft companies of London, like those of other towns, were called upon at first to pay over to the government annually the amount which they had before used for religious purposes. Three years after the confiscation they were required to pay a lump sum representing the capitalized value of this amount, estimated for tne London companies at £20,000. In order to do so they were of course forced to sell or mortgage much of their land. That which they succeeded in retaining, however, or bought subsequently was relieved of all government charges, and being situated for the most part in the heart of London, ultimately became extremely valuable and is still in their possession. So far have the London companies, however, departed from their original purpose that their members have long ceased to have any connection with the occupations from which the bodies take their names.

41. General Causes and Evidences of the Decay of the Gilds.— An analogous narrowing of the interests of the crafts occurred in the form of a cessation of the mystery plays. Dramatic shows continued to be brought out yearly by the crafts in many towns well into the sixteenth century. It is to be noticed, however, that this was no longer done spontaneously. The town governments insisted that the pageants should be provided as of old, and on the approach of Corpus Christi day, or whatever festival was so celebrated in the particular town, instructions were given for their production, pecuniary help being sometimes provided to assist the companies in their expense. The profit which came to the town from the influx of visitors to see the pageants was a great inducement to the town government to insist on their continuance. On the other hand, the competition of dramas played by professional actors tended no doubt to hasten the effect of the impoverishment and loss of vitality of the gilds. In the last half of the sixteenth century the mystery plays seem to have come finally to an end.

Thus the gilds lost the unity of their membership, were weakened by the growth of industry outside of their sphere of control, superseded by the government in many of their economic functions, deprived of their administrative, legislative, and jurisdictional freedom, robbed of their religious duties and of the property which had enabled them to fulfil them, and no longer possessed even the bond of their dramatic interests. So the fraternities which had embodied so much of the life of the people of the towns during the thirteenth, fourteenth, and fifteenth centuries now came to include within their organization fewer and fewer persons and to affect a smaller and smaller part of their interests. Although the companies continued to exist into later times, yet long before the close of the period included in this chapter they had become relatively inconspicuous and insignificant.

One striking evidence of their diminished strength, and apparently a last effort to keep the gild organization in existence, is the curious combination or consolidation of the companies under the influence of the city governments. Numerous instances of the combination of several trades are to be found in the records of every town, as for instance the " company of goldsmiths and smiths and others their brethren," at Hull in 1598, which consisted of goldsmiths, smiths, pewterers, plumbers and glaziers, painters, cutlers, musicians, stationers and bookbinders, and basket-makers. A more striking instance is to be found in Ipswich in 1576, where the various occupations were all drawn up into four companies, as follows: (1) The Mercers; including the mariners, shipwrights, bookbinders, printers, fishmongers, sword-setters, cooks, fletchers, arrowhead-makers, physicians, hatters, cappers, mercers, merchants, and several others. (2) The Drapers; including the joiners, carpenters, innholders, freemasons, bricklayers, tilers, carriers, casket-makers, surgeons, clothiers, and some others. (3) The Tailors; including the cutlers, smiths, barbers, chandlers, pewterers, minstrels, pedlers, plumbers, pinners, millers, millwrights, coopers, shearmen, glaziers, turners, tinkers, tailors, and others. (4) The Shoemakers; including the curriers, collar-makers, saddlers, pointers, cobblers, skinners, tanners, butchers, carters, and laborers. Each of these four companies was to have an alderman and two wardens, and all outsiders who came to the town and wished to set up trade were to be placed by the town officials in one or the other of the four companies. The basis of union in some of these combinations was evidently the similarity of their occupations, as the various workers in leather among the "Shoemakers." In other cases there is no such similarity, and the only foundation that can be surmised for the particular grouping is the contiguity of the streets where the greatest number of particular artisans lived, or their proportionate wealth. Later, this process reached its culmination in such a case as that of Preston in 1628, where all the tradesmen of the town were organized as one company or fraternity called "The Wardens and Company of Drapers, Mercers, Grocers, Salters, Ironmongers, and Haberdashers." The craft and trading gilds in their mediæval character had evidently come to an end.

42. The Growth of Native Commerce. — The most distinctive characteristic of English foreign trade down to the middle of the fifteenth century consisted in the fact that it had been entirely in the hands of foreigners. The period under discussion saw it transferred with quite as great completeness to the hands of Englishmen. Even before 1450 trading vessels had occasionally been sent out from the English seaport towns on more or less extensive voyages, carrying out English goods, and bringing back those of other countries or of other parts of England. These vessels sometimes belonged to the town governments, sometimes to individual merchants. This kind of enterprise became more and more common. Individual merchants grew famous for the number and size of their ships and the extent of their trade ; as for instance, William Canynges of Bristol, who in 1461 had ten vessels at sea, or Sturmys of the same town, who at about the same time sent the first English vessel to trade with the eastern Mediterranean, or John Taverner of Hull, who built in 1449 a new type of vessel modelled on the carracks of Genoa and the galleys of Venice. In the middle of the fourteenth century the longest list of merchants of any substance that could be drawn up contained only 169 names. At the beginning of the sixteenth century there were at least 3000 merchants engaged in foreign trade, and in 1601 there were about 3500 trading to the Netherlands alone. These merchants exported the old articles of English production and to a still greater extent textile goods, the manufacture of which was growing so rapidly in England. The export of wool came to an end during the reign of Queen Elizabeth, but the export of woven cloth was more than enough to take its place. There was not so much cloth now imported, but a much greater variety and quantity of food-stuffs and wines, of articles of fine manufacture, and of the special products of the countries to which English trade extended.

The entrance of English vessels into ports of towns or

countries whose own vessels had been accustomed to the control of the trade with England, or where the old commercial towns of the Hanseatic League, of Flanders, or of Italy had valuable trading concessions, was not obtained without difficulty, and there was a constant succession of conflicts more or less violent, and of disputes between English and foreign sailors and merchants. The progress of English commerce was, however, facilitated by the decay in the prosperity of many of these older trading towns. The growth of strong governments in Denmark, Sweden, Norway, Poland, and Russia resulted in a withdrawal of privileges which the Hanseatic League had long possessed, and internal dissensions made the League very much weaker in the later fifteenth century than it had been during the century and a half before. The most important single occurrence showing this tendency was the capture of Novgorod by the Russian Czar and his expulsion of the merchants of the Hanse from their settlement in that commercial centre. In the same way most of the towns along the south coast of the Baltic came under the control of the kingdom of Poland.

A similar change came about in Flanders, where the semi-independent towns came under the control of the dukes of Burgundy. These sovereigns had political interests too extensive to be subordinated to the trade interests of individual towns in their dominions. Thus it was that Bruges now lost much of its prosperity, while Antwerp became one of the greatest commercial cities of Europe. Trading rights could now be obtained from centralized governments, and were not dependent on the interest or the antagonism of local merchants.

In Italy other influences were leading to much the same results. The advance of Turkish conquests was gradually increasing the difficulties of the Eastern trade, and the discovery of the route around the Cape of Good Hope in 1498 finally diverted that branch of commerce into new lines. English merchants gained access to some of this new Eastern trade through their connection with Portugal, a country advantageously situated to inherit the former trade of Italy and southern Germany. English commerce also profited by the predominance which Florence obtained over Pisa, Genoa, and other trading towns. Thus conditions on the Continent were strikingly favorable to the growing commercial enterprise of England.

43. The Merchants Adventurers. — English merchants who exported and imported goods in their own vessels were, with the exception of the staplers or exporters of wool and other staple articles, usually spoken of as "adventurers," "venturers," or "merchants adventurers." This term is used in three different senses. Sometimes it simply means merchants who entered upon adventure or risk by sending their goods outside of the country to new or unrecognized markets, as the "adventurers to Iceland," "adventurers to Spain." Again, it is applied to groups of merchants in various towns who were organized for mutual protection or other advantage, as the "fishmongers adventurers" who brought their complaints before the Royal Council in 1542, "The Master, Wardens, and Commonalty of Merchant Venturers, of Bristol," existing apparently in the fourteenth century, fully organized by 1467, and incorporated in 1552, "The Society of Merchants Adventurers of Newcastle upon Tyne," or the similar bodies at York and Exeter.

But by far the most frequent use of the term is that by which it was applied to those merchants who traded to the Netherlands and adjacent countries, especially as exporters of cloth, and who came within this period to be recognized and incorporated as the "Merchants Adventurers" in a special sense, with headquarters abroad, a coat of arms of their own, extensive privileges, great wealth, influence, and prominence. These English merchants, trading to the Netherlands in other articles than those controlled by the Staplers, apparently received privileges of trade from the duke of Brabant as early as the thirteenth century, and the right of settling their own disputes before their own "consul" in the fourteenth. But their commercial enterprises must have been quite insignificant, and it was only during the fifteenth century that they became numerous and their trade in English cloth extensive. Just at the beginning of this century, in 1407, the king of England gave a general charter to all merchants trading beyond seas to assemble in definite places and choose for themselves consuls or governors to arrange for their common trade advantage. After this time, certainly by the middle of the century, the regular series of governors of the English merchants in the Netherlands was established, one of the earliest being William Caxton, afterward the founder of printing in England. On the basis of these concessions and of the privileges and charters granted by the home government the "Merchants Adventurers" gradually became a distinct organization, with a definite membership which was obtained by payment of a sum which gradually rose from 6s. 8d. to £20, until it was reduced by a law of Parliament in 1497 to £6 13s. 4d. They had local branches in England and on the Continent. In 1498 they were granted a coat of arms by Henry VII, and in 1503 by royal charter a distinct form of government under a governor and twenty-four assistants. In 1564 they were incorporated by a royal charter by the title of "The Merchants Adventurers of England." Long before that time they had become by far the largest and most influential company of English exporting merchants. It is said that the Merchants Adventurers furnished ten out of the sixteen London ships sent to join the fleet against the Armada.

Most of their members were London mercers, though there were also in the society members of other London companies, and traders whose homes were in other English towns than London. The meetings of the company in London were held for a long while in the Mercers' hall, and their records were kept in the same minute book as those of the Mercers until 1526. On the Continent their principal office, hall, or gathering place, the residence of their Governor and location of the "Court," or central government of the company, was at different times at Antwerp, Bruges, Calais, Hamburg, Stade, Groningen and Middleburg; for the longest time probably at the first of these places. The larger part of the foreign trade of England during the fifteenth and most of the sixteenth century was carried on and extended as well as controlled and regulated by this great commercial company.

During the latter half of the sixteenth century, however, other companies of merchants were formed to trade with various countries, most of them receiving a government charter and patronage. Of these the Russia or Muscovy Company obtained recognition from the government in 1554, and in 1557, when an ambassador from that country came to London, a hundred and fifty merchants trading to Russia received him in state. In 1581 the Levant or Turkey Company was formed, and its members carried their merchandise as far as the Persian Gulf. In 1585 the Barbary or Morocco Company was formed, but seems to have failed. In 1588, however, a Guinea Company began trading, and in 1600 the greatest of all, the East India Company, was chartered. The expeditions sent out by the

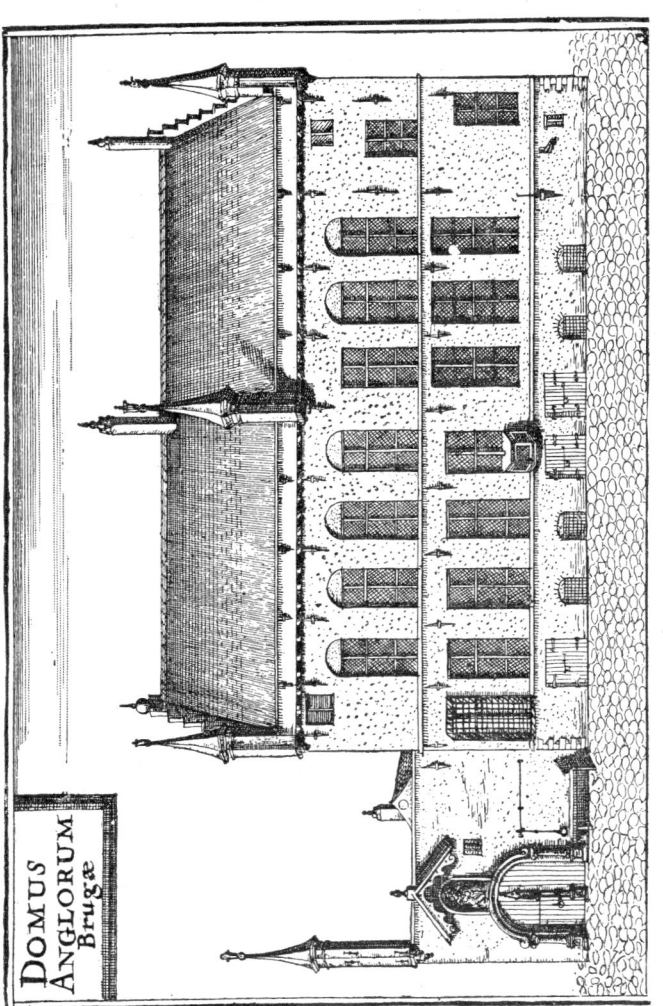

HALL OF THE MERCHANTS ADVENTURERS AT BRUGES.

(Blade: *Life of Caxton*. Published by Kegan Paul, Trench, Trübner & Co.)

Bristol merchants and then by the king under the Cabots, those other voyages so full of romance in search of a northwest or a northeast passage to the Orient, and the no less adventurous efforts to gain entrance to the Spanish possessions in the west, were a part of the same effort of commercial companies or interests to carry their trading into new lands.

44. Government Encouragement of Commerce. — Before the accession of Henry VII it is almost impossible to discover any deliberate or continuous policy of the government in commercial matters. From this time forward, however, through the whole period of the Tudor monarchs a tolerably consistent plan was followed of favoring English merchants and placing burdens and restrictions upon foreign traders. The merchants from the Hanse towns, with their dwellings, warehouses, and offices at the Steelyard in London, were subjected to a narrower interpretation of the privileges which they possessed by old and frequently renewed grants. In 1493 English customs officers began to intrude upon their property; in 1504 especially heavy penalties were threatened if they should send any cloth to the Netherlands during the war between the king and the duke of Burgundy. During the reign of Henry VIII the position of the Hansards was on the whole easier, but in 1551 their special privileges were taken away, and they were put in the same position as all other foreigners. There was a partial regrant of advantageous conditions in the early part of the reign of Elizabeth, but finally, in 1578, they lost their privileges forever. As a matter of fact, German traders now came more and more rarely to England, and their settlement above London Bridge was practically deserted.

The fleet from Venice also came less and less frequently. Under Henry VIII for a period of nine years no fleet came to English ports ; then after an expedition had been sent out from Venice in 1517, and again in 1521, another nine years passed by. The fleet came again in 1531, 1532, and 1533, and even afterward from time to time occasional private Venetian vessels came, till a group of them suffered shipwreck on the southern coast in 1587, after which the Venetian flag disappeared entirely from those waters.

In the meantime a series of favorable commercial treaties were made in various directions by Henry VII and his successors. In 1490 he made a treaty with the king of Denmark by which English merchants obtained liberty to trade in that country, in Norway, and in Iceland. Within the same year a similar treaty was made with Florence, by which the English merchants obtained a monopoly of the sale of wool in the Florentine dominions, and the right to have an organization of their own there, which should settle trade disputes among themselves, or share in the settlement of their disputes with foreigners. In 1496 the old trading relations with the Netherlands were reëstablished on a firmer basis than ever by the treaty which has come in later times to be known as the *Intercursus Magnus*. In the same year commercial advantages were obtained from France, and in 1499 from Spain. Few opportunities were missed by the government during this period to try to secure favorable conditions for the growing English trade. Closely connected as commercial policy necessarily was with political questions, the former was always a matter of interest to the government, and in all the ups and downs of the relations of England with the Continental countries during the sixteenth century the foothold gained by English merchants was always preserved or regained after a temporary loss.

The closely related question of English ship-building was

also a matter of government encouragement. In 1485 a law was passed declaring that wines of the duchies of Guienne and Gascony should be imported only in vessels which were English property and manned for the most part by Englishmen. In 1489 woad, a dyestuff from southern France, was included, and it was ordered that merchandise to be exported from England or imported into England should never be shipped in foreign vessels if sufficient English vessels were in the harbor at the time. Although this policy was abandoned during the short reign of Edward VI it was renewed and made permanent under Elizabeth. By indirect means also, as by the encouragement of fisheries, English seafaring was increased.

As a result of these various forms of commercial influence, the enterprise of individual English merchants, the formation of trading companies, the assistance given by the government through commercial treaties and favoring statutes, English commerce became vastly greater than it had ever been before, reaching to Scandinavia and Russia, to Germany and the Netherlands, to France and Spain, to Italy and the eastern Mediterranean, and even occasionally to America. Moreover, it had come almost entirely into the hands of Englishmen ; and the goods exported and imported were carried for the most part in ships of English build and ownership, manned by English sailors.

45. The Currency. — The changes just described were closely connected with contemporary changes in the gold and silver currency. Shillings were coined for the first time in the reign of Henry VII, a pound weight of standard silver being coined into 37 shillings and 6 pence. In 1527 Henry VIII had the same amount of metal coined into 40 shillings, and later in the year, into 45 shillings. In 1543 coin silver was changed from the old standard of 11 ounces

2 pennyweights of pure silver to 18 pennyweights of alloy, so as to consist of 10 ounces of silver to 2 ounces of alloy; and this was coined into 48 shillings. In 1545 the coin metal was made one-half silver, one-half alloy; in 1546, one-third silver, two-thirds alloy; and in 1550, one-fourth silver, three-fourths alloy. The gold coinage was correspondingly though not so excessively debased. The lowest point of debasement for both silver and gold was reached in 1551. In 1560 Queen Elizabeth began the work of restoring the currency to something like its old standard. The debased money was brought to the mints, where the government paid the value of the pure silver in it. Money of a high standard and permanently established weight was then issued in its place. Much of the confusion and distress prevalent during the reigns of Henry VIII and Edward VI was doubtless due to this selfish and unwise monetary policy.

At about the same time a new influence on the national currency came into existence. Strenuous but not very successful efforts had long been made to draw bullion into England and prevent English money from being taken out. Now some of the silver and gold which was being extorted from the natives and extracted from the mines of Mexico and Peru by the Spaniards began to make its way into England, as into other countries of Europe. These American sources of supply became productive by about 1525, but very little of this came into general European circulation or reached England till the middle of the century. After about 1560, however, through trade, and sometimes by even more direct routes, the amount of gold and silver money in circulation in England increased enormously. No reliable statistics exist, but there can be little doubt that the amount of money in England, as in Europe at

Breaking up of Mediæval System

large, was doubled, trebled, quadrupled, or perhaps increased still more largely within the next one hundred years.

This increase of money produced many effects. One of the most important was its effect on prices. These had begun to rise in the early part of the century, principally as a result of the debasement of the coinage. In the latter part of the century the rise was much greater, due now, no doubt, to the influx of new money. Most commodities cost quite four times as much at the end of the sixteenth century as they did at its beginning.

Another effect of the increased amount of currency appeared in the greater ease with which the use of money capital was obtained. Saving up and borrowing were both more practicable. More capital was now in existence and more persons could obtain the use of it. As a result, manufacturing, trade, and even agriculture could now be conducted on a more extensive scale, changes could be introduced, and production was apt to be profitable, as prices were increasing and returns would be greater even than those calculated upon.

46. Interest. — Any extensive and varied use of capital is closely connected with the payment of interest. In accord with a strict interpretation of certain passages in both the Old and the New Testament, the Middle Ages regarded the payment of interest for the use of money as wicked. Interest was the same as usury and was illegal. As a matter of fact, most regular occupations in the Middle Ages required very little capital, and this was usually owned by the agriculturists, handicraftsmen, or merchants themselves; so that borrowing was only necessary for personal expenses or in occasional exigencies. With the enclosures, sheep farming, consolidation of farms, and other changes in agriculture, with the beginning of manufacturing under the control of capitalist manufacturers, with the more extensive foreign trading and ship owning, and above all with the increase in the actual amount of money in existence, these circumstances were changed. It seemed natural that money which one person had in his possession, but for which he had no immediate use, should be loaned to another who could use it for his own enterprises. These enterprises might be useful to the community, advantageous to himself, and yet profitable enough to allow him to pay interest for the use of the money to the capitalist who loaned it to him. As a matter of fact much money was loaned and, legally or illegally, interest or usury was paid for it. Moreover, a change had been going on in legal opinion parallel to these economic changes, and in 1545 a law was passed practically legalizing interest if it was not at a higher rate than ten per cent. This was, however, strongly opposed by the religious opinion of the time, especially among men of Puritan tendencies. They seemed, indeed, to be partially justified by the fact that the control of capital was used by the rich men of the time in such a way as to cause great hardship. In 1552, therefore, the law of 1545 was repealed, and interest, except in the few forms in which it had always been allowed, was again prohibited. But the tide soon turned, and in 1571 interest up to ten per cent was again made lawful. From that time forward the term usury was restricted to excessive interest, and this alone was prohibited. Yet the practice of receiving interest for the loan of money was still generally condemned by writers on morals till quite the end of this period; though lawyers, merchants, and popular opinion no longer disapproved of it if the rate was moderate.

47. Paternal Government. — In many of the changes which have been described in this chapter, the share which government took was one of the most important influences. In some cases, as in the laws against enclosures, against the migration of industry from the towns to the rural districts, and against usury, the policy of King and Parliament was not successful in resisting the strong economic forces which were at work. In others, however, as in the oversight of industry, in the confiscation of the property of the gilds devoted to religious uses, in the settlement of the relations between employers and employees, in the control of foreign commerce, the policy of the government really decided what direction changes should take.

As has been seen in this chapter, after the accession of Henry VII there was a constant extension of the sphere of government till it came to pass laws upon and provide for and regulate almost all the economic interests of the nation. This was a result, in the first place, of the breaking down of those social institutions which had been most permanent and stable in earlier periods. The manor system in the country, landlord farming, the manor courts, labor dues, serfdom, were passing rapidly away; the old type of gilds, city regulations, trading at fairs, were no longer so general; it was no longer foreigners who brought foreign goods to England to be sold, or bought English goods for exportation. When these old customs were changing or passing away, the national government naturally took charge to prevent the threatened confusion of the process of disintegration. Secondly, the government itself, from the latter part of the fifteenth century onward, became abler and more vigorous, as has been pointed out in the first paragraph of this chapter. The Privy Council of the king exercised larger functions, and extended its jurisdiction into new fields. Under these circumstances, when the functions of the central government were being so widely extended, it was altogether natural that they should come to include the control of all forms of industrial life, including agriculture, manufacturing, commerce, internal trade, labor, and other social and economic relations. Thirdly, the control of economic and social matters by the government was in accordance with contemporary opinions and feelings. An enlightened absolutism seems to have commended itself to the most thoughtful men of that time. A paternalism which regulated a very wide circle of interests was unhesitatingly accepted and approved. As a result of the decay of mediæval conditions, the strengthening of national government, and the prevailing view of the proper functions of government, almost all economic conditions were regulated by the government to a degree quite unknown before. In the early part of the period this regulation was more minute, more intrusive, more evidently directed to the immediate advantage of government; but by the close of Elizabeth's reign a systematic regulation was established, which, while not controlling every detail of industrial life, yet laid down the general lines along which most of industrial life must run. Some parts of this regulation have already been analyzed. Perhaps the best instance and one of the most important parts of it is the Statute of Apprentices of 1563, already described in paragraph 40. In the same year, 1563, a statute was passed full of minute regulations for the fishing and fish-dealing trades. Foreign commerce was carried on by regulated companies; that is, companies having charters from the government, giving them a monopoly of the trade with certain countries, and laying down at least a part of the rules under which that trade should be carried on. The importation of most kinds of finished goods and the exportation of raw materials were prohibited. New industries were encouraged by patents or other government concessions. Many laws were passed, of which that of 1571, to encourage the industry of making caps, is a type. This law laid down the requirement that every person of six years old and upward should wear on every Sunday and holy day a woollen cap made in England.

The conformity to standard of manufactures was enforced either by the officers of companies which were established under the authority of the government or by government officials or patentees, and many of the methods and standards of manufacture were themselves defined by statutes or proclamation. In agriculture, while the policy was less consistent, government regulation was widely applied. There were laws, as has been noted, forbidding the possession of more than two thousand sheep by any one landholder and of more than two farms by any one tenant; laws requiring the keeping of one cow and one calf for every sixty sheep, and the raising a quarter of an acre of flax or hemp for every sixty acres devoted to other crops. The most characteristic laws for the regulation of agriculture, however, were those controlling the export of grain. In order to prevent an excessive price, grain-raisers were not allowed to export wheat or other grain when it was scarce in England. When it was cheap and plenty, they were permitted to do so, the conditions under which it was to be allowed or forbidden being decided, according to a law of 1571, by the justices of the peace of each locality, with the restriction that none should be exported when the prevailing price was more than 1*s*. 3*d*. a bushel, a limit which was raised to 2*s*. 6*d*. in 1592.

Thus, instead of industrial life being controlled and regulated by town governments, merchant and craft gilds, lords of fairs, village communities, lords of manors and their stewards, or other local bodies, it was now regulated in its main features by the all-powerful national government.

48. BIBLIOGRAPHY

Professor Ashley's second volume is of especial value for this period.

Green, Mrs. J. R.: *Town Life in England in the Fifteenth Century*, two volumes.

Cheyney, E. P.: *Social Changes in England in the Sixteenth Century, Part I, Rural Changes*.

A discussion of the legal character of villain tenure in the sixteenth century will be found in articles by Mr. I. S. Leadam, in *The English Historical Review*, for October, 1893, and in the *Transactions of the English Royal Historical Society* for 1892, 1893, and 1894; and by Professor Ashley in the *English Historical Review* for April, 1893, and *Annals of the American Academy of Political Science* for January, 1891. (Reprinted in *English Economic History*, Vol. II, Chap. 4.)

Bourne, H. R. F.: *English Merchants*.

Froude, J. A.: *History of England*. Many scattered passages of great interest refer to the economic and social changes of this period, but they are frequently exaggerated, and in some cases incorrect. Almost the same remark applies to Professor Rogers' *Six Centuries of Work and Wages* and *Industrial and Commercial History of England*.

Busch, Wilhelm: *A History of England under the Tudors*. For the economic policy of Henry VII.

CHAPTER VII

THE EXPANSION OF ENGLAND

Economic Changes of the Seventeenth and Early Eighteenth Centuries

49. National Affairs from 1603 to 1760. — The last three rulers of the Tudor family had died childless. James, king of Scotland, their cousin, therefore inherited the throne and became the first English king of the Stuart family. James reigned from 1603 to 1625. Many of the political and religious problems which had been created by the policy of the Tudor sovereigns had now to come up for solution. Parliament had long been restive under the almost autocratic government of Queen Elizabeth, but the danger of foreign invasion and internal rebellion, long-established habit, Elizabeth's personal popularity, her age, her sex, and her occasional yielding, all combined to prevent any very outspoken opposition. Under King James all these things were changed. Yet he had even higher ideas of his personal rights, powers, and duties as king than any of his predecessors. Therefore during the whole of the reign dispute and ill feeling existed between the king, his ministers, and many of the judges and other officials, on the one hand, and the majority of the House of Commons and among the middle and upper classes of the country, on the other. James would willingly have avoided calling Parliament altogether and would have carried on the government according to his own judgment and that of the ministers he selected, but it was absolutely necessary to assemble it for the passing of certain laws, and above all for the authorization of taxes to obtain the means to carry on the government. The fall in the value of gold and silver and the consequent rise of prices, and other economic changes, had reduced the income of the government just at a time when its necessary expenses were increasing, and when a spendthrift king was making profuse additional outlays. Finances were therefore a constant difficulty during his reign, as in fact they remained during the whole of the seventeenth century.

In religion James wished to maintain the middle course of the established church as it had been under Elizabeth. He was even less inclined to harsh treatment of the Roman Catholics. On the other hand, the tide of Puritan feeling appealing for greater strictness and earnestness in the church and a more democratic form of church government was rising higher and higher, and with this a desire to expel the Roman Catholics altogether. The House of Commons represented this strong Protestant feeling, so that still another cause of conflict existed between King and Parliament. Similarly, in foreign affairs and on many other questions James was at cross purposes with the main body of the English nation.

This reign was the period of foundation of England's great colonial empire. The effort to establish settlements on the North American coast were at last successful in Virginia and New England, and soon after in the West Indies. Still other districts were being settled by other European nations, ultimately to be absorbed by England. On the other side of the world the East India Company began its progress toward the subjugation of India. Nearer home, a new policy was carried out in Ireland, by which large numbers of English and Scotch immigrants were induced to settle in Ulster, the northernmost province. Thus that process was begun by which men of English race and language, living under English institutions and customs, have established centres of population, wealth, and influence in so many parts of the world.

Charles I came to the throne in 1625. Most of the characteristics of the period of James continued until the quarrels between King and Parliament became so bitter that in 1642 civil war broke out. The result of four years of fighting was the defeat and capture of the king. After fruitless attempts at a satisfactory settlement Charles was brought to trial by Parliament in 1649, declared guilty of treason, and executed.

A republican form of government was now established, known as the "Commonwealth," and kingship and the House of Lords were abolished. The army, however, had come to have a will of its own, and quarrels between its officers and the majority of Parliament were frequent. Both Parliament and army had become unpopular, taxation was heavy, and religious disputes troublesome. The majority in Parliament had carried the national church so far in the direction of Puritanism that its excesses had brought about a strong reactionary feeling. Parliament had already sat for more than ten years, hence called the "Long Parliament," and had become corrupt and despotic. Under these circumstances, one modification after another was made in the form of government until in 1653 Oliver Cromwell, the commander of the army and long the most influential man in Parliament, dissolved that body by military force and was made Lord Protector, with powers not very different from those of a king. There was now a period of good order and great military and naval success for England; Scotland and Ireland, both of which had declared against the Commonwealth, were reduced to obedience, and successful foreign wars were waged. But at home the government did not succeed in obtaining either popularity or general acceptance. Parliament after Parliament was called, but could not agree with the Protector. In 1657 Cromwell was given still higher powers, but in 1658 he died. His son, Richard Cromwell, was installed as Protector. The republican government had, however, been gradually drifting back toward the old royal form and spirit, so when the new Lord Protector proved to be unequal to the position, when the army became rebellious again, and the country threatened to fall into anarchy, Monk, an influential general, brought about the reassembling of the Long Parliament, and this body recalled the son of Charles I to take his hereditary seat as king.

This event occurred in 1660, and is known as the Restoration. Charles II reigned for twenty-five years. His reign was in one of its aspects a time of reaction in manners and morals against the over-strictness of the former Puritan control. In government, notwithstanding the independent position of the king, it was the period when some of the most important modern institutions came into existence. Permanent political parties were formed then for the first time. It was then that the custom arose by which the ministers of the government are expected to resign when there proves to be a majority in Parliament against them. It was then that a "cabinet," or group of ministers acting together and responsible for the policy of the king, was first formed. The old form of the established church came again into power, and harsh laws were enacted against Presbyterians, Baptists, Quakers, and members of the other sects which had grown up during the earlier part of the century.

It was to escape these oppressive laws that many emigrated to the colonies in America and established new settlements. Not only was the stream of emigration kept up by religious persecutions, but the prosperity and abundant opportunity for advancement furnished by the colonies attracted great numbers. The government of the Stuart kings, as well as that of the Commonwealth, constantly encouraged distant settlements for the sake of commerce, shipping, the export of English manufactured goods, and the import of raw materials. The expansion of the country through its colonial settlements therefore still continued.

The great literature which reached its climax in the reign of Elizabeth continued in equal variety and abundance throughout the reigns of James and Charles. The greater plays of Shakespeare were written after the accession of James. Milton belonged to the Commonwealth period, and Bunyan, the famous author of *Pilgrim's Progress*, was one of those non-conformists in religion who were imprisoned under Charles II. With this reign, however, quite a new literary type arose, whose most conspicuous representative was Dryden.

In 1685 James II succeeded his brother. Instead of carrying on the government in a spirit of concession to national feeling, he adopted such an unpopular policy that in 1688 he was forced to flee from England, and his son-in-law and daughter, William and Mary, were elected to the throne. On their accession Parliament passed and the king and queen accepted a "Bill of Rights." This declared the illegality of a number of actions which recent sovereigns had claimed the right to do, and guaranteed to Englishmen a number of important individual rights, which have since been included in many other documents, especially in the constitutions of several of the American states and the first ten amendments to the Constitution of the United States. The Bill of Rights is often grouped with the Great Charter, and these two documents, along with several of the Acts of the Parliaments of Charles I accepted by the king, make the principal written elements of the English constitution. The form and powers attained by the English government have been, however, rather the result of slight changes from time to time, often without intention of influencing the constitution, than of any deliberate action. Important examples of this are certain customs of legislation which grew up under William and Mary. The Mutiny Act, by which the army is kept up, was only passed for one year at a time. The grant of taxes was also only made annually. Parliament must therefore be called every year in order to obtain money to carry on the work of government, and in order to keep up the military organization.

As a result of the Revolution of 1688, as the deposition of James II. and the appointment of William and Mary are called, and of the changes which succeeded it, Parliament gradually became the most powerful part of government, and the House of Commons the strongest part of Parliament. The king's ministers came more and more to carry out the will of Parliament rather than that of the king. Somewhat later the custom grew up by which one of the ministers by presiding over the whole Cabinet, nominating its members to the king, representing it in interviews with the king, and in other ways giving unity to its action, created the position of prime minister. Thus the modern Parliamentary organization of the government was practically complete before the middle of the eighteenth century. William and Mary died childless, and Anne, Mary's sister, succeeded, and reigned till 1714. She also left no heir. In the meantime arrangements had been made to set aside the descendants of James II, who were Roman Catholics, and to give the succession to a distant line of Protestant descendants of James I. In this way George I, Elector of Hanover, of the house of Brunswick, became king, reigned till 1727, and was succeeded by George II, who reigned till 1760. The sovereigns of England have been of this family ever since.

The years following the Revolution of 1688 were a time of almost constant warfare on the Continent, in the colonies, and at sea. In many of these wars the real interests of England were but slightly concerned. In others her colonial and native dependencies were so deeply affected as to make them veritable national wars. Just at the close of the period, in 1763, the war known in Europe as the Seven Years' War and in America as the French and Indian War was brought to an end by the peace of Paris. This peace drew the outlines of the widespread empire of Great Britain, for it handed over to her Canada, the last of the French possessions in America, and guaranteed her the ultimate predominance in India.

50. The Extension of Agriculture. — During the seventeenth and the first half of the eighteenth century there are no such fundamental changes in social organization to chronicle as during the preceding century and a half. During the first hundred years of the period the whole energy of the nation seems to have been thrown into political and religious contests. Later there was development and increase of production, but they were in the main an extension or expansion of the familiar forms, not such a change of form as would cause any alteration in the position of the mass of the people.

The practice of enclosing open land had almost ceased before the death of Elizabeth. There was some enclosing under

James I, but it seems to have been quite exceptional. In the main, those common pastures and open fields which had not been enclosed by the beginning of this period, probably one-half of all England, remained unenclosed till the recommencement of the process long afterward. Sheep farming gradually ceased to be so exclusively practised, and mixed agriculture became general, though few if any of those fields which had been surrounded with hedges, and come into the possession of individual farmers, were thrown open or distributed again into scattered holdings. Much new land came into cultivation or into use for pasture through the draining of marshes and fens, and the clearing of forests. This work had been begun for the extensive swampy tracts in the east of England in the latter years of Elizabeth's reign by private purchasers, assisted by an act of Parliament passed in 1601, intended to remove legal difficulties. It proceeded slowly, partly because of the expense and difficulty of putting up lasting embarkments, and partly because of the opposition of the fenmen, or dwellers in the marshy districts, whose livelihood was obtained by catching the fish and water fowl that the improvements would drive away. With the seventeenth and early eighteenth centuries, however, largely through the skill of Dutch engineers and laborers, many thousands of acres of fertile land were reclaimed and devoted to grazing, and even grain raising. Great stretches of old forest and waste land covered with rough underbrush were also reduced to cultivation.

There was much writing on agricultural subjects, and methods of farming were undoubtedly improved, especially in the eighteenth century. Turnips, which could be grown during the remainder of the season after a grain crop had been harvested, and which would provide fresh food for the cattle during the winter, were introduced from the Continent and cultivated to some extent, as were clover and some improved grasses. But these improvements progressed but slowly, and farming on the whole was carried on along very much the same old lines till quite the middle of the eighteenth century. The raising of grain was encouraged by a system of government bounties, as already stated in another connection. From 1689 onward a bounty was given on all grain exported, when the prevailing price was less than six shillings a bushel. The result was that England exported wheat in all but famine years, that there was a steady encouragement even if without much result to improve methods of agriculture, and that landlords were able to increase their rents. In the main, English agriculture and the organization of the agricultural classes of the population did not differ very much at the end of this period from that at the beginning except in the one point of quantity, the amount of produce and the number of the population being both largely increased.

51. The Domestic System of Manufactures. — Much greater skill in manufacturing was acquired, principally, as in earlier periods, through the immigration of foreign artisans. In Queen Elizabeth's time a great number of such men with their families, who had been driven from the Netherlands by the persecutions of the duke of Alva, came to England for refuge. In Sandwich in 1561 some twenty families of Flemings settled and began their manufactures of various kinds of cloth; in 1565 some thirty Dutch and Walloon families settled in Norwich as weavers, in Maidstone a body of similar artisans who were thread-makers settled in 1567; in 1570 a similar group carrying on various forms of manufacture settled at Colchester; and still others settled in some five or six other towns. After 1580 a wave of French Huguenots, principally silk-weavers, fled from their native country and were allowed to settle in London, Canterbury, and Coventry. The renewed persecutions of the Huguenots, culminating in the revocation of the Edict of Nantes in 1685, sent many thousands more into exile, large numbers of silk and linen weavers and manufacturers of paper, clocks, glass, and metal goods coming from Normandy and Brittany into England, and settling not only in London and its suburbs, but in many other towns of England. These foreigners, unpopular as they often were among the populace, and supported in their opportunities of carrying on their industry only by royal authority, really taught new and higher industries to the native population and eventually were absorbed into it as a more gifted and trained component.

There were also some inventions of new processes or devices for manufacture. The "stocking frame," or machine knitting, was invented in the time of Queen Elizabeth, but did not get into actual use until the next century. It then became for the future an extensive industry, especially in London and Nottingham and their vicinity. The weaving of cotton goods was introduced and spread especially in the northwest, in the neighborhood of Manchester and Bolton. A machine for preparing silk thread was invented in 1719. The printing of imported white cotton goods, as calicoes and lawns, was begun, but prohibited by Parliament in the interest of woven goods manufacturers, though the printing of linens was still allowed. Stoneware was also improved. These and other new industries introduced by foreigners or developed by English inventors or enterprising artisans added to the variety and total amount of English manufacture. The old established industries, like the old coarser woollen goods and linen manufacture, increased but slowly in amount and went through no great changes of method.

These industries old and new were in some cases regulated and supervised as to the quality of ware and methods of manufacture, by the remaining gilds or companies, with the authority which they possessed from the national government. Indeed, there were within the later sixteenth and the seventeenth centuries some new companies organized or old ones renewed especially for this oversight, and to

HANDLOOM WEAVING.
(Hogarth: *The Industrious and the Lazy Apprentice*.)

guard the monopoly of their members over certain industries in certain towns. In other cases rules were established for the carrying on of a certain industry, and a patent or monopoly was then granted by the king by which the person or company was given the sole right to carry on a certain industry according to those rules, or to enforce the rules when it was carried on by other people. In still other industries a government official had the oversight and control of quality and method of manufacture. Much production, however, especially such as went on in the country, was not supervised at all.

Far the greater part of manufacturing industry in this period was organized according to the " domestic system," the beginnings of which have been already noticed within the previous period. That is to say, manufacturing was carried on in their own houses by small masters with a journeyman and apprentice or two. Much of it was done in the country villages or suburbs of the larger towns, and such handicraft was very generally connected with a certain amount of cultivation of the soil. A small master weaver or nail manufacturer, or soap boiler or potter, would also have a little farm and divide his time between the two occupations. The implements of manufacture almost always belonged to the small master himself, though in the stocking manufacture and the silk manufacture they were often owned by employing capitalists and rented out to the small manufacturers, or even to journeymen. In some cases the raw material — wool, linen, metal, or whatever it might be — was purchased by the small manufacturer, and the goods were either manufactured for special customers or taken when completed to a neighboring town on market days, there to be sold to a local dealer, or to a merchant who would transport it to another part of the country or export it to other countries. In other cases the raw material, especially in the case of cotton, was the property of a town merchant or capitalist, who distributed it to the small domestic manufacturers in their houses in the villages, paying them for the processes of production, and himself collecting the completed product and disposing of it by sale or export. This domestic manufacture was especially common in the southwest, centre, and northwest of

OLD CLOTH-HALL AT HALIFAX.

England, and manufacturing towns like Birmingham, Halifax, Sheffield, Leeds, Bolton, and Manchester were growing up as centres around which it gathered. Little or no organization existed among such small manufacturers, though their apprentices were of course supposed to be taken and their journeymen hired according to the provisions of the Statute of Apprentices, and their products were sometimes subjected to some governmental or other supervision.

Thus in manufacturing and artisan life as in agricultural the period was marked by an extension and increase of the amount of industry, on the same general lines as had been reached by 1600, rather than by any considerable changes.

52. Commerce under the Navigation Acts. — The same thing is true of commerce, although its vast extension was almost in the nature of a revolution. As far back as the reign of Elizabeth most of the imports into England were brought in English vessels by English importers, and the goods which were exported were sent out by English exporters. The goods which were manufactured in scattered villages or town suburbs by the domestic manufacturers were gathered by these merchants and sent abroad in ever increasing amounts. The total value of English exports in 1600 was about 10 million dollars, at the close of the century it was some 34 millions, and in 1750 about 63 millions. This trade was carried on largely by merchants who were members of those chartered trading companies which have been mentioned as existing already in the sixteenth century. Some of these were "regulated companies"; that is, they had certain requirements laid down in their charters and power to adopt further rules and regulations, to which their members must conform. Others had similar chartered rights, but all their members invested funds in a common capital and traded as a joint stock company. In both kinds of cases each company possessed a monopoly of some certain field of trade, and was constantly engaged in the exclusion of interlopers from its trade. Of these companies the Merchants Adventurers, the oldest and one of the wealthiest, controlled the export of manufactured cloth to the Netherlands and northwestern Germany and remained prominent and active into the eighteenth century. The Levant, the Eastland, the Muscovy, and the Guinea or Royal African, and, greatest of all, the East India Company, continued to exist under various forms, and carried on their distant commerce through the whole of this period. With some of the nearer parts of Europe — France, Spain, Portugal, and Italy — there was much trading by private merchants not organized as companies or only organized among themselves. The "Methuen treaty," negotiated with Portugal in 1703, gave free entry of English manufactured goods into that country in return for a decreased import duty on Portuguese wines brought into England.

The foreign lands with which these companies traded furnished at the beginning of this period the only places to which goods could be exported and from which goods could be brought; but very soon that series of settlements of English colonists was begun, one of the principal inducements for which was that they would furnish an outlet for English goods. The "Plantation of Ulster," or introduction of English and Scotch settlers into the north of Ireland between 1610 and 1620, was the beginning of a long process of immigration into that country. But far the most important plantations as an outlet for trade as in every respect were those made on the coast of North America and in the West Indies. The Virginia and the Plymouth Companies played a part in the early settlement of these colonies, but they were soon superseded by the crown, sin-

PRINCIPAL
ENGLISH TRADE
ROUTES
ABOUT 1700

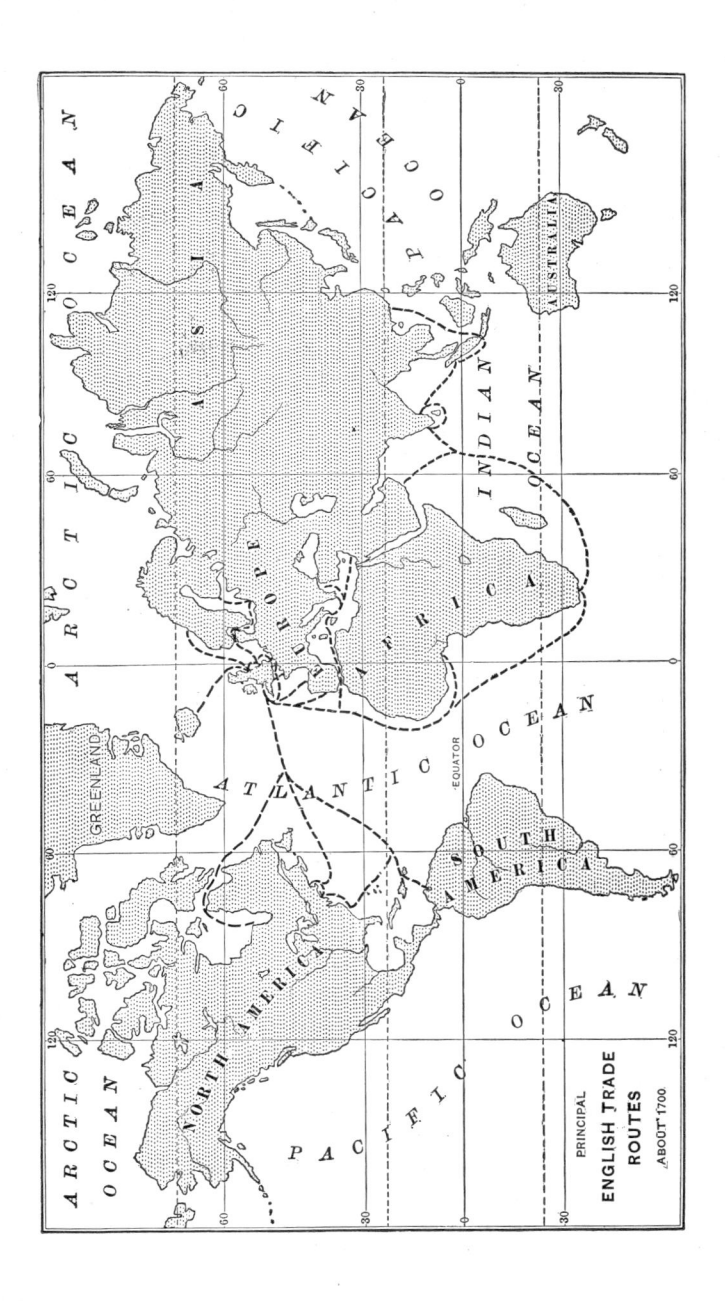

gle proprietaries, or the settlers themselves. Virginia, New England, Maryland, the Carolinas, and ultimately New York, Pennsylvania, and Georgia on the mainland; the islands of Bermudas, Barbadoes, and Jamaica, and ultimately Canada, came to be populous colonies inhabited by Englishmen and demanding an ever increasing supply of English manufactured goods. These colonies were controlled by the English government largely for their commercial and other forms of economic value. The production of goods needed in England but not produced there, such as sugar, tobacco, tar, and lumber, was encouraged, but the manufacture of such goods as could be exported from England was prohibited. The purchase of slaves in Africa and their exportation to the West Indies was encouraged, partly because they were paid for in Africa by English manufactured goods, partly because their use in the colonies made the supply of sugar and some other products plentiful and cheap.

Closely connected with commerce and colonies as a means of disposing of England's manufactured goods and of obtaining those things which were needed from abroad was commerce for its own sake, for the profits which it brought to those engaged in it, and for the indirect value to the nation of having a large mercantile navy.

The most important provision for this end was the passage of the "Navigation Acts." We have seen that as early as 1485 certain kinds of goods could be imported only in English vessels. But in 1651 a law was passed, and in 1660 under a more regular government reënacted in still more vigorous form, which carried this policy to its fullest extent. By these laws all importation of goods into England from any ports of Asia, Africa, or America was forbidden, except in vessels belonging to English owners, built in England and manned by English seamen; and there was the same requirement for goods exported from England to those countries. From European ports goods could be brought to England only in English vessels or in vessels the property of merchants of the country in which the port lay; and similarly for export. These acts were directed especially against the Dutch merchants, who were fast getting control of the carrying trade. The result of the policy of the Navigation Acts was to secure to English merchants and to English shipbuilders a monopoly of all the trade with the East Indies and Africa and with the American colonies, and to prevent the Dutch from competing with English merchants for the greater part of the trade with the Continent of Europe.

The characteristics of English commerce in this period, therefore, were much the same as in the last. It was, however, still more completely controlled by English merchants and was vastly extended in amount. Moreover, this extension bid fair to be permanent, as it was largely brought about by the growth of populous English colonies in Ireland and America, and by the acquisition of great spheres of influence in India.

53. Finance. — The most characteristic changes of the period now being studied were in a field to which attention has been but slightly called before; that is, in finance. Capital had not existed in any large amounts in mediæval England, and even in the later centuries there had not been any considerable class of men whose principal interest was in the investment of saved-up capital which they had in their hands. Agriculture, manufacturing, and even commerce were carried on with very small capital and usually with such capital as each farmer, artisan, or merchant might have of his own; no use of credit to obtain money from individual men or from banks for industrial purposes being ordinarily possible. Questions connected with money, capital, borrowing, and other points of finance came into somewhat greater prominence with the sixteenth century, but they now attained an altogether new and more important notice.

Taxation, which had been looked upon as abnormal and occasional during earlier times, and only justifiable when some special need for large expenditure by the government arose, such as war, a royal marriage, or the entertainment of some foreign visitor, now, after long conflicts between King and Parliament, which are of still greater constitutional than financial importance, came to be looked upon as a regular normal custom. In 1660, at the Restoration, a whole system of excise duties, taxes on imports and exports, and a hearth tax were established as a permanency for paying the expenses of government, besides special taxes of various kinds for special demands.

Borrowing, by merchants and others for ordinary purposes of business, became much more usual. During most of the seventeenth century the goldsmiths were the only bankers. On account of the strong vaults of these merchants, their habitual possession of valuable material and articles, and perhaps of their reputation for probity, persons who had money beyond their immediate needs deposited it with the goldsmiths, receiving from them usually six per cent. The goldsmiths then loaned it to merchants or to the government, obtaining for it interest at the rate of eight per cent or more. This system gradually became better established and the high rates decreased. Payments came to be made by check, and promissory notes were regularly discounted by the goldsmiths.

The greatest extension in the use of credit, however, came from the establishment of the Bank of England. In 1691 the original proposition for the Bank was made to the government by William Patterson. In 1694 a charter for the Bank was finally carried through Parliament by the efforts of the ministry. The Bank consisted of a group of subscribers who agreed to loan to the government £1,200,000, the government to pay them an annual interest of eight and one-half per cent, or £100,000 in cash, guaranteed by the product of a certain tax. The subscribers were at the same time incorporated and authorized to carry on a general business of receiving deposits and lending out money at interest. The capital which was to be loaned to the government was subscribed principally by London merchants, and the Bank began its career in the old Grocers' Hall. The regular income of £100,000 a year gave it a nucleus of strength, and enabled it to discount notes even beyond its actual deposits and to issue its own notes or paper money. Thus money could be borrowed to serve as capital for all kinds of enterprises, and there was an inducement also for persons to save money and thus create capital, since it could always bring them in a return by lending it to the Bank even if they were not in a position to put it to use themselves. Along with the normal effect of such financial inventions in developing all forms of trade and industry, there arose a remarkable series of projects and schemes of the wildest and most unstable character, and the early eighteenth century saw many losses and constant fluctuations in the realm of finance. The most famous instance of this was the "South Sea Bubble," a speculative scheme by which a regulated company, the South Sea Company, was chartered in 1719 to carry on the slave-trade to the West Indies and whale-fishing, and incidentally to loan money to the government. Its shares rose to many fold their par value and fell to almost nothing again within a few months, and the government and vast numbers of investors and speculators were involved in its failure.

The same period saw the creation of the permanent national debt. In earlier times kings and ministers had constantly borrowed money from foreign or native lenders, but it was always provided and anticipated that it would be repaid at a certain period, with the interest. With the later years of the seventeenth century, however, it became customary for the government to borrow money without any definite contract or expectation as to when it should be paid back, only making an agreement to pay a certain rate of interest upon it. This was satisfactory to all parties. The government obtained a large sum at the time, with the necessity of only paying a small sum every year for interest; investors obtained a remunerative use for their money, and if they should need the principal, some one else was always ready to pay its value to them for the sake of receiving the interest. The largest single element of the national debt in its early period was the loan of £1,200,000 which served as the basis for the Bank; but after that time, as for a short time before, sums were borrowed from time to time which were not repaid, but became a permanent part of the debt: the total rising to more than £75,000,000 by the middle of the century. Incidentally, this, like the deposits at the goldsmiths and the Bank, became an opportunity for the investment of savings and an inducement to create more capital.

Fire insurance and life insurance both seem to have had their origin in the later decades of the seventeenth century.

Thus in the realm of finance there was much more of novelty, of actually new development, during this period than in agriculture, manufacturing, or commerce. Yet all these forms of economic life and of the social organization which corresponded to them were alike in one respect, that they were quite minutely regulated by the national government. The fabric of paternal government which we saw rising in the time of the Tudor sovereigns remained almost intact through the whole of this period. The regulation of the conditions of labor, of trade, of importation and exportation, of finance, of agriculture, of manufacture, in more or less detail, was part of the regular work of legislation or administrative action. Either in order to reach certain ulterior ends, such as government power, a large navy, or a large body of money within the country, or simply as a part of what were looked upon at the time as the natural functions of government, laws were constantly being passed, charters formulated, treaties entered into, and other action taken by government, intended to encourage one kind of industry and discourage another, to determine rates of wages and hours of labor, prescribe rules for agriculture, or individual trades or forms of business, to support some kind of industry which was threatened with decay, to restrict certain actions which were thought to be disadvantageous, to regulate the whole economic life of the nation.

It is true that much of this regulation was on the books rather than in actual existence. It would have required a much more extensive and efficient civil service, national and local, than England then possessed to enforce all or any considerable part of the provisions that were made by act of Parliament or ordered by the King and Council. Again, new industries were generally declared to be free from much of the more minute regulation, so that enterprise where it arose was not so apt to be checked, as conservatism where it already existed was apt to be perpetuated. Such regulation and control, moreover, were quite in accord with the feeling and with the economic and political theories of the time, so there was but little sense of interference or tyranny felt by the governed. A regulated industrial organization slowly expanding on well-established lines was as characteristic of the theory as it was of the practice of the period.

54. BIBLIOGRAPHY

Gardiner, S. R.: *The History of England, 1603–1642*, ten volumes.

Many scattered passages in this work and in its continuations, like those in Froude's history, referred to in the last chapter, apply to the economic and social history of the period, and they are always judicious and valuable.

Hewins, W. A. S.: *English Trade and Finance, chiefly in the Seventeenth Century*.

For this period Cunningham, Rogers, and Palgrave, in the books already referred to, are almost the only secondary authorities, except such as go into great detail on individual points. Cunningham's second volume, which includes this period, is extremely full and satisfactory.

Macpherson, D.: *Annals of Commerce* is, however, a book of somewhat broader interest.

CHAPTER VIII

THE PERIOD OF THE INDUSTRIAL REVOLUTION

Economic Changes of the Later Eighteenth and Early Nineteenth Centuries

55. National Affairs from 1760 to 1830. — The seventy years lying between these two dates were covered by the long reign of George III and that of his successor George IV. In the political world this period had by no means the importance that it possessed in the field of economic development. Parliament had already obtained its permanent form and powers, and when George III tried to " be a king," as his mother urged him, the effort to restore personal government was an utter failure. Between 1775 and 1783 occurred the American Revolution, by which thirteen of England's most valued colonies were lost to her and began their progress toward a greater destiny. The breach between the American colonies and the mother country was brought about largely by the obstinacy of the king and his ministers in adopting an arbitrary and unpopular policy. Other political causes no doubt contributed to the result. Yet the greater part of the alienation of feeling which underlay the Revolution was due not to political causes, but to the economic policy already described, by which American commerce and industry were bent to the interests of England.

In the American war France joined the rebellious colonies against England, and obtained advantageous terms at the peace. Within ten years the two countries had again entered upon a war, this time of vastly greater extent, and continuing almost unbroken for more than twenty years. This was a result of the outbreak of the French Revolution. In 1789 the Estates General of France, a body corresponding in its earlier history to the English Parliament, was called for the first time for almost two hundred years. This assembly and its successors undertook to reorganize French government and society. In the course of this radical process principles were enunciated proclaiming the absolute liberty and equality of men, demanding the participation of all in government, the abolition of aristocratic privileges, and finally of royalty itself. In following out these ideas, so different from those generally accepted in Europe, France was brought into conflict with all the other European states, including Great Britain. War broke out in 1793. Fighting took place on sea and land and in various parts of the world. France in her new enthusiasm developed a strength, vigor, and capacity which enabled her to make head against the alliances of almost all the other countries of Europe, and even to gain victories and increase her territory at their expense. No peace seemed practicable. In her successive internal changes of government one of the generals of the army, Napoleon Bonaparte, obtained a more and more influential position, until in 1804 he took the title of Emperor. The wars of the French Revolution therefore were merged in the wars of Napoleon. Alliance after alliance was made against Napoleon, England commonly taking the initiative in the formation of them and paying large monthly subsidies to some of the continental governments to enable them to support their armies. The English navy won several brilliant victories, especially under Nelson, although her land forces played a comparatively small part until the battle of Waterloo in 1815.

The naval supremacy thus obtained made the war a matter of pecuniary profit to the English nation, notwithstanding its enormous expense; for it gave to her vessels almost a complete monopoly of the commerce and the carrying trade of the world, and to her manufactures extended markets which would otherwise have been closed to her or shared with other nations. The cutting off of continental and other sources of supply of grain and the opening of new markets greatly increased the demand for English grain and enhanced the price paid for it. This caused higher rents and further enclosure of open land. Thus the war which had been entered upon reluctantly and with much opposition in 1793, became popular, partly because of the feeling of the English people that it had become a life and death struggle with France, but largely also because English industries were flourishing under it. The wars came to an end with the downfall of Napoleon in 1815, and an unwonted period of peace for England set in and lasted for almost forty years.

The French Revolution produced another effect in England. It awakened a certain amount of admiration for its principles of complete liberty and equality and a desire to apply them to English aristocratic society and government. In 1790 societies began to be formed, meetings held, and pamphlets issued by men who sympathized with the popular movements in France. Indeed, some of these reformers were suspected of wishing to introduce a republic in England. After the outbreak of the war the ministry determined to put down this agitation, and between 1793 and 1795 all public manifestation of sympathy with such principles was crushed out, although at the cost of considerable interference with what had been understood to be established personal rights. Much discontent continued through the whole period of the war, especially among the lower classes, though it did not take the form of organized political agitation. It was a period, as will be seen, of violent economic and social changes, which, although they enriched England as a whole and made it possible for her to support the unprecedented expenses of the long war, were very hard upon the working classes, who were used to the old ways.

After the peace of 1815, however, political agitation began again. The Whig party seemed inclined to resume the effort to carry certain moderate reforms which had been postponed on account of the war, and down below this movement there was a more radical agitation for universal suffrage and for a more democratic type of government generally. On the other hand, the Tory government, which had been in power during almost the whole war period, was determined to oppose everything in the nature of reform or change, on the ground that the outrages accompanying the French Revolution arose from just such efforts to make reforming alterations in the government. The radical agitation was supported by the discontented masses of the people who were suffering under heavy taxes, high prices, irregular employment, and many other evils which they felt to be due to their exclusion from any share in the government. The years intervening between 1815 and 1830 were therefore a period of constant bitterness and contention between the higher and the lower classes. Mass meetings which were called by the popular leaders were dissolved by the government, radical writers were prosecuted by the government for libel, the habeas corpus act was suspended repeatedly, and threatened rioting was met with severe measures. The actions of the ministers, while upheld by the higher classes, were bitterly attacked by others as being unconstitutional and tyrannical.

In 1800 the union of the group of British Islands under one government was completed, at least in form. Scotland had come under the same crown as England in 1603, and the two Parliaments had been united in 1707, the title Great Britain having been adopted for the combined nations. The king of England had held the title of Lord of Ireland from the time of the first conquest, and of King of Ireland since the adoption of the title by Henry VIII. The union which now took place consisted in the abolition of the separate Irish Parliament and the election of Irish members to the combined or "Imperial" Parliament of the three kingdoms sitting at Westminster. The official title of the united countries has since been "The United Kingdom of Great Britain and Ireland."

56. The Great Mechanical Inventions. — As the eighteenth century progressed one form of economic growth seems to have been pressing on the general economic organization. This was the constant expansion of commerce, the steadily increasing demand for English manufactured goods for export.

The great quantities of goods which were every year sent abroad in English ships to the colonies, to Ireland, to the Continent, to Asia and Africa, as well as those used at home, continued to be manufactured in most cases by methods, with instruments, under an organization of labor the same as that which had been in existence for centuries. The cotton and woollen goods which were sold in the West Indies and America were still carded, spun, and woven in the scattered cottages of domestic weavers and weaver-farmers in the rural districts of the west and north of England, by the hand cards, the spinning-wheel, the cumbrous, old-fashioned loom. The pieces of goods were slowly gathered from the hamlets to the towns, from the

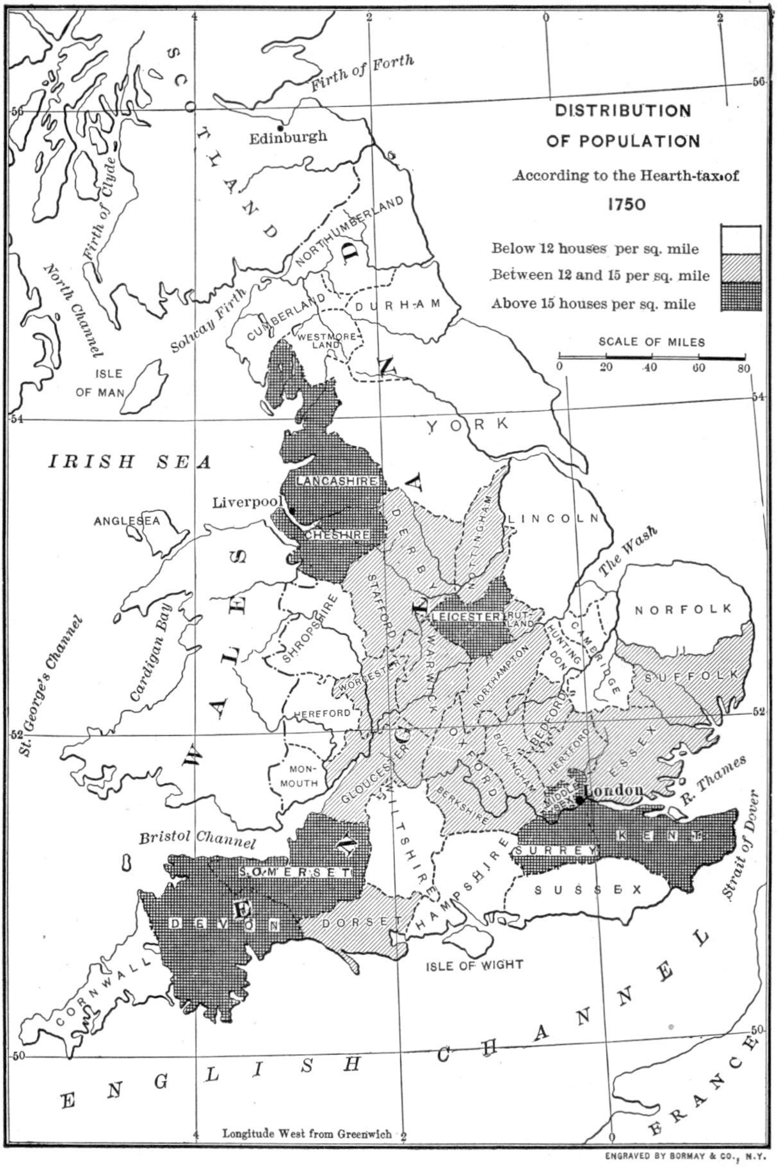
DISTRIBUTION
OF POPULATION
According to the Hearth-tax of
1750
Below 12 houses per sq. mile
Between 12 and 15 per sq. mile
Above 15 houses per sq. mile
SCALE OF MILES
0 20 40 60 80
SCOTLAND
Firth of Forth
Edinburgh
Firth of Clyde
North Channel
Solway Firth
NORTHUMBERLAND
DURHAM
CUMBERLAND
WESTMORELAND
ISLE OF MAN
YORK
IRISH SEA
LANCASHIRE
Liverpool
ANGLESEA
CHESHIRE
DERBY
NOTTINGHAM
LINCOLN
The Wash
NORFOLK
STAFFORD
SHROPSHIRE
LEICESTER
RUTLAND
HUNTINGDON
CAMBRIDGE
SUFFOLK
WALES
Cardigan Bay
St. George's Channel
WORCESTER
WARWICK
NORTHAMPTON
HEREFORD
BEDFORD
OXFORD
BUCKINGHAM
HERTFORD
ESSEX
MONMOUTH
GLOUCESTER
BERKSHIRE
MIDDLESEX
London
R. Thames
WILTSHIRE
KENT
Strait of Dover
Bristol Channel
SURREY
SOMERSET
HAMPSHIRE
SUSSEX
ENGLAND
DEVON
DORSET
ISLE OF WIGHT
CORNWALL
ENGLISH CHANNEL
FRANCE
Longitude West from Greenwich
ENGRAVED BY BORMAY & CO., N.Y.

towns to the seaports, over the poorest of roads, and by the most primitive of conveyances. And these antiquated methods of manufacture and transportation were all the more at variance with the needs and possibilities of the time because there had been, as already pointed out, a steady accumulation of capital, and much of it was not remuneratively employed. The time had certainly come for some improvement in the methods of manufacture.

A closer examination into the process of production in England's principal industry, cloth-making, shows that this pressure on old methods was already felt. The raw material for such uses, as it comes from the back of the sheep, the boll of the cotton plant, or the crushed stems of the flax, is a tangled mass of fibre. The first necessary step is to straighten out the threads of this fibre, which is done in the case of wool by combing, in the others by carding, both being done at that time by hand implements. The next step is spinning, that is drawing out the fibres, which have been made parallel by carding, into a slender cord, and at the same time twisting this sufficiently to cause the individual fibres to take hold one of another and thus make a thread of some strength. This was sometimes done on the old high wheel, which was whirled around by hand and then allowed to come to rest while another section of the cotton, wool, or flax was drawn from the carded mass by hand, then whirled again, twisting this thread and winding it up on the spindle, and so on. Or it was done by the low wheel, which was kept whirling continuously by the use of a treadle worked by the foot, while the material was being drawn out all the time by the two hands, and twisted and wound continuously by the horseshoe-shaped device known as the "flyer." When the thread had been spun it was placed upon the loom; strong, firmly spun material being necessary for the "warp" of upright threads, softer and less tightly spun material for the "woof" or "weft," which was wrapped on the shuttle and thrown horizontally by hand between the two diverging lines of warp threads. After weaving, the fabric was subjected to a number of processes of finishing, fulling, shearing, dyeing, if that had not been done earlier, and others, according to the nature of the cloth or the kind of surface desired.

In these successive stages of manufacture it was the spinning that was apt to interpose the greatest obstacle, as it took the most time. From time immemorial spinning had been done, as explained, on some form of the spinning-wheel, and by women. One weaver continuously at work could easily use up the product of five or six spinners. In the domestic industry the weaving was of course carried on in the dwelling-house by the father of the family with the grown sons or journeymen, while the spinning was done for the most part by the women and younger children of the family. As it could hardly be expected that there would always be as large a proportion as six of the latter class to one of the former, outside help must be obtained and much delay often submitted to. Many a small master who had agreed to weave up the raw material sent him by the master clothier within a given time, or a cloth weaver who had planned to complete a piece by next market day, was obliged to leave his loom and search through the neighborhood for some disengaged laborer's wife or other person who would spin the weft for which he was waiting. One of the very few inventions of the early part of the century intensified this difficulty. Kay's drop box and flying shuttle, invented in 1738, made it possible for a man to sit still and by pulling two cords alternately throw the shuttle to and fro. One man could therefore weave broadcloth instead of its requiring two as before, and consequently weaving was more rapid, while no corresponding change had been introduced into the process of spinning.

Indeed, this particular difficulty was so clearly recognized that the Royal Society offered a prize for the invention of a machine that would spin several threads at the same time.

SPINNING-JENNY.

(Byrn, *Invention in the Nineteenth Century*. Published by the Scientific American Company.)

No one claimed this reward, but the spirit of invention was nevertheless awake, and experiments in more than one mechanical device were being made about the middle of the century. The first to be brought to actual completion was Hargreaves' spinning-jenny, invented in 1764. According to the traditional story James Hargreaves, a small master weaver living near Blackburn, on coming suddenly into the house caused his wife, who was spinning with the old high wheel, to spring up with a start and overset the wheel, which still continued whirling, but horizontally, and with its spindle in a vertical position. He was at once struck with the idea of using one wheel to cause a number of spindles to revolve by means of a continuous band, and by the device

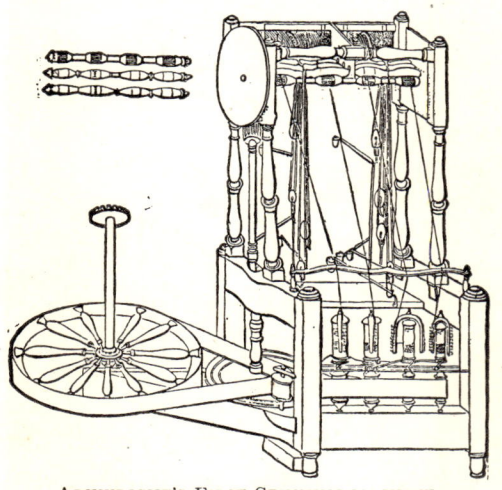

ARKWRIGHT'S FIRST SPINNING-MACHINE.
(Ure: *History of the Cotton Manufacture.*)

of substituting for the human hand a pair of bars which could be successively separated and closed, and which could be brought closer to or removed from the spindles on wheels, to spin several threads at the same time. On the basis of this idea and with the help of a neighboring mechanic he constructed a machine by which a man could spin eight threads at the same time. In honor of his wife he named it the "Spinning-jenny." The secret of this device soon came out and jennies spinning twenty or thirty or more threads at a time came into use here and there through the old spinning districts. At the same time a much more effective method was being brought to perfection by Richard Arkwright, who followed out some old experiments of Wyatt of Northampton. According to this plan the carded material was carried through successive

SIR RICHARD ARKWRIGHT.
(Portrait by Wright.)

pairs of rollers, each pair running more rapidly than the previous pair, thus stretching it out, while it was spun after leaving the last pair by flyers adapted from the old low or treadle spinning-wheel. Arkwright's first patent was taken out in 1769, and from that time forward he invented, patented, and manufactured a series of machines which made possible the spinning of a number of threads at the same time very much more rapidly than even the spinning-jenny. Great numbers of Arkwright's spinning-machines were manufactured and sold by him and his partners. He made others for use in cotton mills carried on by himself with various partners in different parts of the country. His patent was eventually set aside as having been unfairly obtained, and the machines were soon generally manufactured and used. Improvements followed. An ingenious weaver named Samuel Crompton, perceiving that the roller spinning was more rapid but that the jennies would spin the finer thread, combined the two devices into one machine, known from its hybrid origin as the "mule." This was invented in 1779, and as it was not patented it soon came into general use. These inventions in spinning reacted on the earlier processes and led to a rapid development of carding and combing machines. A carding cylinder had been invented by Paul as far back as 1748, and now came into general use, while several wool-combing machines were invented in 1792 and 1793.

So far all these inventions had been in the earlier textile processes. Use for the spun thread was found in giving fuller employment to the old hand looms, in the stocking manufacture, and for export; but no corresponding improvement had taken place in weaving. From 1784 onward a clergyman from the south of England, Dr. Edward Cartwright, was gradually bringing to perfection a power loom which by the beginning of the nineteenth century began to come into general use. The value put upon Cartwright's invention may be judged from the fact that Parliament voted him a gift of £10,000 in 1809. Arkwright had already won a large fortune by his invention, and in 1786 was knighted in recognition of his services to the national industry.

While Cartwright was experimenting on the power loom, an invention was made far from England which was in reality an essential part of the improvement in the manufacture of cotton goods. This was the American cotton gin, for the

REV. EDMUND CARTWRIGHT.
(Portrait by Robert Fulton.)

removal of the seeds from the fibre of the boll, invented by Eli Whitney in 1792. Cotton had been introduced into the Southern states during the Revolutionary war. Its cultivation and export now became profitable, and a source of supply became available at the very time that the inventions for its manufacture were being perfected.

Spinning-jennies could be used in the household of the weaver; but the later spinning-machines were so large and cumbrous that they could not be used in a dwelling-house, and required so much power and rapidity of motion that human strength was scarcely available. Horse power was used to some extent, but water power was soon applied and special buildings came to be put up along streams where water power was available. The next stage was the application of steam power. Although the possibility of using steam for the production of force had long been familiar, and indeed used to some extent in the pumping out of mines, it did not become available for general uses until the improvements of James Watt, patented in 1769 and succeeding years. In partnership with a man named Boulton, Watt began the manufacture of steam-engines in 1781. In 1785 the first steam-engine was used for power in a cotton mill. After that time the use of steam became more and more general and by the end of the century steam power was evidently superseding water power.

57. The Factory System. — But other things were needed to make this new machinery available. It was much too expensive for the old cottage weavers to buy and use. Capital had, therefore, to be brought into manufacturing which had been previously used in trade or other employments. Capital was in reality abundant relatively to existing opportunities for investment, and the early machine spinners and weavers drew into partnership moneyed men from the towns who had previously no connection with manufacturing. Again, the new industry required bodies of laborers working regular hours under the control of their employers and in the buildings where the machines were placed and the

MULE-SPINNING IN 1835.

(Baines: *History of Cotton Manufacture.*)

Power-Loom Weaving in 1835.

(Baines: *History of Cotton Manufacture.*)

power provided. Such groups of laborers or "mill hands" were gradually collected where the new kind of manufacturing was going on. Thus factories, in the modern sense, came into existence — a new phenomenon in the world.

These changes in manufacturing and in the organization of labor came about earliest in the manufacture of cotton goods, but the new machinery and its resulting changes were soon introduced into the woollen manufacture, then other textile lines, and ultimately into still other branches of manufacturing, such as the production of metal, wooden, and leather goods, and, indeed, into nearly all forms of production. Manufacturing since the last decades of the eighteenth century is therefore usually described as being done by the "factory system," as contrasted with the domestic system and the gild system of earlier times.

The introduction of the factory system involved many changes: the adoption of machinery and artificial power, the use of a vastly greater amount of capital, and the collection of scattered laborers into great strictly regulated establishments. It was, comparatively speaking, sudden, all its main features having been developed within the period between 1760 and 1800; and it resulted in the raising of many new and difficult social problems. For these reasons the term "Industrial Revolution," so generally applied to it, is not an exaggerated nor an unsuitable term. Almost all other forms of economic occupation have subsequently taken on the main characteristics of the factory system, in utilizing improved machinery, in the extensive scale on which they are administered, in the use of large capital, and in the organization of employees in large bodies. The industrial revolution may therefore be regarded as the chief characteristic distinguishing this period and the times since from all earlier ages.

214 *Industrial and Social History of England*

58. Iron, Coal, and Transportation. — A vast increase in the production of iron and coal was going on concurrently with the rise of the factory system. The smelting of iron ore was one of the oldest industries of England, but it was a declining rather than an advancing industry. This was due to the exhaustion of the woods and forests that provided fuel, or to their retention for the future needs of ship-building and for pleasure parks. In 1760, however, Mr. Roebuck introduced at the Carron iron-works a new kind of blast furnace by which iron ore could be smelted with coal

A CANAL AND FACTORY TOWN IN 1827.

as fuel. In 1790 the steam-engine was introduced to cause the blast. Production had already begun to advance before the latter date, and it now increased by thousands of tons a year till far into the present century. Improvements were introduced in puddling, rolling, and other processes of the manufacture of iron at about the same time. The production of coal increased more than proportionately. New devices in mining were introduced, such as steam pumps, the custom of supporting the roofs of the veins with timber instead of pillars of coal, and Sir Humphry Davy's safety lamp of 1815. The smelting of iron and the use of the steam-engine made such a demand for coal that capital was applied in large quantities to its production, and more than ten million tons a year were mined before the century closed.

"THE ROCKET" LOCOMOTIVE, 1825.
(Smiles: *Life of George Stephenson*.)

Some slight improvements in roads and canals had been made and others projected during the seventeenth and early eighteenth centuries; but in the last quarter of the century the work of Telford, Macadam, and other engineers, and of the private turnpike companies or public authorities who engaged them, covered England with good roads. The first canal was that from Worsley to Manchester, built by Brindley for the duke of Bridgewater in 1761. Within a few years a system of canals had been constructed which gave ready transportation for goods through all parts of the country. The continuance of this development of transportation and its fundamental modification by the introduction of railways and steamboats has been one of the most striking characteristics of the nineteenth century.

59. The Revival of Enclosures. — The changes which the latter half of the eighteenth century and the early part of the nineteenth brought were as profound in the occupation and use of the land as they were in the production and transportation of manufactured goods. An agricultural revolution was in progress as truly as was the industrial.

The improvements in the methods of farming already referred to as showing themselves earlier in the century became much more extensive. The raising of turnips and other root crops spread from experimental to ordinary farms so that a fallow year with no crop at all in the ground came to be almost unknown. Clover and artificial grasses for hay came to be raised generally, so that the supply of forage for the winter was abundant. New breeds of sheep and cattle were obtained by careful crossing and plentiful feeding, so that the average size was almost doubled, while the meat, and in some cases the wool, was improved in quality in even greater proportion. The names of such men as Jethro Tull, who introduced the "drill husbandry," Bakewell, the great improver of the breeds of cattle, and Arthur Young, the greatest agricultural observer and writer of the century, have become almost as familiar as those of Crompton, Arkwright, Watt, and other pioneers of the factory system. The general improvement in agricultural methods was due, not so much to new discoveries or inventions, as it was to the large amount of capital which was introduced into their practice. Expensive schemes of draining, marling, and other forms of fertilizing were carried out, long and careful investigations were entered upon, and managers of large farms were trained in special processes by landlords and farmers who had the command of large sums of money; and with the high prices prevalent they were abundantly remunerated for the outlay. Great numbers of "gentlemen farmers," such as Lord Townshend, the duke of Bedford, and George III himself, who wrote articles for the agricultural papers signed "Farmer George," were leaders in this agricultural progress. In 1793 a government Board of Agriculture was established, and through the whole latter part of the century numerous societies for the encouragement of scientific tillage and breeding were organized.

In the early years of the eighteenth century there had been signs of a revival of the old process of enclosures, which had been suspended for more than a hundred years. This was brought about by private acts of Parliament. An act would be passed by Parliament giving legal authority to the inhabitants of some parish to throw together the scattered strips, and to redivide these and the common meadows and pastures in such a way that each person with any claim on the land should receive a proportionate share, and should have it separated from all others and entirely in his own control. It was the usual procedure for the lord of the manor, the rector of the parish, and other large landholders and persons of influence to agree on the general conditions of enclosure and draw up a bill appointing commissioners, and providing for survey, compensation, redistribution, and other requirements. They then submitted this bill to Parliament, where, unless there was some special reason to the contrary, it was passed. Its provisions were then carried out, and although legal and parliamentary fees and the expenses of survey and enclosure were large, yet as a result each inhabitant who had been able to make out a legal claim to any of the land of the parish received either some money compensation or a stretch of enclosed land. Such private enclosure acts increased slowly in number till about the middle of the century, when the increase became much more rapid.

The number of enclosure acts passed by Parliament and the approximate extent of land enclosed under their provisions were as follows: —

1700–1759	244 Enclosure Bills	337,877 Acres
1760–1769	385 " "	704,550 "
1770–1779	660 " "	1,207,800 "
1780–1789	246 " "	450,180 "
1790–1799	469 " "	858,270 "
1800–1809	847 " "	1,550,010 "
1810–1819	853 " "	1,560,990 "
1820–1829	205 " "	375,150 "
1830–1839	136 " "	248,880 "
1840–1849	66 " "	394,747 "

In 1756, 1758, and 1773 general acts were passed encouraging the enclosure for common use of open pastures and arable fields, but not enclosing or dividing them permanently, and not providing for any separate ownership.

In 1801 an act was passed to make simpler and easier the passage of private bills for enclosure; and in 1836 another to make possible, with the consent of two-thirds of the persons interested, the enclosing of certain kinds of common fields even without appealing to Parliament in each particular case. Finally, in 1845, the general Enclosure Act of that year carried the policy of 1836 further and appointed a body of Enclosure Commissioners, to determine on the expediency of any proposed enclosure and to attend to carrying it out if approved. Six years afterward, however, an amendment was passed making it necessary that even after an enclosure had been approved by the Commissioners it should go to Parliament for final decision.

By measures such as these the greater part of the lands which had remained unenclosed to modern times were transformed into enclosed fields for separate cultivation or pasture. This process of enclosure was intended to make possible, and no doubt did bring about, much improved agriculture. It exerted incidentally a profound effect on the rural population. Many persons had habitually used the common pastures and open fields for pasture purposes, when they had in reality no legal claim whatever to such use. A poor man whose cow, donkey, or flock of geese had picked up a precarious livelihood on land of undistinguished ownership now found the land all enclosed and his immemorial privileges withdrawn without compensation. Naturally there was much dissatisfaction. A popular piece of doggerel declared that: —

> "The law locks up the man or woman
> Who steals the goose from off the common;
> But leaves the greater villain loose
> Who steals the common from the goose."

Again, a small holder was frequently given compensation in the form of money instead of allotting to him a piece of land which was considered by the commissioners too small for effective use. The money was soon spent, whereas his former claim on the land had lasted because it could not readily be alienated.

A more important effect, however, was the introduction on these enclosed lands of a kind of agriculture which the small landholder was ill fitted to follow. Improved cultivation, a careful rotation of crops, better fertilizers, drainage, farm stock, and labor were the characteristics of the new farming, and these were ordinarily practicable only to the man who had some capital, knowledge, and enterprise. Therefore, coincidently with the enclosures began a process by which the smaller tenants began to give up their holdings to men who could pay more rent for them by consolidating them into larger farms. The freeholders also who owned small farms from time to time sold them to neighboring landowners when difficulties forced them or high prices furnished inducements.

60. Decay of Domestic Manufacture. — This process would have been a much slower one but for the contemporaneous changes that were going on in manufacturing. As has been seen, many small farmers in the rural districts made part of their livelihood by weaving or other domestic manufacture, or, as more properly described, the domestic manufacturers frequently eked out their resources by carrying on some farming. But the invention of machinery for spinning not only created a new industry, but destroyed the old. Cotton thread could be produced vastly more cheaply by machinery. In 1786 a certain quantity of a certain grade of spun yarn was worth 38 shillings; ten years later, in 1796, it was worth only 19 shillings; in 1806 it was worth but 7 shillings 2 pence, and so on down till, in 1832, it was worth but 3 shillings. Part of this reduction in price was due to the decrease in the cost of raw cotton, but far the most of it to the cheapening of spinning.

It was the same a few years later with weaving. Handloom weavers in Bolton, who received 25 shillings a week as wages in 1800, received only 19 shillings and 6 pence in 1810, 9 shillings in 1820, and 5 shillings 6 pence in 1830. Hand work in other lines of manufacture showed the same results. Against such reductions in wages resistance was hopeless. Hand work evidently could not compete with machine work. No amount of skill or industry or determination could enable the hand workers to make their living in the same way as of old. As a matter of fact, a long, sad, desperate struggle was kept up by a whole generation of hand laborers, especially by the hand-loom weavers, but the result was inevitable.

The rural domestic manufacturers were, as a matter of fact, devoting themselves to two inferior forms of industry. As far as they were handicraftsmen, they were competing with a vastly cheaper and better form of manufacture; as far as they were farmers, they were doing the same thing with regard to agriculture. Under these circumstances some of them gave up their holdings of land and drifted away to the towns to keep up the struggle a little longer as hand-loom weavers, and then to become laborers in the factories; others gave up their looms and devoted themselves entirely to farming for a while, but eventually sold their holdings or gave up their leases, and dropped into the class of agricultural laborers. The result was the same in either case. The small farms were consolidated, the class of yeomanry or small farmers died out, and household manufacture gave place to that of the factory. Before the end of the century the average size of English farms was computed at three hundred acres, and soon afterward domestic spinning and weaving were almost unknown.

There was considerable shifting of population. Certain parts of the country which had been quite thickly populated with small farmers or domestic manufacturers now lost the greater part of their occupants by migration to the newer manufacturing districts or to America. As in the sixteenth century, some villages disappeared entirely. Goldsmith in the

Deserted Village described changes that really occurred, however opposed to the facts may have been his description of the earlier idyllic life whose destruction he deplored.

The existence of unenclosed commons and common fields had been accompanied by very poor farming, very thriftless and shiftless habits. The improvement of agriculture, the application of capital to that occupation, the disappearance of the domestic system of industry, and other changes made the enclosure of common land and the accompanying changes inevitable. None the less it was a relatively sudden and complete interference with the established character of rural life, and not only was the process accompanied with much suffering, but the form which took its place was marked by some serious disadvantages. This form was brought about through the rapid culmination of old familiar tendencies. The classes connected with the land came to be quite clearly distinguished into three groups: the landlords, the tenant farmers, and the farm laborers. The landlord class was a comparatively small body of nobility and gentry, a few thousand persons, who owned by far the greater portion of the land of the country. Their estates were for the most part divided up into farms, to the keeping of which in productive condition they contributed the greater part of the expense, to the administration of which trained stewards applied themselves, and in the improvement of which their owners often took a keen and enlightened interest. They received high rents, possessed unlimited local influence, and were the favored governing class of the country. The class of farmers were men of some capital, and frequently of intelligence and enterprise, though rarely of education, who held on lease from the landlords farms of some one, two, or three or more hundred acres, paying relatively large rents, and yet by the excellence of their farming making for themselves a liberal income. The farm laborers were the residuum of the changes which have been traced in the history of landholding; a large class living for the most part miserably in cottages grouped in villages, holding no land, and receiving day wages for working on the farms just described.

Notwithstanding the improvements in agriculture and the increase in the extent of cultivated land, England ceased within the eighteenth century to be a self-supporting country in food products. The form which the "corn laws" had taken in 1689 had been as follows: the raising of wheat was encouraged by prohibiting its importation and paying a bounty of about eightpence a bushel for its exportation so long as the prevailing price was less than six shillings a bushel. When it was between six shillings and six shillings eightpence a bushel its importation was forbidden, but there was no bounty paid for exportation. Between the last price and ten shillings a bushel it could be imported by paying a duty of a shilling a bushel. Above the last price it could be imported free. Nevertheless, during the latter half of the eighteenth century it became evident that there was no longer a sufficient amount of wheat raised for the needs of the English people. Between 1770 and 1790 exports and imports about balanced one another, but after the latter year the imports always exceeded the exports.

This was of course due to the great increase of population and to its employment in the field of manufactures. The population in England in 1700 was about five millions, in 1750 about six millions and a half, in 1800 about nine millions, and in 1850 about eighteen millions. That is to say, its progress was slow during the first half of the eighteenth century, more rapid during the latter half, and vastly more rapid during the nineteenth century.

61. The Laissez-faire Theory. — A scarcely less complete change than that which had occurred in manufactures, in agriculture, and in social life as based upon these, was that which was in progress at the same time in the realm of ideas, especially as applied to questions of economic and social life. The complete acceptance of the view that it was a natural and desirable part of the work of government to regulate the economic life of the people had persisted well past the middle of the eighteenth century. But very different tendencies of thought arose in the latter part of the century. One of these was the prevailing desire for greater liberty. The word liberty was defined differently by different men, but for all alike it meant a resistance to oppression, a revulsion against interference with personal freedom of action, a disinclination to be controlled any more than absolutely necessary, a belief that men had a right to be left free to do as they chose, so far as such freedom was practicable.

As applied to economic interests this liberty meant freedom for each person to make his living in the way he might see fit, and without any external restriction. Adam Smith says: "The patrimony of a poor man lies in the strength and dexterity of his hands; and to hinder him from employing this strength and dexterity in what manner he thinks proper, without injury to his neighbor, is a plain violation of this most sacred property. It is a manifest encroachment upon the just liberty both of the workman and of those who might be disposed to employ him. As it hinders the one from working at what he thinks proper, so it hinders the other from employing whom they think proper." Government regulation, therefore, in as far as it restricted men's freedom of action in working, employing, buying, selling, etc., was an interference with their natural liberty.

A second influence in the same direction was the prevalent belief that most of the evils that existed in society were due to the mistakes of civilization, that if men could get back to a "state of nature" and start again, things might be much better. It was felt that there was too much artificiality, too much interference with natural development. Arthur Young condemned the prevailing policy of government, "because it consists of prohibiting the natural course of things. All restrictive forcible measures in domestic policy are bad." Regulation was unwise because it forced men's actions into artificial lines when it would have been much better to let them follow natural lines. Therefore it was felt not only that men had a right to carry on their economic affairs as they chose, but that it was wise to allow them to do so, because interference or regulation had been tried and found wanting. It had produced evil rather than good.

A third and by far the most important intellectual influence which tended toward the destruction of the system of regulation was the development of a consistent body of economic teaching, which claimed to have discovered natural laws showing the futility and injuriousness of any such attempts. Adam Smith's *Wealth of Nations* was published in 1776, the year of the invention of Crompton's mule, and in the decade when enclosures were more rapid than at any other time, except in the middle years of the Napoleonic wars. This was, therefore, one of the earliest, as it was far the most influential, of a series of books which represent the changes in ideas correlative to the changes in actual life already described. It has been described as having for its main object "to demonstrate that the most effectual plan for advancing a people to greatness is to maintain that order of things which nature has pointed out, by allowing every man, as long as he observes the rules of justice, to pursue his own interests in his own way, and to bring both his industry and his capital into the freest competition with those of his fellow-citizens." But the most distinct influence exercised by the writings of Adam Smith and his successors was not so much in pointing out that it was unjust or unwise to interfere with men's natural liberty in the pursuit of their interests, as in showing, as it was believed, that there were natural laws which made all interference incapable of reaching the ends it aimed at. A series of works were published in the latter years of the eighteenth and the early years of the nineteenth century by Malthus, Ricardo, Macculloch, James Mill, and others, in which principles were enunciated and laws formulated which were believed to explain why all interference with free competition was useless or worse. Not only was the whole subject of economic relations clarified, much that had been regarded as wise brought into doubt, and much that had been only doubted shown to be absurd, but the attainment of many objects previously sought for was, apparently, shown to be impossible, and to lie outside of the realm of human control.

It was pointed out, for instance, that because of the limited amount of capital in existence at any one time, "a demand for commodities is not a demand for labor;" and therefore a law like that which required burial in a woollen shroud did not give added occupation to the people, but only diverted them from one occupation to another. Ricardo developed a law of wages to the effect that they always tend to the amount "necessary to enable the laborer to subsist, and to perpetuate his race without either increase or diminution," and that any artificial raising or lowering of wages is impossible, or else causes an increase or diminution in their number which, through competition, soon brings back the old rate. Rent was also explained by Ricardo as arising from the differences of quality between different pieces of land, and as measured by the difference in the productivity of the land under consideration and that of the poorest land under cultivation at the time; and therefore being in its amount independent of direct human control. The Malthusian law of population showed that population tended to increase in a geometrical ratio, subsistence for the population, on the other hand, only in an arithmetical ratio, and that poverty was, therefore, the natural and inevitable result in old countries of a pressure of population on subsistence. The sanction of science was thus given alike to the desires of the lovers of freedom and to the regrets of those who deplored man's departure from the state of nature.

All these intellectual tendencies and reasonings of the later eighteenth century, therefore, combined to discredit the minute regulation of economic society, which had been the traditional policy of the immediately preceding centuries. The movement of thought was definitely opposed to the continuance or extension of the supervision of the government over matters of labor, wages, hours, industry, commerce, agriculture, or other phenomena of production, distribution, exchange, or consumption. This set of opinions is known as the *laissez-faire* theory of the functions of government, the view that the duties of government should be reduced to the smallest possible number, and that it should keep out of the economic sphere altogether. Adam Smith would have restricted the functions of government to three: to protect the nation from the attacks of other nations, to protect each person in the nation from the injustice or violence of other individuals, and to carry on certain educational or similar institutions which were of general utility, but not to any one's private interest. Many of his successors would have cut off the last duty altogether.

62. Cessation of Government Regulation. — These theoretical opinions came to be more and more widely held, more and more influential over the most thoughtful of English statesmen and other men of prominence, until within the first half of the nineteenth century it may be said that their acceptance was general and their influence dominant. They fell in with the actual tendencies of the times, and as a result of the natural breaking down of old conditions, the rise of new, and the general acceptance of this attitude of *laissez-faire*, a rapid and general decay of the system of government regulation took place.

The old regulation had never been so complete in reality as it was on the statute book, and much of it had died out of itself. Some of the provisions of the Statute of Apprentices were persistently disregarded, and when appeals were made for its application to farm work in the latter part of the eighteenth century Parliament refused to enforce it, as they did in the case of discharged soldiers in 1726 and of certain dyers in 1777. The assize of bread was very irregularly enforced, and that of other victuals had been given up altogether. Many commercial companies were growing up without regulation by government, and in the world of finance the hand of government was very light. The new manufactures and the new agriculture grew up to a large extent apart from government control or influence; while the forms to which the old regulation did apply were dying out. In the new factory industry practically the whole body of the employees were without the qualifications required by the Statute of Apprentices, as well as many of the hand-loom weavers who were drawn into the industry by the abundance and cheapness of machine-spun thread. In the early years of the nineteenth century a strenuous effort was made by the older weavers to have the law enforced against them. The whole matter was investigated by Parliament, but instead of enforcing the old law they modified it by acts passed in 1803 and 1809, so as to allow of greater liberty. The old prohibition of using fulling mills passed in 1553 was also repealed in 1809. The Statute of Apprentices after being weakened piecemeal as just mentioned, and by a further amendment removing the wages clauses in 1813, and after being referred to by Lord Mansfield as "against the natural rights and contrary to the common law rights of the land," was finally removed from the statute book in 1814. Even the "Combination Acts," which had forbidden laborers to unite to settle wages and hours, were repealed in 1824. Similar changes took place in other fields than those of the relations between employers and employees. The leading characteristics of legislation on questions of commerce, manufactures, and agriculture during the last quarter of the eighteenth century and the first half of the nineteenth consist in the fact that it almost wholly tended toward freedom from government control. The proportions in which the influence of the natural breaking down of an outgrown system, of the new conditions which were arising, and of pure theory were combined cannot of course be distinguished. All were present. Besides this there is always a large number of persons in the community who would be primarily benefited by a change, and who therefore take the initiative or exercise a special pressure in favor of it.

The Navigation Acts began to go to pieces in 1796, when the old rule restricting importations from America, Asia, and Africa to British vessels was withdrawn in favor of the United States; in 1811 the same permission to send goods to England in other than British vessels was given to Brazil, and in 1822 to the Spanish-American countries. The whole subject was investigated by a Parliamentary Commission in 1820, at the request of the London Chamber of Commerce, and a policy of withdrawal from control determined upon. In 1823 a measure was passed by which the crown was empowered to form reciprocity treaties with any other country so far as shipping was concerned, and agreements were immediately entered into with Prussia, Denmark, Hamburg, Sweden, and within the next twenty years with most other important countries. The old laws of 1660 were repealed in 1826, and a freer system substituted, while in 1849 the Navigation Acts were abolished altogether. In the meantime the monopoly of the old regulated companies was being withdrawn, the India trade being thrown open in 1813 and given up entirely by the Company in 1833. Gradually the commerce of England and of all the English colonies was opened equally to the vessels of all nations.

A beginning of removal of the import and export duties, which had been laid for the purpose of encouraging or discouraging or otherwise influencing certain lines of production or trade, was made in a commercial treaty entered into by Pitt with France in 1786. The work was seriously taken up again in 1824 and 1825 by Mr. Huskisson, and in 1842 by Sir Robert Peel. In 1845 the duty was removed from four hundred and thirty articles, partly raw materials, partly manufactures. But the most serious struggle in the movement for free trade was that for the repeal of the corn laws. A new law had been passed at the close of the Napoleonic wars in 1815, by which the importation of wheat was forbidden so long as the prevailing price was not above ten shillings a bushel. This was in pursuance of the old traditional policy of encouraging the production of grain in order that England might be at least partially self-supporting, and was further justified on the ground that the landowners paid the great bulk of the taxes, which they could not do if the price of grain were allowed to be brought down by foreign competition. Nevertheless an active propaganda for the abolition of this law was begun by the formation of the "Anti-Corn Law League," in 1839. Richard Cobden became the president and the most famous representative of this society, which carried on an active agitation for some years. The chief interest in the abolition of the law would necessarily be taken by the manufacturing employers, the wages of whose employees could thus be made lower and more constant, but there were abundant other arguments against the laws, and their abandonment was entirely in conformity with the spirit of the age. At the close of 1845, therefore, Peel proposed their repeal, the matter was brought up in Parliament in the early months of 1846, and a sliding scale was adopted by which a slight temporary protection should continue until 1849, when any protective tariff on wheat was to cease altogether, though a nominal duty of about one and a half pence a bushel was still to be collected. This is known as the "adoption of free trade."

It remains to be noted in this connection that "free trade in land" was an expression often used during the same period, and consisted in an effort marked by a long series of acts of Parliament and regulations of the courts to simplify the title to land, the processes of buying and selling it, and in other ways making its use and disposal as simple and uncontrolled by external regulation as was commerce or any form of industry.

Thus the structure of regulation of industry, which had

been built up in the sixteenth and seventeenth centuries, or which had survived from the Middle Ages, was now torn down; the use of the powers of government to make men carry on their economic life in a certain way, to buy and sell, labor and hire, manufacture and cultivate, export and import, only in such ways as were thought to be best for the nation, seemed to be entirely abandoned. The *laissez-faire* view of government was to all appearances becoming entirely dominant.

63. Individualism. — But the prevailing tendencies of thought and the economic teaching of the period were not merely negative and opposed to government regulation; they contained a positive element also. If there was to be no external control, what incentive would actuate men in their industrial existence? What force would hold economic society together? The answer was a plain one. Enlightened self-interest was the incentive, universal free competition was the force. James Anderson, in his *Political Economy*, published in 1801, says, "Private interest is the great source of public good, which, though operating unseen, never ceases one moment to act with unabating power, if it be not perverted by the futile regulations of some short-sighted politician." Again, Malthus, in his *Essay on Population*, in 1817, says: "By making the passion of self-love beyond comparison stronger than the passion of benevolence, the more ignorant are led to pursue the general happiness, an end which they would have totally failed to attain if the moving principle of their conduct had been benevolence. Benevolence, indeed, as the great and constant source of action, would require the most perfect knowledge of causes and effects, and therefore can only be the attribute of the Deity. In a being so short-sighted as man it would lead to the grossest errors, and soon transform the fair and cultivated soil of human society into a dreary scene of want and confusion."

In other words, a natural and sufficient economic force was always tending to act and to produce the best results, except in as far as it was interfered with by external regulation. If a man wishes to earn wages, to receive payment, he must observe what work another man wants done, or what goods another man desires, and offer to do that work or furnish those goods, so that the other man may be willing to remunerate him. In this way both obtain what they want, and if all others are similarly occupied all wants will be satisfied so far as practicable. But men must be entirely free to act as they think best, to choose what and when and how they will produce. The best results will be obtained where the greatest freedom exists, where men may compete with one another freed from all trammels, at liberty to pay or ask such wages, to demand or offer such prices, to accept or reject such goods, as they wish or can agree upon. If everybody else is equally free the man who offers the best to his neighbor will be preferred. Effort will thus be stimulated, self-reliance encouraged, production increased, improvement attained, and economy guaranteed. Nor should there be any special favor or encouragement given by government or by any other bodies to any special individuals or classes of persons or kinds of industry, for in this way capital and labor will be diverted from the direction which they would naturally take, and the self-reliance and energy of such favored persons diminished.

Therefore complete individualism, universal freedom of competition, was the ideal of the age, as far as there is ever any universal ideal. There certainly was a general belief among the greater number of the intelligent and influential classes, that when each person was freely seeking his own best interest he was doing the best for himself and for all. Economic society was conceived of as a number of freely competing units held in equilibrium by the force of competition, much as the material universe is held together by the attraction of gravitation. Any hindrance to this freedom of the individual to compete freely with all others, any artificial support or encouragement that gives him an advantage over others, is against his own real interest and that of society.

This ideal was necessarily as much opposed to voluntary combinations, and to restrictions imposed by custom or agreement, as it was to government regulation. Individualism is much more than a mere *laissez-faire* policy of government. It believes that every man should remain and be allowed to remain free, unrestricted, undirected, unassisted, so that he may be in a position at any time to direct his labor, ability, capital, enterprise, in any direction that may seem to him most desirable, and may be induced to put forth his best efforts to attain success. The arguments on which it was based were drawn from the domain of men's natural right to economic as to other freedom; from experience, by which it was believed that all regulation had proved to be injurious; and from economic doctrine, which was believed to have discovered natural laws that proved the necessary result of interference to be evil, or at best futile.

The changes of the time were favorable to this ideal. Men had never been so free from external control by government or any other power. The completion of the process of enclosure left every agriculturist at liberty to plant and raise what he chose, and when and how he chose. The reform of the poor law in 1834 abolished the act of settlement of 1662, by which the authorities of each parish had the power to remove to the place from which they came any laborers who entered it, and so far as the law was concerned, farm laborers were now free to come and go where they chose to seek for work. In the new factories, systems of transportation, and other large establishments that were taking the places of small ones, employees were at liberty to leave their engagements at any time they chose, to go to another employer or another occupation; and the employer had the same liberty of discharging at a moment's notice. Manufacturers were at liberty to make anything they chose, and hire laborers in whatever proportion they chose. And just as early modern regulation had been given up, so the few fragments of mediæval restrictive institutions that had survived the intervening centuries were now rapidly abandoned in the stress of competitive society. Later forms of restriction, such as trade unions and trusts, had not yet grown up. Actual conditions and the theoretical statement of what was desirable approximated to one another more nearly than they usually have in the world's history.

64. Social Conditions at the Beginning of the Nineteenth Century. — Yet somehow the results were disappointing. More and better manufactured goods were produced and foreign goods sold, and at vastly lower prices. The same result would probably have been true in agriculture had not the corn laws long prevented this consummation, and instead distributed the surplus to paupers and the holders of government bonds through the medium of taxes. There was no doubt of English wealth and progress. England held the primacy of the world in commerce, in manufactures, in agriculture. Her rapid increase in wealth had enabled her to bear the burden, not only of her own part in the Napoleonic wars, but of much of the expense of the armament of the continental countries. Population also was increasing more rapidly than ever before. She stood before the world as the most prominent and successful modern nation in all material respects. Yet a closer examination into her internal condition shows much that was deeply unsatisfactory. The period of transition from the domestic to the factory system of industry and from the older to the new farming conditions was one of almost unrelieved misery to great masses of those who were wedded to the old ways, who had neither the capital, the enterprise, nor the physical nor mental adaptability to attach themselves to the new. The hand-loom weavers kept up a hopeless struggle in the garrets and cellars of the factory towns, while their wages were sinking lower and lower till finally the whole generation died out. The small farmers who lost the support of spinning and other by-industries succumbed in the competition with the larger producers. The cottagers whose commons were lost to them by enclosures frequently failed to find a niche for themselves in their own part of the country, and became paupers or vagabonds. Many of the same sad incidents which marked the sixteenth century were characteristic of this period of analogous change, when ultimate improvement was being bought at the price of much immediate misery.

Even among those who were supposed to have reaped the advantages of the changes of the time many unpleasant phenomena appeared. The farm laborers were not worse, perhaps were better off on the average, in the matter of wages, than those of the previous generation, but they were more completely separated from the land than they had ever been before, more completely deprived of those wholesome influences which come from the use of even a small portion of land, and of the incitement to thrift that comes from the possibility of rising. Few classes of people have ever been more utterly without enjoyment or prospects than the modern

CARDING, DRAWING, AND ROVING IN 1835.

(Baines: *History of Cotton Manufacture.*)

English farm laborers. And one class, the yeomen, somewhat higher in position and certainly in opportunities, had disappeared entirely, recruited into the class of mere laborers.

In the early factories, women and children were employed more extensively and more persistently than in earlier forms of industry. Their labor was in greater demand than that of men. In 1839, of 31,632 employees in worsted mills, 18,416, or considerably more than half, were under eighteen years of age, and of the 13,216 adults, 10,192 were women, leaving only 3024 adult men among more than 30,000 laborers. In 1832, in a certain flax spinning mill near Leeds, where about 1200 employees were engaged, 829 were below eighteen, only 390 above; and in the flax spinning industry generally, in 1835, only about one-third were adults, and only about one-third of these were men. In the still earlier years of the factory system the proportion of women and children was even greater, though reliable general statistics are not available. The cheaper wages, the easier control, and the smaller size of women and children, now that actual physical power was not required, made them more desirable to employers, and in many families the men clung to hand work while the women and children went into the factories.

The early mills were small, hot, damp, dusty, and unhealthy. They were not more so perhaps than the cottages where domestic industry had been carried on; but now the hours were more regular, continuous, and prolonged in which men, women, and children were subjected to such labor. All had to conform alike to the regular hours, and these were in the early days excessive. Twelve, thirteen, and even fourteen hours a day were not unusual. Regular hours of work, when they are moderate in length, and a systematized life, when it is not all labor, are probably wholesome, physically and morally; but when the summons to cease from work and that to begin it again are separated by such a short interval, the factory bell or whistle represents mere tyranny.

Wages were sometimes higher than under the old conditions, but they were even more irregular. Greater ups and downs occurred. Periods of very active production and of restriction of production alternated more decidedly than before, and introduced more irregularity into industry for both employers and employees. The town laborer engaged in a large establishment was, like the rural laborer on a large farm, completely separated from the land, from capital, from any active connection with the administration of industry, from any probable opportunity of rising out of the laboring class. His prospects were, therefore, as limited as his position was laborious and precarious.

The rapid growth of the manufacturing towns, especially in the north, drawing the scattered population of other parts of the country into their narrow limits, caused a general breakdown in the old arrangements for providing water, drainage, and fresh air; and made rents high, and consequently living in crowded rooms necessary. The factory towns in the early part of the century were filthy, crowded, and demoralizing, compared alike with their earlier and their present condition.

In the higher grades of economic society the advantages of the recent changes were more distinct, the disadvantages less so. The rise of capital and business enterprise into greater importance, and the extension of the field of competition, gave greater opportunity to employing farmers, merchants, and manufacturers, as well as to the capitalists pure and simple. But even for them the keenness of com-

COTTON FACTORIES IN MANCHESTER.
(Baines: *History of Cotton Manufacture.*)

petition and the exigencies of providing for the varying conditions of distant markets made the struggle for success a harder one, and many failed in it.

In many ways therefore it might seem that the great material advances which had been made, the removal of artificial restrictions, the increase of liberty of action, the extension of the field of competition, the more enlightened opinions on economic and social relations, had failed to increase human happiness appreciably; indeed, for a time had made the condition of the mass of the people worse instead of better.

It will not, therefore, be unexpected if some other lines of economic and social development, especially those which have become more and more prominent during the later progress of the nineteenth century, prove to be quite different in direction from those that have been studied in this chapter.

65. BIBLIOGRAPHY

Toynbee, Arnold: *The Industrial Revolution of the Eighteenth Century in England.*

Lecky, W. E. H.: *History of England in the Eighteenth Century,* Vol. VI, Chap. 23.

Baines, E.: *History of the Cotton Manufacture in Great Britain.*

Cooke-Taylor, R. W.: *The Modern Factory System.*

Levi, L.: *History of British Commerce and of the Economic Progress of the British Nation.*

Prothero, R. E.: *The Pioneers and Progress of English Farming.*

Rogers, J. E. T.: *Industrial and Commercial History.*

Smith, Adam: *An Inquiry into the Nature and Causes of the Wealth of Nations.*

CHAPTER IX

THE EXTENSION OF GOVERNMENT CONTROL

Factory Laws, the Modification of Land Ownership, Sanitary Regulations, and New Public Services

66. National Affairs from 1830 to 1900. — The English government in the year 1830 might be described as a complete aristocracy. The king had practically no powers apart from his ministers, and they were merely the representatives of the majority in Parliament. Parliament consisted of the House of Lords and the House of Commons. The first of these Houses was made up for the most part of an hereditary aristocracy. The bishops and newly created peers, the only element which did not come in by inheritance, were appointed by the king and usually from the families of those who already possessed inherited titles. The House of Commons had originally been made up of two members from each county, and two from each important town. But the list of represented towns was still practically the same as it had been in the fifteenth century, while intervening economic and other changes had, as has been seen, made the most complete alteration in the distribution of population. Great manufacturing towns had grown up as a result of changes in commerce and of the industrial revolution, and these had no representation in Parliament separate from the counties in which they lay. On the other hand, towns once of respectable size had dwindled until they had only a few dozen inhabitants, and in some cases had reverted to open farming country ; but these, or the landlords who owned the land on which they had been built, still retained their two representatives in Parliament. The county representatives were voted for by all " forty shilling freeholders," that is, landowners whose farms would rent for forty shillings a year. But the whole tendency of English landholding, as has been seen, had been to decrease the number of landowners in the country, so that the actual number of voters was only a very small proportion of the rural population.

Such great irregularities of representation had thus grown up that the selection of more than a majority of the members of the House of Commons was in the hands of a very small number of men, many of them already members of the House of Lords, and all members of the aristocracy.

Just as Parliament represented only the higher classes, so officers in the army and to a somewhat less extent the navy, the officials of the established church, the magistrates in the counties, the ambassadors abroad, and the cabinet ministers at home, the holders of influential positions in the Universities and endowed institutions generally, were as a regular thing members of the small class of the landed or mercantile aristocracy of England. Perhaps one hundred thousand out of the fourteen millions of the people of England were the veritable governing classes. They alone had any control of the national and local government, or of the most important political and social institutions.

The " Reform of Parliament," which meant some degree of equalization of the representation of districts, an extension of the franchise, and the abolition of some of the irregularities in elections, had been proposed from time to time, but had awakened little interest until it was advocated by the Radicals under the influence of the French Revolution, along with some much more far-reaching propositions. Between the years 1820 and 1830, however, a moderate reform of Parliament had been advocated by the leaders of the Whig party. In 1830 this party rather unexpectedly obtained a majority in Parliament, for the first time for a long while, and the ministry immediately introduced a reform bill. It proposed to take away the right of separate representation from fifty-six towns, and to reduce the number of representatives from two to one in thirty-one others; to transfer these representatives to the more populous towns and counties; to extend the franchise to a somewhat larger number and to equalize it; and finally to introduce lists of voters, to keep the polls open for only two days, and to correct a number of such minor abuses. There was a bitter contest in Parliament and in the country at large on the proposed change, and the measure was only carried after it had been rejected by one House of Commons, passed by a new House elected as a test of the question, then defeated by the House of Lords, and only passed by them when submitted a second time with the threat by the ministry of requiring the king to create enough new peers to pass it, if the existing members refused to do so. Its passage was finally secured in 1832. It was carried by pressure from below through all its stages. The king signed it reluctantly because it had been sent to him by Parliament, the House of Lords passed it under threats from the ministry, who based their power on the House of Commons. This body in turn had to be reconstructed by a new election before it would agree to it, and there is no doubt that the voters as well as Parliament itself were much influenced by the cry of "the Bill, the whole Bill, and nothing but the Bill," raised by mobs, associations, and meetings, consisting largely of the masses of the people who possessed no votes at all. In the last resort, therefore, it was a victory won by the masses, and, little as they profited by it immediately, it proved to be the turning point, the first step from aristocracy toward democracy.

In 1867 a second Reform Bill was passed, mainly on the lines of the first, but giving what amounted to almost universal suffrage to the inhabitants of the town constituencies, which included the great body of the workingmen. Finally, in 1884 and 1885, the third Reform Bill was passed which extended the right of voting to agricultural laborers as well, and did much toward equalizing the size of the districts represented by each member of the House of Commons. Other reforms have been adopted during the same period, and Parliament has thus come to represent the whole population instead of merely the aristocracy. But there have been even greater changes in local government. By laws passed in 1835 and 1882 the cities and boroughs have been given a form of government in which the power is in the hands of all the taxpayers. In 1888 an act was passed through Parliament forming County Councils, elected by universal suffrage and taking over many of the powers formerly exercised by the magistrates and large landholders. In 1894 this was followed by a Parish Council Bill creating even more distinctly local bodies, by which the people in each locality, elected by universal suffrage, including that of women, may take charge of almost all their local concerns under the general legislation of Parliament.

Corresponding to these changes in general and local government the power of the old ruling classes has been diminished in all directions, until it has become little more than that degree of prominence and natural leadership which the national sentiment or their economic and intellectual advantages give to them. It may be said that England, so far as its government goes, has come nearer to complete democracy than any other modern country.

In the rapidity of movement, the activity, the energy, the variety of interests, the thousand lines of economic, political, intellectual, literary, artistic, philanthropic, or religious life which characterize the closing years of the ninteenth century, it seems impossible to choose a few facts to typify or describe the period, as is customary for earlier times.

Little can be done except to point out the main lines of political movement, as has been done in this paragraph, or of economic and social development, as will be done in the remaining paragraphs of this and the next chapter. The great mass of recent occurrences and present conditions are as yet rather the human atmosphere in which we are living, the problem which we are engaged in solving, than a proper subject for historical description and analysis.

67. The Beginning of Factory Legislation. — One of the greatest difficulties with which the early mill owners had to contend was the insufficient supply of labor for their factories. Since these had to be run by water power, they were placed along the rapid streams in the remote parts of Yorkshire, Lancashire, Derbyshire, and Nottinghamshire, which were sparsely populated, and where such inhabitants as there were had a strong objection to working in factories. However abundant population might be in some other parts of England, in the northwest where the new manufacturing was growing up, and especially in the hilly rural districts, there were but few persons available to perform the work which must be done by human hands in connection with the mill machinery. There was, however, in existence a source of supply of laborers which could furnish almost unlimited numbers and at the lowest possible cost. The parish poorhouses or workhouses of the large cities were overcrowded

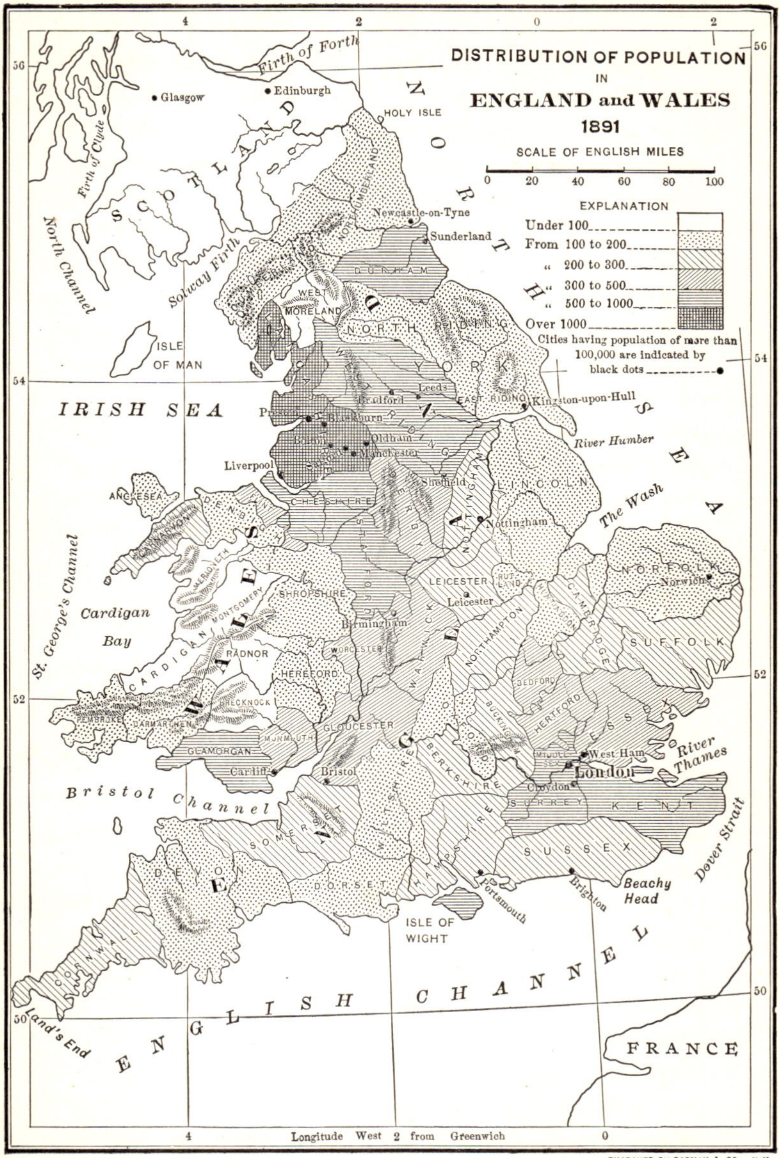

ENGRAVED BY BORMAY & CO., N.Y.

with children. The authorities always had difficulty in finding occupation for them when they came to an age when they could earn their own living, and any plan of putting them to work would be received with welcome. This source of supply was early discovered and utilized by the manufacturers, and it soon became customary for them to take as apprentices large numbers of the poorhouse children. They signed indentures with the overseers of the poor by which they agreed to give board, clothing, and instruction for a certain number of years to the children who were thus bound to them. In return they put them to work in the factories. Children from seven years of age upward were engaged by hundreds from London and the other large cities, and set to work in the cotton spinning factories of the north. Since there were no other facilities for boarding them, " apprentice houses " were built for them in the vicinity of the factories, where they were placed under the care of superintendents or matrons. The conditions of life among these pauper children were, as might be expected, very hard. They were remotely situated, apart from the observation of the community, left to the burdens of unrelieved labor and the harshness of small masters or foremen. Their hours of labor were excessive. When the demands of trade were active they were often arranged in two shifts, each shift working twelve hours, one in the day and another in the night, so that it was a common saying in the north that " their beds never got cold," one set climbing into bed as the other got out. When there was no night work the day work was the longer. They were driven at their work and often abused. Their food was of the coarsest description, and they were frequently required to eat it while at their work, snatching a bite as they could while the machinery was still in motion. Much of the time which should have been devoted to rest was spent in cleaning the machinery, and there seems to have been absolutely no effort made to give them any education or opportunity for recreation.

The sad life of these little waifs, overworked, underfed, neglected, abused, in the factories and barracks in the remote glens of Yorkshire and Lancashire, came eventually to the notice of the outside world. Correspondence describing their condition began to appear in the newspapers, a Manchester Board of Health made a presentment in 1796 calling attention to the unsanitary conditions in the cotton factories where they worked, contagious fevers were reported to be especially frequent in the apprentice houses, and in 1802 Sir Robert Peel, himself an employer of nearly a thousand such children, brought the matter to the attention of Parliament. An immediate and universal desire was expressed to abolish the abuses of the system, and as a result the "Health and Morals Act to regulate the Labor of Bound Children in Cotton Factories" was passed in the same year. It prohibited the binding out for factory labor of children younger than nine years, restricted the hours of labor to twelve actual working hours a day, and forbade night labor. It required the walls of the factories to be properly whitewashed and the buildings to be sufficiently ventilated, insisted that the apprentices should be furnished with at least one new suit of clothes a year, and provided that they should attend religious service and be instructed in the fundamental English branches. This was the first of the "Factory Acts," for, although its application was so restricted, applying only to cotton factories, and for the most part only to bound children, the subsequent steps in the formation of the great code of factory legislation were for a long while simply a development of the same principle, that factory labor involved conditions which it was desirable for government to regulate.

At the time of the passage of this law the introduction of steam power was already causing a transfer of the bulk of factory industry from the rural districts to which the need for water power had confined it to the towns where every other requisite for carrying on manufacturing was more easily obtainable. Here the children of families resident in the town could be obtained, and the practice of using apprentice children was largely given up. Many of the same evils, however, continued to exist here. The practice of beginning to work while extremely young, long hours, night work, unhealthy surroundings, proved to be as common among these children to whom the law did not apply as they had been among the apprentice children. These evils attracted the attention of several persons of philanthropic feeling. Robert Owen, especially, a successful manufacturer who had introduced many reforms in his own mills, collected a large body of evidence as to the excessive labor and early age of employees in the factories even where no apprentice labor was engaged. He tried to awaken an interest in the matter by the publication of a pamphlet on the injurious consequences of the factory system, and to influence various members of Parliament to favor the passage of a law intended to improve the condition of laboring children and young people. In 1815 Sir Robert Peel again brought the matter up in Parliament. A committee was appointed to investigate the question, and a legislative agitation was thus begun which was destained to last for many years and to produce a series of laws which have gradually taken most of the conditions of employment in large establishments under the control of the government. In debates in Parliament, in testimony before government commissions of investigation, in petitions, pamphlets, and newspapers, the conditions of factory labor were described and discussed. Successive laws to modify these conditions were introduced into Parliament, debated at great length, amended, postponed, reintroduced, and in some cases passed, in others defeated.

68. Arguments for and against Factory Legislation. — The need for regulation which was claimed to exist arose from the long hours of work which were customary, from the very early age at which many children were sent to be employed in the factories, and from various incidents of manufacturing which were considered injurious, or as involving unnecessary hardship. The actual working hours in the factories in the early part of the century were from twelve and a half to fourteen a day. That is to say, factories usually started work in the morning at 6 o'clock and continued till 12, when a period from a half-hour to an hour was allowed for dinner, then the work began again and continued till 7.30 or 8.30 in the evening. It was customary to eat breakfast after reaching the mill, but this was done while attending the machinery, there being no general stoppage for the purpose. Some mills ran even longer hours, opening at 5 A.M. and not closing till 9 P.M. In some exceptional cases the hours were only 12 ; from 6 to 12 and from 1 to 7. The inducements to long hours were very great. The profits were large, the demand for goods was constantly growing, the introduction of gas made it possible to light the factories, and the use of artificial power, either water or steam, seemed to make the labor much less severe than when the power had been provided by human muscles. Few or no holidays were regarded, except Sunday, so that work went on in an unending strain of protracted, exhausting labor, prolonged for much of the year far into the night.

To these long hours all the hands alike conformed, the children commencing and stopping work at the same time as the grown men and women. Moreover, the children often began work while extremely young. There was a great deal of work in the factories which they could do just as well, in some cases even better, than adults. They were therefore commonly sent into the mills by their parents at about the age of eight years, frequently at seven or even six. As has been before stated, more than half of the employees in many factories were below eighteen years, and of these a considerable number were mere children. Thirdly, there were certain other evils of factory labor that attracted attention and were considered by the reformers to be remediable. Many accidents occurred because the moving machinery was unprotected, the temperature in the cotton mills had to be kept high, and ventilation and cleanliness were often entirely neglected. The habit of keeping the machinery in motion while meals were being eaten was a hardship, and in many ways the employees were practically at the mercy of the proprietors of the factories so long as there was no form of oversight or of united action to prevent harshness or unfairness.

In the discussions in Parliament and outside there were of course many contradictory statements concerning the facts of the case, and much denial of general and special charges. The advocates of factory laws drew an extremely sombre picture of the evils of the factory system. The opponents of such legislation, on the other hand, declared that their statements were exaggerated or untrue, and that the condition of the factory laborer was not worse than that of other workingmen, or harder than that of the domestic worker and his family had been in earlier times.

But apart from these recriminations and contradictions,

there were certain general arguments used in the debates which can be grouped into three classes on each side. For the regulating laws there was in the first place the purely sentimental argument, repulsion against the hard, unrelieved labor, the abuse, the lack of opportunity for enjoyment or recreation of the children of the factory districts; the feeling that in wealthy, humane, Christian England, it was unendurable that women and little children should work longer hours, be condemned to greater hardships, and more completely cut off from the enjoyments of life than were the slaves of tropical countries. This is the argument of Mrs. Browning's *Cry of the Children:* —

> "Do ye hear the children weeping, O my brothers,
>   Ere the sorrow comes with years?
> They are leaning their young heads against their mothers,
>   And that cannot stop their tears.
> The young lambs are bleating in the meadows;
>   The young birds are chirping in the nest;
> The young fawns are playing with the shadows;
>   The young flowers are blowing toward the west;
> But the young, young children, O my brothers!
>   They are weeping bitterly.
> They are weeping in the play-time of the others
>   In the country of the free.
>   *   *   *   *   *   *
> 'For oh!' say the children, 'we are weary,
>   And we cannot run or leap:
> If we cared for any meadows, it were merely
>   To drop down in them and sleep.'
>   *   *   *   *   *   *
> They look up with their pale and sunken faces,
>   And their look is dread to see,
> For they mind you of their angels in high places,
>   With eyes turned on Deity.
> 'How long,' they say, 'how long, O cruel nation,
>   Will you stand, to move the world on a child's heart,
> Stifle down with a mailed heel its palpitation
>   And tread onward to your throne amid the mart?'"

Secondly, it was argued that the long hours for the children cut them off from all intellectual and moral training, that they were in no condition after such protracted labor to profit by any opportunities of education that should be supplied, that with the diminished influence of the home, and the demoralizing effects that were supposed to result from factory labor, ignorance and vice alike would continue to be its certain accompaniments, unless the age at which regular work was begun should be limited, and the number of hours of labor of young persons restricted. Thirdly, it was claimed that there was danger of the physical degeneracy of the factory population. Certain diseases, especially of the joints and limbs, were discovered to be very prevalent in the factory districts. Children who began work so early in life and were subjected to such long hours of labor did not grow so rapidly, nor reach their full stature, nor retain their vigor so late in life, as did the population outside of the factories. Therefore, for the very physical preservation of the race, it was declared to be necessary to regulate the conditions of factory labor.

On the other hand, apart from denials as to the facts of the case, there were several distinct arguments used against the adoption of factory laws. In the first place, in the interests of the manufacturers, such laws were opposed as an unjust interference with their business, an unnecessary and burdensome obstacle to their success, and a threat of ruin to a class who by giving employment to so many laborers and furnishing so much of the material for commerce were of the greatest advantage to the country. Secondly, from a somewhat broader point of view, it was declared that if such laws were adopted England would no longer be able to compete with other countries and would lose her preeminence in manufactures. The factory system was being introduced into France, Belgium, the United States, and other countries, and in none of these was there any legal restriction on the hours of labor or the age of the employees. If English manufacturers were forced to reduce the length of the day in which production was carried on, they could not produce as cheaply as these other countries, and English exports would decrease. This would reduce the national prosperity and be especially hard on the working classes themselves, as many would necessarily be thrown out of work. Thirdly, as a matter of principle it was argued that the policy of government regulation had been tried and found wanting, that after centuries of existence it had been deliberately given up, and should not be reintroduced. Laws restricting hours would interfere with the freedom of labor, with the freedom of capital, with the freedom of contract. If the employer and the employee were both satisfied with the conditions of their labor, why should the government interfere? The reason also why such regulation had failed in the past and must again, if tried now, was evident. It was an effort to alter the action of the natural laws which controlled employment, wages, profits, and other economic matters, and was bad in theory, and would therefore necessarily be injurious in practice. These and some other less general arguments were used over and over again in the various forms of the discussion through almost half a century. The laws that were passed were carried because the majority in Parliament were either not convinced by these reasonings or else determined that, come what might, the evils and abuses connected with factory labor should be abolished. As a matter of fact, the factory laws were carried by the rank and file of the voting members of Parliament, not only against the protests of the manufacturers especially interested, but in spite of the warnings of those who spoke in the name of established teaching, and frequently against the opposition of the political leaders of both parties. The greatest number of those who voted for them were influenced principally by their sympathies and feelings, and yielded to the appeals of certain philanthropic advocates, the most devoted and influential of whom was Lord Ashley, afterward earl of Shaftesbury, who devoted many years to investigation and agitation on the subject both inside and out of Parliament.

69. Factory Legislation to 1847. — The actual course of factory legislation was as follows. The bill originally introduced in 1815, after having been subjected to a series of discussions, amendments, and postponements, was passed in June, 1819, being the second "Factory Act." It applied only to cotton mills, and was in the main merely an extension of the act of 1802 to the protection of children who were not pauper apprentices. It forbade the employment of any child under nine years of age, and prohibited the employment of those between nine and sixteen more than twelve hours a day, or at night. In addition to the twelve hours of actual labor, at least a half-hour must be allowed for breakfast and an hour for dinner. Other minor acts amending or extending this were passed from time to time, till in 1833, after two successive commissions had made investigations and reports on the subject, an important law was passed. It applied practically to all textile mills, not merely to those for the spinning of cotton. The prohibition of employment of all below nine years was continued, children between nine and thirteen were to work only eight hours per day, and young persons between thirteen and eighteen only twelve hours, and none of these at night. Two whole and eight half holidays were required to be given within the year, and each child must have a surgeon's certificate of fitness for labor. There were also clauses for the education of the children and the cleanliness of the factories. But the most important clause of this statute was the provision of a corps of four inspectors with assistants who were sworn to their duties, salaried, and provided with extensive powers of making rules for the execution of the act, of enforcing it, and prosecuting for its violation. The earlier laws had not been efficiently carried out. Under this act numerous prosecutions and convictions took place, and factory regulation began to become a reality. The inspectors calculated during their first year of service that there were about 56,000 children between nine and thirteen, and about 108,000 young persons between thirteen and eighteen, in the factories under their supervision.

The decade lying between 1840 and 1850 was one of specially great activity in social and economic agitation. Chartism, the abolition of the corn laws, the formation of trade unions, mining acts, and further extensions of the factory acts were all alike under discussion, and they all created the most intense antagonism between parties and classes. In 1844 the law commonly known as the "Children's Half-time Act" was passed. It contained a large number of general provisions for the fencing of dangerous machinery, for its stoppage while being cleaned, for the report of accidents to inspectors and district surgeons, for the public prosecution for damages of the factory owner when he should seem to be responsible for an accident, and for the enforcement of the act. Its most distinctive clause, however, was that which restricted the labor of children to a half-day, or the whole of alternate days, and required their attendance at school for the other half of their time. All women were placed by this act in the same category as young persons between thirteen and eighteen, so far as the restriction of hours of labor to twelve per day and the prohibition of night work extended.

The next statute to be passed was an extension of this regulation, though it contained the provision which had long been the most bitterly contested of any during the whole factory law agitation. This was the "Ten-hour Act" of 1847. From an early period in the century there had been a strong agitation in favor of restricting by law the hours of young persons, and from somewhat later, of women, to ten hours per day, and this proposition had been repeatedly introduced and defeated in Parliament. It was now carried. By this time the more usual length of the working day even when unrestricted had been reduced to twelve hours, and in some trades to eleven. It was now made by law half-time for children, and ten hours for young persons and women, or as rearranged by another law passed three years afterward, ten and a half hours for five days of the week and a half-day on Saturday. The number of persons to whom the Ten-hour Act applied was estimated at something over 360,000. That is, including the children, at least three-fourths of all persons employed in textile industries had their hours and some other conditions of labor directly regulated by law. Moreover, the work of men employed in the same factories was so dependent on that of the women and the children, that many of these restrictions applied practically to them also.

Further minor changes in hours and other details were made from time to time, but there was no later contest on the principle of factory legislation. The evil results which had been feared had not shown themselves, and many of its strongest opponents had either already, or did eventually, acknowledge the beneficial results of the laws.

70. The Extension of Factory Legislation. — By the suc-

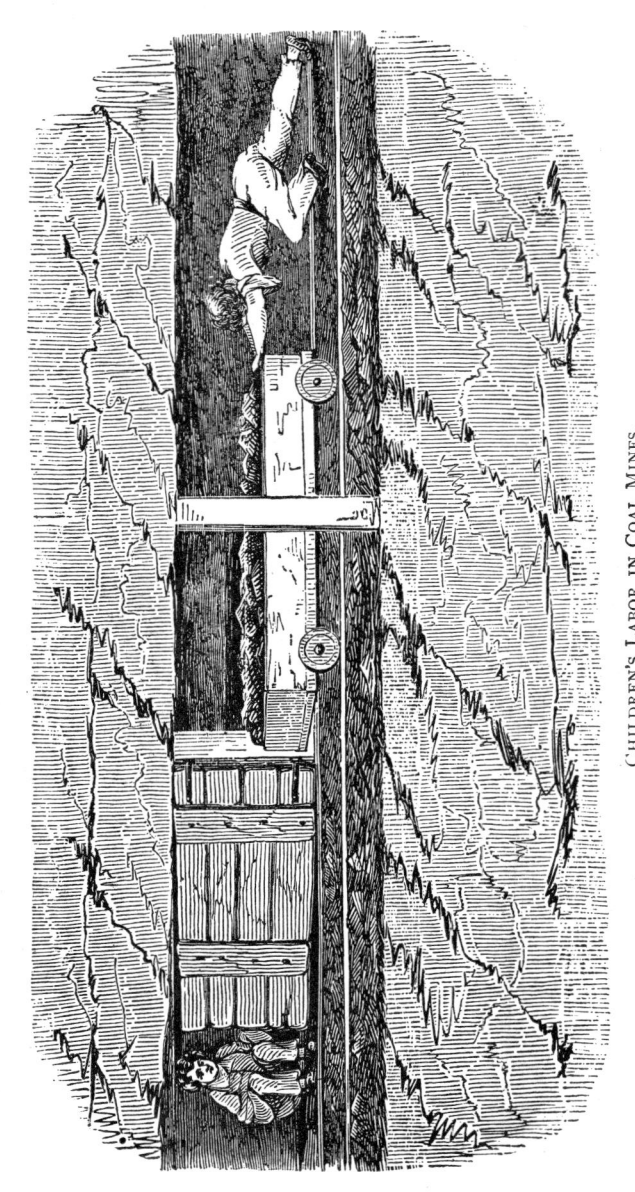

CHILDREN'S LABOR IN COAL MINES.
Report of Children's Employment Commission of 1842.

cessive acts of 1819, 1833, 1844, and 1847, a normal length of working day and regulated conditions generally had been established by government for the factories employing women and children. The next development was an extension of the regulation of hours and conditions of labor from factories proper to other allied fields. Already in 1842 a

WOMEN'S LABOR IN COAL MINES.
(*Report of Children's Employment Commission, 1842.*)

law had been passed regulating labor in mines. This act was passed in response to the needs shown by the report of a commission which had been appointed in 1840. They made a thorough investigation of the obscure conditions of labor underground, and reported a condition of affairs which was heart-sickening. Children began their life in the coal mines at five, six, or seven years of age. Girls and women worked like boys and men, they were less than half clothed, and worked alongside of men who were stark naked. There were from twelve to fourteen working hours in the twenty-four, and these were often at night. Little girls of six or eight years of age made ten to twelve trips a day up steep ladders to the surface, carrying half a hundred weight of coal in wooden buckets on their backs at each journey. Young women appeared before the commissioners, when summoned from their work, dressed merely in a pair of trousers, dripping wet from the water of the mine, and already weary with the labor of a day scarcely more than begun. A common form of labor consisted of drawing on hands and knees over the inequalities of a passageway not more than two feet or twenty-eight inches high a car or tub filled with three or four hundred weight of coal, attached by a chain and hook to a leather band around the waist. The mere recital of the testimony taken precluded all discussion as to the desirability of reform, and a law was immediately passed, almost without dissent, which prohibited for the future all work underground by females or by boys under thirteen years of age. Inspectors were appointed, and by subsequent acts a whole code of regulation of mines as regards age, hours, lighting, ventilation, safety, licensing of engineers, and in other respects has been created.

In 1846 a bill was passed applying to calico printing works regulations similar to the factory laws proper. In 1860, 1861, and 1863 similar laws were passed for bleaching and dyeing for lace works, and for bakeries. In 1864 another so-called factory act was passed applying to at least six other industries, none of which had any connection with textile factories. Three years later, in 1867, two acts for factories and workshops respectively took a large number of additional industries under their care; and finally, in 1878, the "Factory and Workshop Consolidation Act" repealed all the former special laws and substituted a veritable factory code containing a vast number of provisions for the regulation of industrial establishments. This law covered more than fifty printed pages of the statute book. Its principle provisions were as follows: The limit of prohibited labor was raised from nine to ten years, children in the terms of the statute being those between ten and fourteen, and "young persons" those between fourteen and eighteen years of age. For all such the day's work must begin either at six or seven, and close at the same hour respectively in the evening, two hours being allowed for meal-times. All Saturdays and eight other days in the year must be half-holidays, while the whole of Christmas Day and Good Friday, or two alternative days, must be allowed as holidays. Children could work for only one-half of each day or on the whole of alternate days, and must attend school on the days or parts of days on which they did not work. There were minute provisions governing sanitary conditions, safety from machinery and in dangerous occupations, meal-times, medical certificates of fitness for employment, and reports of accidents. Finally there were the necessary body of provisions for administration, enforcement, penalties, and exceptions.

Since 1878 there have been a number of extensions of the principle of factory legislation, the most important of which are the following. In 1891 and 1895, amending acts were passed bringing laundries and docks within the provisions of the law, making further rules against overcrowding and other unsanitary conditions, increasing the age of prohibited labor to eleven years, and making a beginning of the regulation of "outworkers" or those engaged by "sweaters." "Sweating" is manufacturing carried on by contractors or subcontractors on a small scale, who usually have the work done in their own homes or in single hired rooms by members of their families, or by poorly paid employees who by one chance or another are not in a free and independent relation to them. Many abuses exist in these " sweatshops." The law so far is scarcely more than tentative, but in these successive acts provisions have been made by which all manufacturers or contractors must keep lists of outworkers engaged by them, and submit these to the factory inspectors for supervision.

In 1892 a " Shop-hours Act " was passed prohibiting the employment of any person under eighteen years of age more than seventy-four hours in any week in any retail or wholesale store, shop, eating-house, market, warehouse, or other similar establishment; and in 1893 the "Railway Regulation Act" gave power to the Board of Trade to require railway companies to provide reasonable and satisfactory schedules of hours for all their employees. In 1894 a bill for a compulsory eight-hour day for miners was introduced, but was withdrawn before being submitted to a vote. In 1899 a bill was passed requiring the provision of a sufficient number of seats for all female assistants in retail stores. In 1900 a government bill was presented to Parliament carrying legislation somewhat farther on the lines of the acts of 1891 and 1893, but it did not reach its later stages before the adjournment.

71. Employers' Liability Acts. — Closely allied to the problems involved in the factory laws is the question of the liability of employers to make compensation for personal injuries suffered by workmen in their service. With the increasing use of machinery and of steam power for manufacturing and transportation, and in the general absence of precaution, accidents to workmen became much more numerous. Statistics do not exist for earlier periods, but in 1899 serious or petty accidents to the number of 70,760 were reported from such establishments. By Common Law, in the case of negligence on the part of the proprietor or servant of an establishment, damages for accident could be sued for and obtained by a workman, not guilty of contributory negligence, as by any other person, except in one case. If the accident was the result of the negligence of a fellow-employee, no compensation for injuries would be allowed by the courts; the theory being that in the implied contract between employer and employee, the latter agreed to accept the risks of the business, at least so far as these arose from the carelessness of his fellow-employees.

In the large establishments of modern times, however, vast numbers of men were fellow-employees in the eyes of the law, and the doctrine of "common employment," as it was called, prevented the recovery of damages in so many cases as to attract widespread attention. From 1865 forward this provision of the law was frequently complained of by leaders of the workingmen and others, and as constantly upheld by the courts.

In 1876 a committee of the House of Commons on the relations of master and servant took evidence on this matter and recommended in its report that the common law be amended in this respect. Accordingly in 1880 an Employers' Liability Act was passed which abolished the doctrine of "common employment" as to much of its application, and made it possible for the employee to obtain compensation for accidental injury in the great majority of cases.

In 1893 a bill was introduced in Parliament by the ministry of the time to abolish all deductions from the responsibility of employers, except that of contributory negligence on the part of workmen, but it was not passed. In 1897, however, the "Workmen's Compensation Act" was passed, changing the basis of the law entirely. By this Act it was provided that in case of accident to a workman causing death or incapacitating him for a period of more than two weeks, compensation in proportion to the wages he formerly earned should be paid by the employer as a matter of course, unless "serious and wilful misconduct" on the part of the workman could be shown to have existed. The liability of employers becomes, therefore, a matter of insurance of workmen against accidents arising out of their employment, imposed by the law upon employers. It is no longer damages for negligence, but a form of compulsory insurance. In other words, since 1897 a legal, if only an implied part of the contract between employer and employee in all forms of modern industry in which accidents are likely to occur is that the employer insures the employee against the dangers of his work.

72. Preservation of Remaining Open Lands. — Turning from the field of manufacturing labor to that of agriculture and landholding it will be found that there has been some legislation for the protection of the agricultural laborer analogous to the factory laws. The Royal Commission of 1840–1844 on trades then unprotected by law included a report on the condition of rural child labor, but no law followed until 1873, when the "Agricultural Children's Act" was passed, but proved to be ineffective. The evils of "agricultural gangs," which were bodies of poor laborers, mostly children, engaged by a contractor and taken from place to place to be hired out to farmers, were reported on by a commission in 1862, and partly overcome by the "Agricultural Gangs Act" of 1867. There is, however, but little systematic government oversight of the farm-laboring class.

Government regulation in the field of landholding has taken a somewhat different form. The movement of enclosing which had been in progress from the middle of the eighteenth century was brought to an end, and a reversal of tendency took place, by which the use and occupation of the land was more controlled by the government in the interest of the masses of the rural population. By the middle of the century the process of enclosing was practically complete. There had been some 3954 private enclosure acts passed, and under their provisions or those of the Enclosure Commissioners more than seven million acres had been changed from mediæval to modern condition. But now a reaction set in. Along with the open field farming lands it was perceived that open commons, village greens, gentlemen's parks, and the old national forest lands were being enclosed, and frequently for building or railroad, not for agricultural uses, to the serious detriment of the health and of the enjoyment of the people, and to the destruction of the beauty of the country. The dread of interference by the government with matters that might be left to private settlement was also passing away. In 1865 the House of Commons appointed a commission to investigate the question of open spaces near the city of London, and the next year on their recommendation passed a law by which the Enclosure Commissioners were empowered to make regulations for the use of all commons within fifteen miles of London as public parks, except so far as the legal rights of the lords of the manors in which the commons lay should prevent. A contest had already arisen between many of these lords of manors having the control of open commons, whose interest it was to enclose and sell them, and other persons having vague rights of pasturage and other use of them, whose interest it was to preserve them as open spaces. To aid the latter in their legal resistance to proposed enclosures, the "Commons Preservation Society" was formed in 1865. As a result a number of the contests were decided in the year 1866 in favor of those who opposed enclosures.

The first case to attract attention was that of Wimbledon Common, just west of London. Earl Spencer, the lord of the manor of Wimbledon, had offered to give up his rights on the common to the inhabitants of the vicinity in return for a nominal rent and certain privileges; and had proposed that a third of the common should be sold, and the money obtained for it used to fence, drain, beautify, and keep up the remainder. The neighboring inhabitants, however, preferred the spacious common as it stood, and when a bill to carry out Lord Spencer's proposal had been introduced into Parliament, they contended that they had legal rights on the common which he could not disregard, and that they objected to its enclosure. The parliamentary committee practically decided in their favor, and the proposition was dropped. An important decision in a similar case was made by the courts in 1870. Berkhamstead Common, an open stretch some three miles long and half a mile wide, lying near the town of Berkhamstead, twenty-five miles north of London, had been used for pasturing animals, cutting turf, digging gravel, gathering furze, and as a place of general recreation and enjoyment by the people of the two manors in which it lay, from time immemorial. In 1866 Lord Brownlow, the lord of these two manors, began making enclosures upon it, erecting two iron fences across it so as to enclose 434 acres and to separate the remainder into two entirely distinct parts. The legal advisers of Lord Brownlow declared that the inhabitants had no rights which would prevent him from enclosing parts of the common, although to satisfy them he offered to give to them the entire control over one part of it. The Commons Preservation Society, however, advised the inhabitants differently, and encouraged them to make a legal contest. One of their number, Augustus Smith, a wealthy and obstinate man, a member of Parliament, and a possessor of rights on the common both as a freeholder and a copyholder, was induced to take action in his own name and as a representative of other claimants of common rights. He engaged in London a force of one hundred and twenty laborers, sent them down at night by train, and before morning had broken down Lord Brownlow's two miles of iron fences, on which he had spent some £5000, and piled their sections neatly up on another part of the common. Two lawsuits followed: one by Lord Brownlow against Mr. Smith for trespass, the other a cross suit in the Chancery Court by Mr. Smith to ascertain the commoner's rights, and prevent the enclosure of the common. After a long trial the decision was given in Mr. Smith's favor, and not only was Berkhamstead Common thus preserved as an open space, but a precedent set for the future decision of other similar cases. Within the years between 1866 and 1874 dispute after dispute analogous to this arose, and decision after decision was given declaring the illegality of enclosures by a lord of a manor where there were claims of commoners which they still asserted and valued and which could be used as an obstacle to enclosure. Hampstead Heath, Ashdown Forest, Malvern Hills, Plumstead, Tooting, Wandsworth, Coulston, Dartford, and a great many other commons, village greens, roadside wastes, and other open spaces were saved from enclosure, and some places were partly opened up again, as a result either of lawsuits, of parliamentary action, or of voluntary agreements and purchase.

Perhaps the most conspicuous instance was that of Epping Forest. This common consisted of an open tract about thirteen miles long and one mile wide, containing in 1870 about three thousand acres of open common land. Enclosure was being actively carried on by some nineteen lords of manors, and some three thousand acres had been enclosed by rather high-handed means within the preceding twenty years. Among the various landowners who claimed rights of common upon a part of the Forest was, however, the City of London, and in 1871 this body began suit against the various lords of manors under the claim that it possessed pasture rights, not only in the manor of Ilford, in which its property of two hundred acres was situated, but, since the district was a royal forest, over the whole of it. The City asked that the lords of manors should be prevented from enclosing any more of it, and required to throw open again what they had enclosed during the last twenty years. After a long and expensive legal battle and a concurrent investigation by a committee of Parliament, both extending over three years, a decision was given in favor of the City of London and other commoners, and the lords of manors were forced to give back about three thousand acres. The whole was made permanently into a public park. The old forest rights of the crown proved to be favorable to the commoners, and thus obtained at least one tardy justification to set against their long and dark record in the past.

In 1871, in one of the cases which had been appealed, the Lord Chancellor laid down a principle indicating a reaction in the judicial attitude on the subject, when he declared that no enclosure should be made except when there was a manifest advantage in it; as contrasted with the policy of enclosing unless there was some strong reason against it, as had formerly been approved. In 1876 Parliament passed a law amending the acts of 1801 and 1845, and directing the Enclosure Commissioners to reverse their rule of action in the same direction. That is to say, they were not to approve any enclosure unless it could be shown to be to the manifest advantage of the neighborhood, as well as to the interest of the parties directly concerned. Finally, in 1893, by the Commons Law Amendment Act, it was required that every proposed enclosure of any kind should first be advertised and opportunity given for objection, then submitted to the Board of Agriculture for its approval, and this approval should only be given when such an enclosure was for the general benefit of the public. No desire of a lord of a manor to enclose ground for his private park or game preserve, or to use it for building ground, would now be allowed to succeed. The interest of the community at large has been placed above the private advantage and even liberty of action of landholders. The authorities do not merely see that justice is done between lord and commoners on the manor, but that both alike shall be restrained from doing what is not to the public advantage. Indeed, Parliament went one step further, and by an order passed in 1893 set a precedent for taking a common entirely out of the hands of the lord of the manor, and putting it in the hands of a board to keep it for public uses. Thus not only had the enclosing movement diminished for lack of open farming land to enclose, but public opinion and law between 1864 and 1893 interposed to preserve such remaining open land as had not been already divided. Whatever land remained that was not in individual ownership and occupancy was to be retained under control for the community at large.

73. Allotments. — But this change of attitude was not

merely negative. There were many instances of government interposition for the encouragement of agriculture and for the modification of the relations between landlord and tenant. In 1875, 1882, and 1900 the "Agricultural Holdings Acts" were passed, by which, when improvements are made by the tenant during the period in which he holds the land, compensation must be given by the landlord to the tenant when the latter retires. No agreement between the landlord and tenant by which the latter gives up this right is valid. This policy of controlling the conditions of landholding with the object of enforcing justice to the tenant has been carried to very great lengths in the Irish Land Bills and the Scotch Crofters' Acts, but the conditions that called for such legislation in those countries have not existed in England itself. There has been, however, much effort in England to bring at least some land again into the use of the masses of the rural population. In 1819, as part of the administration of the poor law, Parliament passed an act facilitating the leasing out by the authorities of common land belonging to the parishes to the poor, in small "allotments," as they were called, by the cultivation of which they might partially support themselves. Allotments are small pieces of land, usually from an eighth of an acre to an acre in size, rented out for cultivation to poor or working-class families. In 1831 parish authorities were empowered to buy or enclose land up to as much as five acres for this purpose. Subsequently the formation of allotments began to be advocated, not only as part of the system of supporting paupers, but for its own sake, in order that rural laborers might have some land in their own occupation to work on during their spare times, as their forefathers had during earlier ages. To encourage this plan of giving the mass of the people again an interest in the land the "Allotments and Small Holdings Association" was formed in 1885. Laws which were passed in 1882 and 1887 made it the duty of the authorities of parishes, when there seemed to be a demand for allotments, to provide all the land that was needed for the purpose, giving them, if needed, and under certain restrictions, the right of compulsory purchase of any particular piece of land which they should feel to be desirable. This was to be divided up and rented out in allotments from one quarter of an acre to an acre in size. By laws passed in 1890 and 1894 this plan of making it the bounden duty of the local government to provide sufficient allotments for the demand, and giving them power to purchase land even without the consent of its owners, was carried still further and put in the hands of the parish council. The growth in numbers of such allotments was very rapid and has not yet ceased. The approximate numbers at several periods are as follows: —

1873	246,398
1888	357,795
1890	455,005
1895	579,133

In addition to those formed and granted out by the public local authorities, many large landowners, railroad companies, and others have made allotments to their tenants or employees. Large tracts of land subdivided into such small patches are now a common sight in England, simulating in appearance the old open fields of the Middle Ages and early modern times.

74. Small Holdings. — Closely connected with the extension of allotments is the movement for the creation of "small holdings," or the reintroduction of small farming. One form of this is that by which the local authorities in

1892 were empowered to buy land for the purpose of renting it out in small holdings of not more than fifteen acres each to persons who would themselves cultivate it.

A still further and much more important development in the same direction is the effort to introduce " peasant proprietorship," or the ownership of small amounts of farming land by persons who would otherwise necessarily be mere laborers on other men's land. There has been an old dispute as to the relative advantages of a system of large farms, rented by men who have some considerable capital, knowledge, and enterprise, as in England; and of a system of small farms, owned and worked by men who are mere peasants, as in France. The older economists generally advocated the former system as better in itself, and also pointed out that a policy of withdrawal by government from any regulation was tending to make it universal. Others have been more impressed with the good effects of the ownership of land on the mental and moral character of the population, and with the desirability of the existence of a series of steps by which a thrifty and ambitious workingman could rise to a higher position, even in the country. There has, therefore, since the middle of the century, been a widespread agitation in favor of the creation of smaller farms, of giving assistance in their purchase, and of thus introducing a more mixed system of rural land occupancy, and bringing back something of the earlier English yeoman farming.

This movement obtained recognition by Parliament in the Small Holdings Act of 1892, already referred to. This law made it the duty of each county council, when there seemed to be any sufficient demand for small farms from one to fifty acres in size, to acquire in any way possible, though not by compulsory purchase, suitable land, to adapt

The Extension of Government Control 271

it for farming purposes by fencing, making roads, and, if necessary, erecting suitable buildings; and then to dispose of it by sale, or, as a matter of exception, as before stated, on lease, to such parties as will themselves cultivate it. The terms of sale were to be advantageous to the purchaser. He must pay at least as much as a fifth of the price down, but one quarter of it might be left on perpetual ground-rent, and the remainder, slightly more than one-half, might be repaid in half-yearly instalments during any period less than fifty years. The county council was also given power to loan money to tenants of small holdings to buy from their landlords, where they could arrange terms of purchase but had not the necessary means.

Through the intervention of government, therefore, the strict division of those connected with the land into landlords, tenant farmers, and farm laborers has been to a considerable extent altered, and it is generally possible for a laborer to obtain a small piece of land as an allotment, or, if more ambitious and able, a small farm, on comparatively easy terms. In landholding and agriculture, as in manufacturing and trade, government has thus stepped in to prevent what would have been the effect of mere free competition, and to bring about a distribution and use of the land which have seemed more desirable.

75. Government Sanitary Control. — In the field of buying and selling the hand of government has been most felt in provisions for the health of the consumer of various articles. Laws against adulteration have been passed, and a code of supervision, registry, and enforcement constructed. Similarly in broader sanitary lines, by the "Housing of the Working Classes Act" of 1890, when it is brought to the attention of the local authorities that any street or district is in such a condition that its houses or alleys are unfit for human habitation, or that the narrowness, want of light or air, or bad drainage makes the district dangerous to the health of the inhabitants or their neighbors, and that these conditions cannot be readily remedied except by an entire rearrangement of the district, then it becomes the duty of the local authorities to take the matter in hand. They are bound to draw up and, on approval by the proper superior authorities, to carry out a plan for widening the streets and approaches to them, providing proper sanitary arrangements, tearing down the old houses, and building new ones in sufficient number and suitable character to provide dwelling accommodation for as many persons of the working class as were displaced by the changes. Private rights or claims are not allowed to stand in the way of any such public action in favor of the general health and well-being, as the local authorities are clothed by the law with the right of purchase of the land and buildings of the locality at a valuation, even against the wishes of the owners, though they must obtain parliamentary confirmation of such a compulsory purchase. Several acts have been passed to provide for the public acquisition or building of workingmen's dwellings. In 1899 the "Small Dwellings Acquisition Act" gave power to any local authority to loan four-fifths of the cost of purchase of a small house, to be repaid by the borrower by instalments within thirty years.

Laws for the stamping out of cattle disease have been passed on the same principle. In 1878, 1886, 1890, 1893, and 1896 successive acts were passed which have given to the Board of Agriculture the right to cause the slaughter of any cattle or swine which have become infected or been subjected to contagious diseases; Parliament has also set apart a sufficient sum of money and appointed a large corps of inspectors to carry out the law. Official analysts of fertilizers and food-stuffs for cattle have also since 1893 been regularly appointed by the government in each county. Adulteration has been taken under control by the "Sale of Food and Drugs Act" of 1875, with its later amendments and extensions, especially that of 1899.

76. Industries Carried on by Government. — In addition to the regulation in these various respects of industries carried on by private persons, and intervention for the protection of the public health, the government has extended its functions very considerably by taking up certain new duties or services, which it carries out itself instead of leaving to private hands.

The post-office is such an old and well-established branch of the government's activity as not in itself to be included among newly adopted functions, but its administration has been extended since the middle of the century over at least four new fields of duty: the telegraph, the telephone, the parcels post, and the post-office savings-bank.

The telegraph system of England was built up in the main and in its early stages by private persons and companies. After more than twenty-five years of competitive development, however, there was widespread public dissatisfaction with the service. Messages were expensive and telegraphing inconvenient. Many towns with populations from three thousand to six thousand were without telegraphic facilities nearer than five or ten miles, while the offices of competing companies were numerous in busy centres. In 1870, therefore, all private telegraph companies were bought up by the government at an expense of £10,130,000. A strict telegraphic monopoly in the hands of the government was established, and the telegraph made an integral part of the post-office system.

In 1878 the telephone began to compete with the telegraph, and its relation to the government telegraphic monopoly became a matter of question. At first the government adopted the policy of collecting a ten per cent royalty on all messages, but allowed telephones to be established by private companies. In the meantime the various companies were being bought up successively by the National Telephone Company which was thus securing a virtual monopoly. In 1892 Parliament authorized the Postmaster General to spend £1,000,000, subsequently raised to £1,300,000, in the purchase of telephone lines, and prohibited any private construction of new lines. As a result, by 1897 the government had bought up all the main or trunk telephone lines and wires, leaving to the National Telephone Company its monopoly of all telephone communication inside of the towns. This monopoly was supposed to be in its legal possession until 1904, when it was anticipated that the government would buy out its property at a valuation. In 1898, however, there was an inquiry by Parliament, and a new "Telegraph Act" was passed in 1899. The monopoly of the National Company was discredited and the government began to enter into competition with it within the towns, and to authorize local governments and private companies under certain circumstances to do the same. It was provided that every extension of an old company and every new company must obtain a government license and that on the expiring of this license the plant could be bought by the government. In the meantime the post-office authorities have power to restrict rates. An appropriation of £2,000,000 was put in the hands of the Postmaster General to extend the government telephone system. It seems quite certain that by 1925, at latest, all telephones will be in the hands of the government.

The post-office savings-bank was established in 1861.

Any sum from one shilling upward is accepted from any depositor until his deposits rise to £50 in any one year, or a total of £200 in all. It presents great attractions from its security and its convenience. The government through the post-office pays two and one-half per cent interest. In 1870 there was deposited in the post-office savings-banks approximately £14,000,000, in 1880 £31,000,000, and ten years later £62,000,000. In 1880 arrangements were made by which government bonds and annuities can be bought through the post-office. In 1890 some £4,600,000 was invested in government stock in this way.

The parcels post was established in 1883. This branch of the post-office does a large part of the work that would otherwise be done by private express companies. It takes charge of packages up to eleven pounds in weight and under certain circumstances up to twenty-one pounds, presented at any branch post-office, and on prepayment of regular charges delivers them to their consignees.

In these and other forms each year within recent times has seen some extension of the field of government control for the good of the community in general, or for the protection of some particular class in the community, and there is at the same time a constant increase in the number and variety of occupations that the government undertakes. Instead of withdrawing from the field of intervention in economic concerns, and restricting its activity to the narrowest possible limits, as was the tendency in the last period, the government is constantly taking more completely under its regulation great branches of industry, and even administering various lines of business that formerly were carried on by private hands.

77. BIBLIOGRAPHY

Jevons, Stanley: *The State in Relation to Labor.*

"Alfred" (Samuel Kydd): *The History of the Factory Movement from the Year 1802 to the Enactment of the Ten Hours Bill in 1847.*

Von Plener, E.: *A History of English Factory Legislation.*

Cooke-Taylor, R. W.: *The Factory System and the Factory Acts.*

Redgrave, Alexander: *The Factory Acts.*

Shaftesbury, The Earl of: *Speeches on Labour Questions.*

Birrell, Augustine: *Law of Employers' Liability.*

Shaw-Lefevre, G.: *English Commons and Forests.*

Far the best sources of information for the adoption of the factory laws, as for other nineteenth-century legislation, are the debates in Parliament and the various reports of Parliamentary Commissions, where access to them can be obtained. The early reports are enumerated in the bibliography in Cunningham's second volume. The later can be found in the appropriate articles in Palgrave's *Dictionary*. For recent legislation, the action of organizations, and social movements generally, the articles in *Hazell's Annual*, in its successive issues since 1885, are full, trustworthy, and valuable.

CHAPTER X

THE EXTENSION OF VOLUNTARY ASSOCIATION

Trade Unions, Trusts, and Coöperation

78. The Rise of Trade Unions. — One of the most manifest effects of the introduction of the factory system was the intensification of the distinction between employers and employees. When a large number of laborers were gathered together in one establishment, all in a similar position one to the other and with common interests as to wages, hours of labor, and other conditions of their work, the fact that they were one homogeneous class could hardly escape their recognition. Since these common interests were in so many respects opposed to those of their employers, the advantages of combination to obtain added strength in the settlement of disputed questions was equally evident. As the Statute of Apprentices was no longer in force, and freedom of contract had taken its place, a dispute between an employer and a single employee would result in the discharge of the latter. If the dispute was between the employer and his whole body of employees, each one of the latter would be in a vastly stronger position, and there would be something like equality in the two sides of the contest.

Under the old gild conditions, when each man rose successively from apprentice to journeyman, and from journeyman to employer, when the relations between the employing master and his journeymen and apprentices were very close, and the advantages of the gild were participated in by all grades of the producing body, organizations of the employed against the employers could hardly exist. It has been seen that the growth of separate combinations was one of the indications of a breaking down of the gild system. Even in the later times, when establishments were still small and scattered, when the government required that engagements should be made for long periods, and that none should work in an industry except those who had been apprenticed to it, and when rates of wages and hours of labor were supposed to be settled by law, the opposition between the interests of employers and employees was not very strongly marked. The occasion or opportunity for union amongst the workmen in most trades still hardly existed. Unions had been formed, it is true, during the first half of the eighteenth century and spasmodically in still earlier times. These were, however, mostly in trades where the employers made up a wealthy merchant class and where the prospect of the ordinary workman ever reaching the position of an employer was slight.

The changes of the Industrial Revolution, however, made a profound difference. With the growth of factories and the increase in the size of business establishments the employer and employee came to be farther apart, while at the same time the employees in any one establishment or trade were thrown more closely together. The hand of government was at about the same time entirely withdrawn from the control of wages, hours, length of engagements, and other conditions of labor. Any workman was at liberty to enter or leave any occupation under any circumstances that he chose, and an employer could similarly hire or discharge any laborer for any cause or at any time he saw fit. Under these circumstances of homogeneity of the interests of the laborers, of opposition of their interests to those of the employer, and of the absence of any external control, combinations among the workmen, or trade unions, naturally sprang up.

79. Opposition of the Law and of Public Opinion. The Combination Acts. — Their growth, however, was slow and interrupted. The poverty, ignorance, and lack of training of the laborers interposed a serious obstacle to the formation of permanent unions; and a still more tangible difficulty lay in the opposition of the law and of public opinion. A trade union may be defined as a permanent organized society, the object of which is to obtain more favorable conditions of labor for its members. In order to retain its existence a certain amount of intelligence and self-control and a certain degree of regularity of contributions on the part of its members are necessary, and these powers were but slightly developed in the early years of this century. In order to obtain the objects of the union a "strike," or concerted refusal to work except on certain conditions, is the natural means to be employed. But such action, or in fact the existence of a combination contemplating such action, was against the law. A series of statutes known as the "Combination Acts" had been passed from time to time since the sixteenth century, the object of which had been to prevent artisans, either employers or employees, from combining to change the rate of wages or other conditions of labor, which should be legally established by the government. The last of the combination acts were passed in 1799 and 1800, and were an undisguised exercise of the power of the employing class to use their membership in Parliament to legislate in their own interest. It provided that all agreements whatever between journeymen or other workmen for obtaining an advance in wages for themselves or for other workmen, or for decreasing the number of hours of labor, or for endeavoring to prevent any employer from engaging any one whom he might choose, or for persuading any other workmen not to work, or for refusing to work with any other men, should be illegal. Any justice of the peace was empowered to convict by summary process and sentence to two months' imprisonment any workmen who entered into such a combination.

The ordinary and necessary action of trade unions was illegal by the Common Law also, under the doctrine that combined attempts to influence wages, hours, prices, or apprenticeship were conspiracies in restraint of trade, and that such conspiracies had been repeatedly declared to be illegal.

In addition to their illegality, trade unions were extremely unpopular with the most influential classes of English society. The employers, against whose power they were organized, naturally antagonized them for fear they would raise wages and in other ways give the workmen the upper hand; they were opposed by the aristocratic feeling of the country, because they brought about an increase in the power of the lower classes; the clergy deprecated their growth as a manifestation of discontent, whereas contentment was the virtue then most regularly inculcated upon the lower classes; philanthropists, who had more faith in what should be done for than by the workingmen, distrusted their self-interested and vaguely directed efforts. Those who were interested in England's foreign trade feared that they would increase prices, and thus render England incapable of competing with other nations, and those who were influenced by the teachings of political economy opposed them as being harmful, or at best futile efforts to interfere with the free action of those natural forces which, in the long run, must govern all questions of labor and wages. If the average rate of wages at any particular time was merely the quotient obtained by dividing the number of laborers into the wages fund, an organized effort to change the rate of wages would necessarily be a failure, or could at most only result in driving some other laborers out of employment or reducing their wages. Finally, there was a widespread feeling that trade unions were unscrupulous bodies which overawed the great majority of their fellow-workmen, and then by their help tyrannized over the employers and threw trade into recurring conditions of confusion. That same great body of uninstructed public opinion, which, on the whole, favored the factory laws, was quite clearly opposed to trade unions. With the incompetency of their own class, the power of the law, and the force of public opinion opposed to their existence and actions, it is not a matter of wonder that the development of these working-class organizations was only very gradual.

Nevertheless these obstacles were one by one removed, and the growth of trade unions became one of the most characteristic movements of modern industrial history.

80. Legalization and Popular Acceptance of Trade Unions. —During the early years of the century combinations, more or less long lived, existed in many trades, sometimes secretly because of their illegality, sometimes openly, until it became of sufficient interest to some one to prosecute them or their officers, sometimes making the misleading claim of being benefit societies. Prosecutions under the combination laws were, however, frequent. In the first quarter of the century there were many hundred convictions of workmen or their delegates or officers. Yet these laws were clear instances of interference with the perfect freedom which ought theoretically to be allowed to each person to employ his labor or capital in the manner he might deem most advantageous. Their inconsistency with the general movement of abolition of restrictions then in progress could hardly escape observation. Thus the philosophic tendencies of the time combined with the aspirations of the leaders of the working classes to rouse an agitation in favor of the repeal of the combination laws. The matter was brought up in Parliament in 1822, and two successive committees were appointed to investigate the questions involved. As a result, a thoroughgoing repeal law was passed in 1824, but this in turn was almost immediately repealed, and another substituted for it in 1825, a great series of strikes having impressed the legislature with the belief that the former had gone too far. The law, as finally adopted, repealed all the combination acts which stood upon the statute book, and relieved from punishment men who met together for the sole purpose of agreeing on the rate of wages or the number of hours they would work, so long as this agreement referred to the wages or hours of those only who were present at the meeting. It declared, however, the illegality of any violence, threats, intimidation, molestation, or obstruction, used to induce any other workmen to strike or to join their association or take any other action in regard to hours or wages. Any attempt to bring pressure to bear upon an employer to make any change in his business was also forbidden, and the common law opposition was left unrepealed. The effect of the legislation of 1824 and 1825 was to enable trade unions to exist if their activity was restricted to an agreement upon their own wages or hours. Any effort, however, to establish wages and hours for other persons than those taking part in their meetings, or any strike on questions of piecework or number of apprentices or machinery or non-union workmen, was still illegal, both by this statute and by Common Law.

The vague words, "molestation," "obstruction," and "intimidation," used in the law were also capable of being construed, as they actually were, in such a way as to prevent any considerable activity on the part of trade unions. Nevertheless a great stimulus was given to the formation of organizations among workingmen, and the period of their legal growth and development now began, notwithstanding the narrow field of activity allowed them by the law as it then stood. Combinations were continually formed for further objects, and prosecutions, either under the statute or under Common Law, were still very numerous. In 1859 a further change in the law was made, by which it became lawful to combine to demand a change of wages or hours, even if the action involved other persons than those taking part in the agreement, and to exercise peaceful persuasion upon others to join the strikers in their action. Within the bounds of the limited legal powers granted by the laws of 1825 and 1859, large numbers of trade unions were formed, much agitation carried on, strikes won and lost, pressure exerted upon Parliament, and the most active and capable of the working classes gradually brought to take an interest in the movement. This growth was unfortunately accompanied by much disorder. During times of industrial struggle non-strikers were beaten, employers were assaulted, property was destroyed, and in certain industrial communities confusion and outrage occurred every few years. The complicity of the trade unions as such in these disorders was constantly asserted and as constantly denied; but there seems little doubt that while by far the greatest amount of disorder was due to individual strikers or their sympathizers, and would have occurred, perhaps in even more intense form, if there had been no trade unions, yet there were cases where the organized unions were themselves responsible. The frequent recurrence of rioting and assault, the losses from industrial conflicts, and the agitation of the trade unionists for further legalization, all combined to bring the matter to attention, and four successive Parliamentary commissions of investigation, in addition to those of 1824 and 1825, were appointed in 1828, 1856, 1860, and 1867, respectively. The last of these was due to a series of prolonged strikes and accompanying outrages in Sheffield, Nottingham, and Manchester. The committee consisted of able and influential men. It made a full investigation and report, and finally recommended, somewhat to the public surprise, that further laws for the protection and at the same time for the regulation of trade unions be passed. As a result, two laws were passed in the year 1871, the Trade Union Act and the Criminal Law Amendment Act. By the first of these it was declared that trade unions were not to be declared illegal because they were "in restraint of trade," and that they might be registered as benefit societies, and thereby become quasi-corporations, to the extent of having their funds protected by law, and being able to hold property for the proper uses of their organization. At the same time the Liberal majority in Parliament, who had only passed this law under pressure, and were but half hearted in their approval of trade unions, by the second law of the same year, made still more clear and vigorous the prohibition of "molesting," "obstructing," "threatening," "persistently following," "watching or besetting" any workmen who had not voluntarily joined the trade union. As these terms were still undefined, the law might be, and it was, still sufficiently elastic to allow magistrates or judges who disapproved of trade unionism to punish men for the most ordinary forms of persuasion or pressure used in industrial conflicts. An agitation was immediately begun for the repeal or modification of this later law. This was accomplished finally by the Trade Union Act of 1875, by which it was declared that no action committed by a group of workmen was punishable unless the same act was criminal if committed by a single individual. Peaceful persuasion of non-union workmen was expressly permitted, some of the elastic words of disapproval used in previous laws were omitted altogether, other offences especially likely to occur in such disputes were relegated to the ordinary criminal law, and a new act was passed, clearing up the whole question of the illegality of conspiracy in such a way as not to treat trade unions in any different way from other bodies, or to interfere with their existence or normal actions.

Thus, by the four steps taken in 1825, 1859, 1871, and 1875, all trace of illegality has been taken away from trade unions and their ordinary actions. They have now the same legal right to exist, to hold property, and to carry out the objects of their organization that a banking or manufacturing company or a social or literary club has.

The passing away of the popular disapproval of trade unions has been more gradual and indefinite, but not less real. The employers, after many hard-fought battles in their own trades, in the newspapers, and in Parliament, have come, in a great number of cases, to prefer that there should be a well-organized trade union in their industry rather than a chaotic body of restless and unorganized laborers. The aristocratic dread of lower-class organizations and activity has become less strong and less important, as political violence has ceased to threaten and as English society as a whole has become more democratic. The Reform Bill of 1867 was a voluntary concession by the higher and middle classes to the lower, showing that political dread of the working classes and their trade unions had disappeared. The older type of clergymen of the established church, who had all the sympathies and prejudices of the aristocracy, has been largely superseded, since the days of Kingsley and Maurice, by men who have taken the deepest interest in working-class movements, and who teach struggle and effort rather than acceptance and contentment.

The formation of trade unions, even while it has led to higher wages, shorter hours, and a more independent and self-assertive body of laborers, has made labor so much more efficient that, taken in connection with other elements of English economic activity, it has led to no resulting loss of her industrial supremacy. As to the economic arguments against trade unions, they have become less influential with the discrediting of much of the theoretical teaching on which they were based. In 1867 a book by W. T. Thornton, *On Labor, its Wrongful Claims and Rightful Dues*, successfully attacked the wages-fund theory, since which time the belief that the rate of wages was absolutely determined by the amount of that fund and the number of laborers has gradually been given up. The belief in the possibility of voluntary limitation of the effect of the so-called "natural laws" of the economic teachers of the early and middle parts of the century has grown stronger and spread more widely. Finally, the general popular feeling of dislike of trade unions has much diminished within the last twenty-five years, since their lawfulness has been acknowledged, and since their own policy has become more distinctly orderly and moderate.

Much of this change in popular feeling toward trade unions was so gradual as not to be measurable, but some of its stages can be distinguished. Perhaps the first very noticeable step in the general acceptance of trade unions, other than their mere legalization, was the interest and approval given to the formation of boards of conciliation or arbitration from 1867 forward. These were bodies in which representatives elected by the employers and representatives elected by trade unions met on equal terms to discuss differences, the unions thus being acknowledged as the normal form of organization of the working classes. In 1885 the Royal Commission on the depression of trade spoke with favor of trade unions. In 1889 the great London Dockers' strike called forth the sympathy and the moral and pecuniary support of representatives of classes which had probably never before shown any favor to such organizations. More than $200,000 was subscribed by the public, and every form of popular pressure was brought to bear on the employers. In fact, the Dock Laborers' Union was partly created and almost entirely supported by outside public influence. In the same year the London School Board and County Council both declared that all contractors doing their work must pay "fair wages," an expression which was afterward defined as being union wages. Before 1894 some one hundred and fifty town and county governments had adopted a rule that fair wages must be paid to all workmen employed directly or indirectly by them. In 1890 and 1893 and subsequently the government has made the same declaration in favor of the rate of wages established by the unions in each industry. In 1890 the report of the House of Lords Committee on the sweating system recommends in certain cases " well-considered combinations among the laborers." Therefore public opinion, like the formal law of the country, has passed from its early opposition to the trade unions, through criticism and reluctant toleration, to an almost complete acceptance and even encouragement. Trade unions have become a part of the regularly established institutions of the country, and few persons probably would wish to see them go out of existence or be seriously weakened.

81. The Growth of Trade Unions. — The actual growth of trade unionism has been irregular, interrupted, and has spread from many scattered centres. Hundreds of unions have been formed, lived for a time, and gone out of existence; others have survived from the very beginning of the century to the present; some have dwindled into insignificance and then revived in some special need. The workmen in some parts of the country and in certain trades were early and strongly organized, in others they have scarcely even yet become interested or made the effort to form unions. In the history of the trade-union movement as a whole there have been periods of active growth and multiplication and strengthening of organizations. Again, there have been times when trade unionism was distinctly losing ground, or when internal dissension seemed likely to deprive the whole movement of its vigor. There have been three periods when progress was particularly rapid, between 1830 and 1834, in 1873 and 1874, and from 1889 to the present time. But before the middle of the century trade unions existed in almost every important line of industry. By careful computation it is estimated that there were in Great Britain and Ireland in 1892 about 1750 distinct unions or separate branches of unions, with some million and a half members. This would be about twenty per cent of the adult male working-class population, or an average of about one man who is a member of a trade union out of five who might be. But the great importance and influence of the trade unionists arises not from this comparatively small general proportion, but from the fact that the organizations are strongest in the most highly skilled and best-paid industries, and in the most thickly settled, highly developed parts of the country, and that they contain the picked and ablest men in each of the industries where they do exist.

In some occupations, as cotton spinning in Lancashire, boiler making and iron ship building in the seaport towns, coal mining in Northumberland, glass making in the Midland counties, and others, practically every operative is a member of a trade union. Similarly in certain parts of the country much more than half of all workingmen are trade unionists. Their influence also is far more than in proportion to their numbers, since from their membership are chosen practically all workingmen representatives in Parliament and local governments and in administrative positions. The unions also furnish all the most influential leaders of opinion among the working classes.

82. Federation of Trade Unions.— From the earliest days of trade-union organization there have been efforts to extend the unions beyond the boundaries of the single occupation or the single locality. The earliest form of union was a body made up of the workmen of some one industry in some one locality, as the gold beaters of London, or the cutlers of Sheffield, or the cotton spinners of Manchester. Three forms of extension or federation soon took place: first, the formation of national societies composed of men of the same trade through the whole country; secondly, the formation of "trades councils," — bodies representing all the different trades in any one locality; and, thirdly, the formation of a great national organization of workingmen or trade unionists. The first of these forms of extension dates from the earliest years of the century, though such bodies had often only a transitory existence. The Manchester cotton spinners took the initiative in organizing a national body in that industry in 1829; in 1831 a National Potters' Union is heard of, and others in the same decade. The largest and most permanent national bodies, however, such as the compositors, the flint-glass makers, miners, and others were formed after 1840 ; the miners in 1844 numbering 70,000 voting members. Several of these national bodies were formed by an amalgamation of a number of different but more or less closely allied trades. The most conspicuous example of this was the Amalgamated Society of Engineers, the formation of which was completed in 1850, and which, beginning in that year with 5000 members, had more than doubled them in the next five years, doubled them again by 1860, and since then has kept up a steady increase in numbers and strength, having 67,928 members in 1890. The increasing ease of travel and cheapness of postage, and the improved education and intelligence of the workingmen, made the formation of national societies more practicable, and since the middle of the century most of the important societies have become national bodies made up of local branches.

The second form of extension, the trades council, dates from a somewhat later period. Such a body arose usually when some matter of common interest had happened in the labor world, and delegates from the various unions in each locality were called upon to organize and to subscribe funds, prepare a petition to Parliament, or take other common action. In this temporary form they had existed from a much earlier date. The first permanent local board, made up of representatives of the various local bodies, was that of Liverpool, formed in 1848 to protect trade unionists from prosecutions for illegal conspiracy. In 1857 a permanent body was formed in Sheffield, and in the years immediately following in Glasgow, London, Bristol, and other cities. They have since come into existence in most of the larger industrial towns, 120 local trades councils existing in 1892. Their influence has been variable and limited.

The formation of a general body of organized workingmen of all industries and from all parts of the country is an old dream. Various such societies were early formed only to play a more or less conspicuous rôle for a few years and then drop out of existence. In 1830 a "National Association for the Protection of Labor" was formed, in 1834 a "Grand National Consolidated Trades Union," in 1845 a "National Association of United Trades for the Protection of Labor," and in 1874 a "Federation of Organized Trade Societies," each of which had a short popularity and influence, and then died.

In the meantime, however, a more practicable if less ambitious plan of unification of interests had been discovered in the form of an "Annual Trade Union Congress." This institution grew out of the trades councils. In 1864 the Glasgow Trades Council called a meeting of delegates from all trade unions to take action on the state of the law of employment, and in 1867 the Sheffield Trades Council called a similar meeting to agree upon measures of opposition to lockouts. The next year, 1868, the Manchester Trades Council issued a call for "a Congress of the Representatives of Trades Councils, Federations of Trades, and Trade Societies in general." Its plan was based on the annual meetings of the Social Science Association, and it was contemplated that it should meet each year in a different city and sit for five or six days. This first general Congress was attended by 34 delegates, who claimed to represent some 118,000 trade unionists. The next meeting, at Birmingham, in 1869, was attended by 48 delegates, representing 40 separate societies, with some 250,000 members. With the exception of the next year, 1870, the Congress has met annually since, the meetings taking place at Nottingham, Leeds, Sheffield, and other cities, with an attendance varying between one and two hundred delegates, representing members ranging from a half-million to eight or nine hundred thousand. It elects each year a Parliamentary Committee consisting of ten members and a secretary, whose duty is to attend in London during the sittings of Parliament and exert what influence they can on legislation or appointments in the interests of the trade unionists whom they represent. In fact, most of the activity of the Congress was for a number of years represented by the Parliamentary Committee, the meetings themselves being devoted largely to commonplace discussions, points of conflict between the unions being intentionally ruled out. In recent years there have been some heated contests in the Congress on questions of general policy, but on the whole it and its Parliamentary Committee remain a somewhat loose and ineffective representation of the unity and solidarity of feeling of the great army of trade unionists. As a result, however, of the efforts of the unions in their various forms of organization there have always, since 1874, been a number of "labor members" of Parliament, usually officers of the great national trade unions, and many trade unionist members of local government bodies and school boards. Representative trade unionists have been appointed as government inspectors and other officials, and as members of government investigating commissions. Many changes in the law in which as workingmen the trade unionists are interested have been carried through Parliament or impressed upon the ministry through the influence of the organized bodies or their officers.

The trade-union movement has therefore resulted in the formation of a powerful group of federated organizations, including far the most important and influential part of the working classes, acknowledged by the law, more or less fully approved by public opinion, and influential in national policy. It is to be noticed that while the legalization of trade unions was at first carried out under the claim and with the intention that the workingmen would thereby be relieved from restrictions and given a greater measure of freedom, yet the actual effect of the formation of trade unions has been a limitation of the field of free competition as truly as was the passage of the factory laws. The control of the government was withdrawn, but the men voluntarily limited their individual freedom of action by combining into organizations which bound them to act as groups, not as individuals. The basis of the trade unions is arrangement by the collective body of wages, hours, and other conditions of labor for all its members instead of leaving them to individual contract between the employer and the single employee. The workman who joins a trade union therefore divests himself to that extent of his individual freedom of action in order that he may, as he believes, obtain a higher good and a more substantial liberty through collective or associated action. Just in as far, therefore, as the trade-union movement has extended and been approved of by law and public opinion, just so far has the ideal of individualism been discredited and its sphere of applicability narrowed. Trade unions therefore represent the same reaction from complete individual freedom of industrial action as do factory laws and the other extensions of the economic functions of government discussed in the last chapter.

83. Employers' Organizations. — From this point of view there has been a very close analogy between the actions of workingmen and certain recent action among manufacturers and other members of the employing classes. In the first place, employers' associations have been formed from time to time to take common action in resistance to trade unions or for common negotiations with them. As early as 1814 the master cutlers formed, notwithstanding the combination laws, the "Sheffield Mercantile and Manufacturing Union," for the purpose of keeping down piece-work wages to their existing rate. In 1851 the "Central Association of Employers of Operative Engineers" was formed to resist the strong union of the "Amalgamated Engineers." They have also had their national bodies, such as the "Iron Trade Employers' Association," active in 1878, and their general federations, such as the "National Federation of Associated Employers of Labor," which was formed in 1873, and included prominent shipbuilders, textile manufacturers, engineers, iron manufacturers, and builders. Many of these organizations, especially the national or district organizations of the employers in single trades, exist for other and more general purposes, but incidentally the representatives of the masters' associations regularly arrange wages and other labor conditions with the representatives of the workingmen's associations. There is, therefore, in these cases no more competition among employers as to what wages they shall pay than among the workmen as to what wages they shall receive. In both cases it is a matter of arrangement between the two associations, each representing its own membership. The liberty both of the individual manufacturer and of the workman ceases in this respect when he joins his association.

84. Trusts and Trade Combinations. — But the competition among the great producers, traders, transportation companies, and other industrial leaders has been diminished in recent times in other ways than in their relation to their employees. In manufacturing, mining, and many wholesale trades, employers' associations have held annual or more frequent meetings at which agreements have been made as to prices, amount of production, terms of sale, length of credit, and other such matters. In some cases formal combinations have been made of all the operators in one trade, with provisions for enforcing trade agreements. In such a case all competition comes to an end in that particular trade, so far as the subjects of agreement extend. The culminating stage in this development has been the formation of "trusts," by which the stock of all or practically all the producers in some one line is thrown together, and a company formed with regular officers or a board of management controlling the whole trade. An instance of this is the National Telephone Company, already referred to. In all these fields unrestricted competition has been tried and found wanting, and has been given up by those most concerned, in favor of action which is collective or previously agreed upon. In the field of transportation, boards of railway presidents or other combinations have been formed, by which rates of fares and freight rates have been established, "pooling" or the proportionate distribution of freight traffic made, "car trusts" formed, and other non-competitive arrangements made. In banking, clearing-house agreements have been made, a common policy adopted in times of financial crisis, and through gatherings of bankers a common influence exerted on legislation and opinion. Thus in the higher as in the lower stages of industrial life, in the great business interests, as among workingmen, recent movements have all been away from a competitive organization of economic society, and in the direction of combination, consolidation, and union. Where competition still exists it is probably more intense than ever before, but its field of application is much smaller than it has been in the past. Government control and voluntary regulation have alike limited the field in which competition acts.

85. Coöperation in Distribution. — Another movement in

the same direction is the spread of coöperation in its various forms. Numerous coöperative societies, with varying objects and methods, formed part of the seething agitation, experimentation, and discussion characteristic of the early years of the nineteenth century; but the coöperative movement as a definite, continuous development dates from the organization of the "Rochdale Equitable Pioneers" in 1844. This society was composed of twenty-eight working weavers of that town, who saved up one pound each, and thus created a capital of twenty-eight pounds, which they invested in flour, oatmeal, butter, sugar, and some other groceries. They opened a store in the house of one of their number in Toad Lane, Rochdale, for the sale of these articles to their own members under a plan previously agreed to. The principal points of their scheme, afterward known as the "Rochdale Plan," were as follows: sale of goods at regular market prices, division of profits to members at quarterly intervals in proportion to purchases, subscription to capital in instalments by members, and payment of five per cent interest. There were also various provisions of minor importance, such as absolute purity and honesty of goods, insistance on cash payments, devoting a part of their earnings to educational or other self-improvement, settling all questions by equal vote. These arrangements sprang naturally from the fact that they proposed carrying on their store for their own benefit, alike as proprietors, shareholders, and consumers of their goods.

The source of the profits they would have to divide among their members was the same as in the case of any ordinary store. The difference between the wholesale price, at which they would buy, and the retail market price, at which they would sell, would be the gross profits. From this would have to be paid, normally, rent for their store, wages for their salesmen, and interest on their capital. But after these were paid there should still remain a certain amount of net profit, and this it was which they proposed to divide among themselves as purchasers, instead of leaving it to be taken by an ordinary store proprietor. The capital they furnished themselves, and consequently paid themselves the interest. The first two items also amounted to nothing at first, though naturally they must be accounted for if their store rose to any success. As a matter of fact, their success was immediate and striking. They admitted new members freely, and at the end of the first year of their existence had increased in numbers to seventy-four with £187 capital. During the year they had done a business of £710, and distributed profits of £22. A table of the increase of this first successful coöperative establishment at succeeding ten years' periods is as follows: —

Date	Members	Capital	Business	Profits
1855	1,400	£ 11,032	£ 44,902	£ 3,109
1865	5,326	78,778	196,234	25,156
1875	8,415	225,682	305,657	48,212
1885	11,084	324,645	252,072	45,254
1898	12,719	———	292,335	———

They soon extended their business in variety as well as in total amount. In 1847 they added the sale of linen and woollen goods, in 1850 of meat, in 1867 they began baking and selling bread to their customers. They opened eventually a dozen or more branch stores in Rochdale, the original Toad Lane house being superseded by a great distributing building or central store, with a library and reading room. They own much property in the town, and have spread their activity into many lines.

The example of the Rochdale society was followed by many others, especially in the north of England and south of Scotland. A few years after its foundation two large and successful societies were started in Oldham, having between them by 1860 more than 3000 members, and doing a business of some £80,000 a year. In Liverpool, Manchester, Birmingham, and other cities similar societies grew up at the same period. In 1863 there were some 454 coöperative societies of this kind in existence, 381 of them together having 108,000 members and doing an annual business of about £2,600,000. One hundred and seventeen of the total number of societies were in Lancashire and 96 in Yorkshire. Many of these eventually came to have a varied and extensive activity. The Leeds Coöperative Society, for instance, had in 1892 a grist mill, 69 grocery and provision stores, 20 dry goods and millinery shops, 9 boot and shoe shops, and 40 butcher shops. It had 12 coal depots, a furnishing store, a bakery, a tailoring establishment, a boot and shoe factory, a brush factory, and acted as a builder of houses and cottages. It had at that time 29,958 members. The work done by these coöperative stores is known as "distributive coöperation," or "coöperation in distribution." It combines the seller and the buyer into one group. From one point of view the society is a store-keeping body, buying goods at wholesale and selling them at retail. From another point of view, exactly the same group of persons, the members of the society, are the customers of the store, the purchasers and consumers of the goods. Whenever any body of men form an association to carry on an establishment which sells them the goods they need, dividing the profits of the buying and selling among the members of the association, it is a society for distributive coöperation.

A variation from the Rochdale plan is that used in three or perhaps more societies organized in London between 1856 and 1875 by officials and employees of the government. These are the Civil Service Supply Association, the Civil Service Coöperative Society, and the Army and Navy Stores. In these, instead of buying at wholesale and selling at retail rates, sharing the profits at the end of a given term, they sell as well as buy at wholesale rates, except for the slight increase necessary to pay the expenses of carrying on the store. In other words, the members obtain their goods for use at cheap rates instead of dividing up a business profit.

But these and still other variations have had only a slight connection with the working-class coöperative movement just described. A more direct development of it was the formation, in 1864, of the Wholesale Coöperative Society, at Manchester, a body holding much the same relation to the coöperative societies that each of them does to its individual members. The shareholders are the retail coöperative societies, which supply the capital and control its actions. During its first year the Wholesale Society possessed a capital of £2456 and did a business of £51,858. In 1865 its capital was something over £7000 and business over £120,000. Ten years later, in 1875, its capital was £360,527 and yearly business £2,103,226. In 1889 its sales were £7,028,994. Its purchasing agents have been widely distributed in various parts of the world. In 1873 it purchased and began running a cracker factory, shortly afterward a boot and shoe factory, the next year a soap factory. Subsequently it has taken up a woollen goods factory, cocoa works, and the manufacture of ready-made clothing. It employs something over 5000 persons, has large branches in London, Newcastle, and Leicester, agencies and depots in various countries, and runs six steamships. It possesses also a banking department. Coöperative stores, belonging to wholesale and retail distributive coöperative societies, are thus a well-established and steadily, if somewhat slowly, extending element in modern industrial society.

86. Coöperation in Production. — But the greatest problems in the relations of modern industrial classes to one another are not connected with buying and selling, but with employment and wages. The competition between employer and employee is more intense than that between buyer and seller and has more influence on the constitution of society. This opposition of employer and employee is especially prominent in manufacturing, and the form of coöperation which is based on a combination or union of these two classes is therefore commonly called "coöperation in production," as distinguished from coöperation in distribution. Societies have been formed on a coöperative basis to produce one or another kind of goods from the earliest years of the century, but their real development dates from a period somewhat later than that of the coöperative stores, that is, from about 1850. In this year there were in existence in England bodies of workmen who were carrying on, with more or less outside advice, assistance, or control, a coöperative tailoring establishment, a bakery, a printing shop, two building establishments, a piano factory, a shoe factory, and several flour mills. These companies were all formed on the same general plan. The workmen were generally the members of the company. They paid themselves the prevailing rate of wages, then divided among themselves either equally or in proportion to their wages the net profits of the business, when there were any, having first reserved a sufficient amount to pay interest on capital.

As a matter of fact, the capital and much of the direction was contributed from outside by persons philanthropically interested in the plans, but the ideal recognized and desired was that capital should be subscribed, interest received, and all administration carried on by the workmen-coöperators themselves. In this way, in a coöperative productive establishment, there would not be two classes, employer and employee. The same individuals would be acting in both capacities, either themselves or through their elected managers. All of these early companies failed or dissolved, sooner or later, but in the meantime others had been established. By 1862 some 113 productive societies had been formed, including 28 textile manufacturing companies, 8 boot and shoe factories, 7 societies of iron workers, 4 of brush makers, and organizations in various other trades. Among the most conspicuous of these were three which were much discussed during their period of prosperity. They were the Liverpool Working Tailors' Association, which lasted from 1850 to 1860, the Manchester Working Tailors' Association, which flourished from 1850 to 1872, and the Manchester Working Hatters' Association, 1851–1873. These companies had at different times from 6 to 30 members each. After the great strike of the Amalgamated Society of Engineers, in 1852, a series of iron workers' coöperative associations were formed. In the next twenty years, between 1862 and 1882, some 163 productive societies were formed, and in 1892 there were 143 societies solely for coöperative production in existence, with some 25,000 members. Coöperative production has been distinctly less prosperous than coöperative distribution. Most purely coöperative productive societies have had a short and troubled existence, though their dissolution has in many cases been the result of contention rather than ordinary failure and has not always involved pecuniary loss. In addition to the usual difficulties of all business, insufficiency of capital, incompetency of buying and selling agents and of managers, dishonesty of trusted officials or of debtors, commercial panics, and other adversities to which coöperative, quite as much as or even more than individual companies have been subject, there are peculiar dangers often fatal to their coöperative principles. For instance, more than one such association, after going through a period of struggle and sacrifice, and emerging into a period of prosperity, has yielded to the temptation to hire additional employees just as any other employer might, at regular wages, without admitting them to any share in the profits, interest, or control of the business. Such a concern is little more than an ordinary joint-stock company with an unusually large number of shareholders. As a matter of fact, plain, clear-cut coöperative production makes up but a small part of that which is currently reported and known as such. A fairer statement would be that there is a large element of coöperation in a great many productive establishments. Nevertheless, productive societies more or less consistent to coöperative principles exist in considerable numbers and have even shown a distinct increase of growth in recent years.

87. Coöperation in Farming. — Very much the same statements are true of another branch of coöperative effort, — coöperation in farming. Experiments were made very early, they have been numerous, mostly short-lived, and yet show a tendency to increase within the last decade. Sixty or more societies have engaged in coöperative farming, but only half a dozen are now in existence. The practicability and desirability of the application of coöperative ideals to agriculture is nevertheless a subject of constant discussion among those interested in coöperation, and new schemes are being tried from time to time.

The growth of coöperation, like that of trade unions, has been dependent on successive modifications of the law; though it was rather its defects than its opposition that caused the difficulty in this case. When coöperative organizations were first formed it was found that by the common law they could not legally deal as societies with non-members; that they could not hold land for investment, or for any other purpose than the transaction of their own business, or more than one acre even for this purpose; that they could not loan money to other societies; that the embezzlement or misuse of their funds by their officers was not punishable; and that each member was responsible for the debts of the whole society. Eight or ten statutes have been passed to cure the legal defects from which coöperative associations suffered. The most important of these were the "Frugal Investment Clause" in the Friendly Societies Act of 1846, by which such associations were allowed to be formed and permitted to hold personal property for the purposes of a society for savings; the Industrial and Provident Societies Act, of 1852, by which coöperative societies were definitely authorized and obtained the right to sue as if they were corporations; the Act of 1862, which repealed the former acts, gave them the right of incorporation, made each member liable for debt only to the extent of his own investment, and allowed them greater latitude for investments; the third Industrial and Provident Societies Act of 1876, which again repealed previous acts and established a veritable code for their regulation and extension; and the act of 1894, which amends the law in some further points in which it had proved defective. All the needs of the coöperative movement, so far as they have been discovered and agreed upon by those interested in its propagation, have thus been provided for, so far as the law can do so.

Coöperation has always contained an element of philanthropy, or at least of enthusiastic belief on the part of those especially interested in it, that it was destined to be of great service to humanity, and to solve many of the problems of modern social organization. Advocates of coöperation have not therefore been content simply to organize societies which would conduce to their own profit, but have kept up a constant propaganda for their extension. There was a period of about twenty years, from 1820 to 1840, before coöperation was placed on a solid footing, when it was advocated and tried in numerous experiments as a part of the agitation begun by Robert Owen for the establishment of socialistic communities. Within this period a series of congresses of delegates of coöperative associations was held in successive years from 1830 to 1846, and numerous periodicals were published for short periods. In 1850 a group of philanthropic and enthusiastic young men, including such able and prominent men as Thomas Hughes, Frederick D. Maurice, and others who have since been connected through long lives with coöperative effort, formed themselves into a "Society for promoting Working Men's Associations," which sent out lecturers, published tracts and a newspaper, loaned money, promoted legislation, and took other action for the encouragement of coöperation. Its members were commonly known as the "Christian Socialists." They had but scant success, and in 1854 dissolved the Association and founded instead a "Working Men's College" in London, which long remained a centre of coöperative and reformatory agitation.

So far, this effort to extend and regulate the movement came rather from outside sympathizers than from coöperators themselves. With 1869, however, began a series of annual Coöperative Congresses which, like the annual Trade Union Congresses, have sprung from the initiative of workingmen themselves and which are still continued. Papers are read, addresses made, experiences compared, and most important of all a Central Board and a Parliamentary Committee elected for the ensuing year. At the thirty-first annual Congress, held in Liverpool in 1899, there were 1205 delegates present, representing over a million members of coöperative societies. Since 1887 a "Coöperative Festival," or exhibition of the products of coöperative workshops and factories, has been held each year in connection with the Congress. This exhibition is designed especially to encourage coöperative production. At the first Congress, in 1869, a Coöperative Union was formed which aims to include all the coöperative societies of the country, and as a matter of fact does include about three-fourths of them. The Central Coöperative Board represents this Union. It is divided into seven sections, each having charge of the affairs of one of the seven districts into which the country is divided for coöperative work. The Board issues a journal, prints pamphlets, keeps up correspondence, holds public examinations on auditing, book-keeping, and the principles of coöperation, and acts as a statistical, propagandist, and regulative body. There is also a "Coöperative Guild" and a "Women's Coöperative Guild," the latter with 262 branches and a membership of 12,537, in 1898.

The total number of recognized coöperative societies in existence at the beginning of the year 1900 has been estimated at 1640, with a combined membership of 1,640,078, capital of £19,759,039, and investments of £11,681,296.

The sale of goods in the year 1898 was £65,460,871, and net profits had amounted to £7,165,753. During the year 1898, 181 new societies of various kinds were formed.

88. Coöperation in Credit. — In England building societies are not usually recognized as a form of coöperation, but they are in reality coöperative in the field of credit in the same way as the associations already discussed are in distribution, in production, or in agriculture. Building societies are defined in one of the statutes as bodies formed " for the purpose of raising by the subscription of the members a stock or fund for making advances to members out of the funds of the society." The general plan of one of these societies is as follows : A number of persons become members, each taking one or more shares. Each shareholder is required to pay into the treasury a certain sum each month. There is thus created each month a new capital sum which can be loaned to some member who may wish to borrow it and be able and willing to give security and to pay interest. The borrower will afterward have to pay not only his monthly dues, but the interest on his loan. The proportionate amount of the interest received is credited to each member, borrower and non-borrower alike, so that after a certain number of months, by the receipts from dues and interest, the borrower will have repaid his loan, whilst the members who have not borrowed will receive a corresponding sum in cash. Borrowers and lenders are thus the same group of persons, just as sellers and consumers are in distributive, and employers and employees in productive coöperation. The members of such societies are enabled to obtain loans when otherwise they might not be able to ; the periodical dues create a succession of small amounts to be loaned, when otherwise this class of persons could hardly save up a sufficient sum to be used as capital; and finally by paying the interest to their collective group, so that a proportionate part of it is returned to the borrower, and by the continuance of the payment of dues, the repayment of the loan is less of a burden than in ordinary loans obtained from a bank or a capitalist. Loans to their members have been usually restricted to money to be used for the building of a dwelling-house or store or the purchase of land; whence their name of "building societies." Their formation dates from 1815, their extension, from about 1834. The principal laws authorizing and regulating their operations were passed in 1836, 1874, and 1894. The total number of building societies in England to-day is estimated at about 3000, their membership at about 600,000 members with £52,000,000 of funds. The history of these societies has been marked by a large number of failures, and they have lacked the moral elevation of the coöperative movement in its other phases. The codifying act of 1894 established a minute oversight and control over these societies on the part of the government authorities while at the same time it extended their powers and privileges.

The one feature common to all forms of coöperation is the union of previously competing economic classes. In a coöperative store, competition between buyer and seller does not exist; and the same is true for borrower and lender in a building and loan association and for employer and employee in a coöperative factory. Coöperation is therefore in line with other recent movements in being a reaction from competition.

89. Profit Sharing. — There is a device which has been introduced into many establishments which stands midway between simple competitive relations and full coöperation. It diminishes, though it does not remove, the opposition between employer and employee. This is "profit sharing."

In the year 1865 Henry Briggs, Son and Co., operators of collieries in Yorkshire, after long and disastrous conflicts with the miners' trade unions, offered as a measure of conciliation to their employees that whenever the net profit of the business should be more than ten per cent on their investment, one-half of all such surplus profit should be divided among the workmen in proportion to the wages they had earned in the previous year. The expectation was that the increased interest and effort and devotion put into the work by the men would be such as to make the total earnings of the employers greater, notwithstanding their sacrifice to the men of the half of the profits above ten per cent. This anticipation was justified. After a short period of suspicion on the part of the men, and doubt on the part of the employers, both parties seemed to be converted to the advantages of profit sharing, a sanguine report of their experience was made by a member of the firm to the Social Science Association in 1868, sums between one and six thousand pounds were divided yearly among the employees, while the percentage of profits to the owners rose to as much as eighteen per cent. This experiment split on the rock of dissension in 1875, but in the meantime others, either in imitation of their plan or independently, had introduced the same or other forms of profit sharing. Another colliery, two iron works, a textile factory, a millinery firm, a printing shop, and some others admitted their employees to a share in the profits within the years 1865 and 1866. The same plan was then introduced into certain retail stores, and into a considerable variety of occupations, including several large farms where a share of all profits was offered to the laborers as a "bonus" in addition to their wages. The results were very various, ranging all the way from the most extraordinary success to complete and discouraging failure.

Up to 1897 about 170 establishments had introduced some form of profit sharing, 75 of which had subsequently given it up, or had gone out of business. In that year, however, the plan was still in practice in almost a hundred concerns, in some being almost twenty years old.

A great many other employers, corporate or individual, provide laborers' dwellings at favorable rents, furnish meals at cost price, subsidize insurance funds, offer easy means of becoming shareholders in their firms, support reading rooms, music halls, and gymnasiums, or take other means of admitting their employees to advantages other than the simple receipt of competitive wages. But, after all, the entire control of capital and management in the case of firms which share profits with their employees remains in the hands of the employers, so that there is in these cases an enlightened fulfilment of the obligations of the employing class rather than a combination of two classes in one.

With the exception of profit sharing, however, all the economic and social movements described in this chapter are as truly collective and as distinctly opposed to individualism, voluntary though they may be, as are the various forms of control exercised by government, described in the preceding chapter. In as far as men have combined in trade unions, in business trusts, in coöperative organizations, they have chosen to seek their prosperity and advantage in united, collective action, rather than in unrestricted individual freedom. And in as far as such organizations have been legalized, regulated by government, and encouraged by public opinion, the confidence of the community at large has been shown to rest rather in associative than in competitive action. Therefore, whether we look at the rapidly extending sphere of government control and service, or at the spread of voluntary combinations which restrict individual liberty, it is evident that the tendencies of social development at the close of the nineteenth century are as strongly toward association and regulation as they were at its beginning toward individualism and freedom from all control.

90. Socialism. — All of these changes are departures from the purely competitive ideal of society. Together they constitute a distinct movement toward a quite different ideal of society — that which is described as socialistic. Socialism in this sense means the adoption of measures directed to the general advantage, even though they diminish individual freedom and restrict enterprise. It is the tendency to consider the general good first, and to limit individual rights or introduce collective action wherever this will subserve the general good.

Socialism thus understood, the process of limiting private action and introducing public control, has gone very far, as has been seen in this and the preceding chapter. How far it is destined to extend, to what fields of industry collective action is to be applied, and which fields are to be left to individual action can only be seen as time goes on. Many further changes in the same direction have been advocated in Parliament and other public bodies in recent years and failed of being agreed to by very small majorities only. It seems almost certain from the progress of opinion that further socialistic measures will be adopted within the near future. The views of those who approve this socialistic tendency and would extend it still further are well indicated in the following expressions used in the minority report of the Royal Commission on Labor of 1895. "The whole force of democratic statesmanship must, in our opinion, henceforth be directed to the substitution as fast as possible of public for capitalist enterprise, and where the substitution is not yet practicable, to the strict and detailed regulation of all industrial operations so as to secure to every worker the conditions of efficient citizenship."

There is a somewhat different use of the word socialism, according to which it means the deliberate adoption of such an organization of society as will rid it of competition altogether. This is a complete social and philosophic ideal, involving the consistent reorganization of all society, and is very different from the mere socialistic tendency described above. In the early part of the century, Robert Owen developed a philosophy which led him to labor for the introduction of communities in which competition should be entirely superseded by joint action. He had many adherents then, and others since have held similar views. There has, indeed, been a series of more or less short-lived attempts to found societies or communities on this socialistic basis. Apart from these efforts, however, socialism in this sense belongs to the history of thought or philosophic speculation, not of actual economic and social development. Professed socialists, represented by the Fabyan Society, the Socialist League, the Social Democratic Federation, and other bodies, are engaged in the spread of socialistic doctrines and the encouragement of all movements of associative, anti-individualistic character rather than in efforts to introduce immediate practical socialism.

91. BIBLIOGRAPHY

Webb, Sidney and Beatrice : *The History of Trade Unionism.* This excellent history contains, as an Appendix, an extremely detailed bibliography on its own subject and others closely allied to it.

Howell, George : *Conflicts of Labor and Capital.*
Rousiers, P. de : *The Labour Question in Britain.*

Holyoake, G. I.: *History of Coöperation*, two volumes. This is the classical work on the subject, but its plan is so confused, its style so turgid, and its information so scattered, that, however amusing it may be, it is more interesting and valuable as a history of the period than as a clear account of the movement for which it is named. Mr. Holyoake has written two other books on the same subject: *A History of the Rochdale Pioneers* and *The Coöperative Movement of To-day*.

Pizzamiglio, L.: *Distributing Coöperative Societies*.

Jones, Benjamin: *Coöperative Production*.

Gilman, N. P.: *Profit Sharing between Employer and Employee;* and *A Dividend to Labor*.

Webb, Sidney and Beatrice: *Problems of Modern Industry*.

Verhaegen, P.: *Socialistes Anglais*.

A series of small modern volumes known as the Social Science Series, most of which deal with various phases of the subject of this chapter, is published by Swan, Sonnenschein and Co., London, and the list of its eighty or more numbers gives a characteristic view of recent writing on the subject, as well as further references.

INDEX

Acres, 33.
Adventurers, 164.
Agincourt, 97.
Agricultural Children's Act, 262.
Agricultural Gangs Act, 262.
Agricultural Holdings Acts, 268.
Alderman, 63.
Ale-taster, 49.
Alfred, 13.
Alien immigrants, 90.
Allotments and Small Holdings Association, 269.
Amalgamated Society of Engineers, 290.
Angevin period, 22.
Anti-Corn Law League, 231.
Apprentice, 65.
Apprentice houses, 246.
Apprentices, Statute of, 156, 228.
Arkwright, Sir Richard, 209.
Armada, 141.
Army and navy stores, 299.
Arras, 81, 87.
Ashley, Lord, 254.
Assize of Bread and Beer, 68, 228.
Assize, rents of, 41, 49.

Bailiff, 40, 141.
Balk, 35.
Ball, John, 112.
Bank of England, 194.
Barbary Company, 166.
Bardi, 91.
Berkhamstead Common, 264.
Beverly, 71.
Birmingham, 189.
Black Death, 99.
Blackheath, 115.
Bolton, 189.
Boon-works, 41.
Boston, 76.
Bridgewater Canal, 216.

Bristol, 80, 148, 162.
Britons, 4.
Bryan, Chief-Justice, 143.
Building Societies, 306.
Burgage Tenure, 59.
Burgesses, 59.

Calais, 89, 97.
Cambridge, 117.
Canterbury, 11, 115.
Canynges, William, 162.
Carding, 205, 210.
Carta Mercatoria, 81.
Cartwright, Edmund, 210.
Cavendish, John, 117.
Chaucer, 98.
Chester, 70.
Chevage, 44.
Children's Half-time Act, 255.
Children's labor, 237, 246.
Church, organization of the, 11.
Civil Service Supply Association, 299.
Climate, 2.
Clothiers, 153.
Coal, 3, 214.
Coal mines, labor in, 257.
Cobden, Richard, 231.
Cologne, 80.
Colonies, 178, 190.
Combination Acts, 279.
Combinations, legalization of, 282.
Commerce, 81, 134, 161, 189.
Common employment, doctrine of, 261.
Commons, 37, 263.
Commons Preservation Society, 264.
Commutation of services, 125.
Competition, 226, 233, 311.
Coöperation in credit, 306.
Coöperation in distribution, 295.
Coöperation in farming, 302.
Coöperation in production, 300.

313

Index

Coöperative congresses, 305.
Coöperative legislation, 303.
Copyholders, 143.
Corn Laws, 185, 223, 230.
Corpus Christi day, 70.
Cotters, 40.
Cotton gin, 211.
Cotton manufacture, 188, 203.
County councils, 243.
Court of Assistants, 150.
Court rolls, 46.
Coventry, 70, 148.
Craft gilds, 64, 147.
Crafts, 64, 147.
Crafts, combination of, 160.
Crécy, 97.
Crompton, Samuel, 210.
Cromwell, 179.
Cry of the Children, 251.
Currency, 169.
Customary tenants, 41, 143.

Danes, 12.
Dartford, 115.
Davy, Sir Humphry, 215.
Dean, 63.
Decaying of towns, 144, 154.
Demesne farming, abandonment of, 128, 141.
Demesne lands, 39, 104, 131.
Dockers' strike, 287.
Domesday Book, 18, 29.
Domestic system, 153, 185, 188, 220.
Drapers, 149, 161.
Droitwich, 155.

Eastern trade, 84, 164.
East India Company, 166, 190.
Employer's Liability Acts, 260.
Enclosure commissioners, 218, 263.
Enclosures, 141, 216.
Engrossers, 68.
Epping Forest, 266.
Essay on Population, 232.
Essex, 114.
Evesham, 155.

Fabyan Society, 311.
Factory Acts, 244.
Factory and Workshop Consolidation Act, 258.

Factory system, 212.
Fairs, 75.
Farmers, 129, 144.
Federation of trade unions, 289.
Fens, 184.
Feudalism, 20.
Finance, 169, 193.
Flanders, 163.
Flanders fleet, 86, 167.
Flanders trade, 87, 168.
Flemish artisans in England, 94, 116.
Flemish Hanse of London, 88.
Florence, 90, 168.
Forestallers, 68.
Foreign artisans in England, 94.
Foreign trade, 81, 134, 161, 189, 203, 230.
Forty-shilling freeholders, 241.
Frank pledge, 46.
Fraternities, 62, 71.
Freeholders, 41, 124, 241.
Free-tenants, 41.
Free trade in land, 231.
French Revolution, 200.
Fugitive villains, 59, 130.
Fulling mills, 229.
Furlong, 34.

Gascony, 90, 94, 169.
Geography of England, 1.
Ghent, 87.
Gildhall, 69, 92.
Gild merchant, 59.
Gilds, craft, 64.
Gilds, non-industrial, 71.
Government policy toward gilds, 65, 154.
Greater Companies of London, 153.
Grocyn, 136.
Groningen, 166.
Guienne, 90, 169.
Guinea Company, 166.

Hales, Robert, 116.
Hamburg, 89, 166, 230.
Hamlet, 31.
Hand-loom weavers, 188, 203, 220.
Hanseatic League, 89, 163.
Hanse trade, 89, 167.
Hargreaves, James, 207.
Health and Morals Act, 247.

Index

Heriot, 41.
Hospitallers, 91, 116.
Hostage, 81.
Houses of the Working Classes Act, 271.
Huguenots, 185.
Hull, 160.
Hundred Years' War, 96.

Iceland, 168.
Individualism, 232.
Industrial revolution, 213.
Insular situation of England, 2.
Insurance, 196.
Intercursus Magnus, 168.
Interest, 171.
Ireland, conquest of, 24.
Irish union, 203.
Iron, 3, 214.
Italian trade, 84, 164, 167.
Italians in England, 90.

Jack Straw, 116.
Jews, 59, 91.
John of Gaunt, 114.
Journeymen, 66, 147.
Journeymen gilds, 148.

Kay, 206.
Kempe, John, 94.
Kent, 9, 114.
Kidderminster, 155.

Laborers, Statutes of, 106.
Laissez-faire, 224, 228.
Land, reclamation of, 6.
Latimer, Hugh, 145.
Law merchant, 78.
Law of wages, 226.
Lawyers, hostility to, 124.
Lead, 3, 83, 88.
Leather, 83, 88.
Leeds, 189.
Leet, 46.
Leicester, 62, 79.
Lesser Companies of London, 151.
Levant Company, 166.
Leyr, 44.
Lister, Geoffrey, 117.
Livery Companies, 149.

Location of industries, change of, 151.
Lollards, 98, 111.
London, 149.
Lord of manor, 39, 103, 125, **143**.
Lubeck, 89.
Lynn, 93.
Lyons, Richard, **117**.

Macadam, 215.
Magna Carta, 26.
Malthus, 232.
Manchester, 189, 247, 284.
Manor, 31.
Manor-courts, 123, 141.
Manor-house, 31, 123.
Manufacturing towns, 189, 238.
Manumissions, 120, 129.
Markets, 75.
Market towns, 75.
Masters, 65.
Mechanical inventions, 203.
Mercers, 147, 150, 166.
Merchant gilds, 59.
Merchants adventurers, 164.
Merchet, 44.
Methuen Treaty, 190.
Mile End, 120.
Mill-hands, 213, 221.
Misteries, 64.
Monopolies, 187.
More, Sir Thomas, 145.
Morocco Company, 166.
Morrowspeche, 63.
Mule spinning, 210.
Muscovy Company, 166.
Mushold Heath, 117.
Mutiny Act, 182.
Mystery plays, 70.

Napoleon, 200.
National debt, 196.
Native commerce, 161.
Nativus, 43.
Navigation laws, 169, 189, 192, **229.**
Newcastle-on-Tyne, 164.
Non-industrial gilds, 71.
Norman Conquest, 15.
Norway, 163.
Norwich, 117.
Novgorod, 163.

Open-fields, 33, 142, **217.**
Origin of the manor, 55.
Owen, Robert, 248, **311.**
Oxford, 102, 147.

Pageants, 159.
Parcels post, 275.
Parish councils, 243, 269.
Parliament, foundation of, 26.
Paternal government, 173.
Peasant proprietorship, 270.
Peasants' rebellion, 111.
Peel, Sir Robert (the elder), 247.
Peel, Sir Robert (the younger), 230.
Peruzzi, 91.
Pie Powder Courts, 78.
Pilgrimage of Grace, 146.
Plymouth Company, 190.
Poitiers, 97.
Poll tax, 113.
Poor Priests, 112.
Portugal, 83, 190.
Post-office Savings Bank, **274.**
Power-loom, 210.
Prehistoric Britain, 4.
Private Enclosure Acts, **217.**
Privy Council, 138.
Profit-sharing, 307.
Puritans, 140, 178.

Railway Regulation Act, **260.**
Reaper, 49.
Reeve, 40.
Reformation, 138.
Reform of Parliament, 241.
Regrators, 68.
Regulated Companies, 174.
Relief, 21, 41.
Religious gilds, 71, 158.
Rents of Assize, 41.
Reorganized Companies, 187.
Restoration, 180.
Revolution, Industrial, 213.
Revolution of 1688, 181.
Ricardo, David, 226.
Rochdale Pioneers, 296.
Rochdale plan, 296.
Romans in Britain, 5.
Roses, Wars of the, 99.
Russia Company, 166.
Rusticus, 43.

St. Albans, 118.
St. Edmund's Abbey, **117.**
St. Helen of Beverly, 71.
St. Ives' Fair, 76, 79.
Sale of Food and Drugs Act, **273.**
Savoy Palace, 116.
Saxon invasion, 8.
Scattered strips, 38.
Scotland, contest with, 24.
Serfdom, 43, 120, 124.
Serfdom, decay of, **129.**
Servus, 43.
Sheep-raising, 142.
Sheffield, 189, 284.
Shop Hours Act, **260.**
Shrewsbury, 147.
Skevin, 63.
Sliding scale, 231.
Small Dwellings Acquisition Act, 272.
Small holdings, 269.
Smith, Adam, 224.
Smithfield, 121.
Social Democratic Federation, **311.**
Social gilds, 71, 158.
Socialism, 310.
Socialist League, **311.**
Sources, 54.
Southampton, 61.
South Sea Bubble, **195.**
Spain, 82, 168.
Spencer, Henry de, **122.**
Spices, 84.
Spinning, 205.
Spinning-jenny, **207.**
Stade, 166.
Staple, 87.
Statute of Apprentices, 156, 228.
Statutes of Laborers, 106.
Steelyard, 92, 167.
Sterling, 89.
Steward, 40, 46.
Stourbridge Fair, **76.**
Sturmys, 162.
Sudbury, 116.
Sweating, 260.

Tallage, 44.
Taverner, John, 162.
Taxation, 194.
Telegraph, government, **273.**

Index

Telephone, government, 273.
Telford, 215.
Temple Bar, 116.
Ten-hour Act, 256.
Three-field system, 36.
Tin, 3, 83, 88, 91, 93.
Tolls, 57, 78, 82.
Town government, 57.
Towns, 57, 79, 154.
Trade combinations, 294.
Trade routes, 84.
Trade unions, 279.
Trades councils, 289.
Transportation, 214.
Trusts, 294.
Turkey Company, 166.

Ulster, Plantation of, 190.
Usury, 171.
Utopia, 145.

Venice, 84.
Venturers, 164.
Vill, 31.
Village community, 54.
Villages, 31, 114.
Villain, 40, 111, 125.
Villainage, 130.
Villanus, 43.
Virgate, 38.

Virginia Company, 190.
Vision of Piers Plowman, 98, 111.

Wages in hand occupations, 220.
Wages, law of, 226.
Wales, conquest of, 24.
Walloons, 185.
Walworth, Sir William, 121.
Wardens, 69, 161.
Watt, James, 212.
Wat Tyler, 116, 121.
Wealth of Nations, 225.
Weavers, 65, 152, 188.
Weaving, 205.
Week-work, 42.
Whitney, Eli, 211.
Wholesale Coöperative Society, 299.
Wilburton, 128.
Wimbledon Common, 264.
Winchester Fair, 76.
Wolsey, Cardinal, 145.
Women's labor, 237.
Woodkirk, 70.
Wool, 83, 87, 142, 205, 210, 216.
Worcester, 155.
Wycliffe, 97.

Yeomen, 129, 221, 237.
Yeomen gilds, 148.
York, 65, 70.
Young, Arthur, 225.
Ypres, 87.

Printed in the United States of America.